Collector's Guide to

ONLINE AUCTIONS

Nancy L. Hix

COLLECTOR BOOKS

A Division of Schroeder Publishing Co., Inc.

Searching for a Publisher?

We are always looking for knowledgeable people considered to be experts within their fields. If you feel there is a real need for a book on your collectible subject and have a large comprehensive collection, contact Collector Books.

Cover Design: **Beth Summers**
Book Design: **Ben Faust**

COLLECTOR BOOKS
P.O. Box 3009
Paducah, Kentucky 42002-3009

www.collectorbooks.com

☛Contents

For George

See you in the bether, my friend.

☞Acknowledgments

As always, I must first thank my husband, Jeffrey A. Hix, who taught me enough about computers and the Internet to impart knowledge to others. Jeff provided much of the technical information included in this book.

Warm thanks to Harmony Ball Company, Antiquark, Ltd., and Martin R. Perry, who generously donated many of his personal artist prototypes so I could run charity auctions on eBay through the HK House of Peers.

No research happens unassisted. I'm grateful to a special Internet collector community known as CollectorNet.com. Several helpful and willing people proffered their experiences, knowledge, anecdotes, and advice in response to my posted questions. Others let me hammer them in e-mail for the information. My heartfelt thanks to Michael Trenteseau, Kelly Bloom, Charlynn Muehle, Stephen Llano, Donna Paul, Sally Simmons, Catherine Leicester, Bret M. Graves, Karen Gilbert, Chris and Davey Flanagan, Sandy Robinson, Andrius Gerulis, Patrick Harbert, Gina Ottaviani, Cyndra Henry, Sylvia Richards, Sharon Radosevich, Angie Jones, Bernadette Lambert, and Elaine Dowdin.

I acknowledge and appreciate professional input from Dave D'Archangelo (Live Auction Online), Chris Downie (Up4Sale), Beth Karkosak (Auctions.com), Kevin Pursglove (eBay), Colin Webster (eDeal), the CityAuction Support Team, Netscape Communications, Noel Wiggins (Harmony Ball Company), and James C. Armstrong, Jr. (Netscape Communications).

I'm grateful for information from online auction users Jim Turney, Dennis Becker, Franziska Tinner, Christina Russell, Heather Golden, Cliff Baker, Stan Allen, Monica Goben, R.B., Lydia A., Billy B., Teri Post, Janie Rice, Emily Bandi, Randy C. Jones, Steve Blount, Jim Smriga, and Barth Richards. Thanks also to Larry Riccio for the joke about angels in Heaven that I used in Chapter 2.

I must also thank Nancy J. Davies for teaching me more about writing than I ever dreamed I didn't know.

Many thanks to Sandy K. Doran for her real-life Internet experiences. No book about collecting will ever be complete without input from Sandy.

To the folks at Collector Books: Lisa Stroup, Billy Schroeder, Amy Hopper, Beth Summers, and Ben Faust. Thanks for countless hours given to these Collecting on the Internet projects.

Special thanks to my favorite ladybug, Mindy Smith, for "being there" with cyber bug hugs when the days and nights dragged on and the low-carb snacks didn't cut it.

Last but not least, thanks again to my sons, Chris J. Colucci and Jeffrey J. Hix, for being old enough to take themselves out to dinner. I am definitely one lucky — and very tired — person.

☞Foreword

We are lucky to be living in one of the most exciting times in the history of our culture. The changes the Internet has brought and will continue to bring to our lives were unthinkable twenty years ago. We now have the technology to interact instantly with people all over the globe. You can go to remote places like Madagascar, and there is someone capable of hooking you up to the World Wide Web.

Nancy Hix has been involved in the Internet for well over a decade. We first met electronically by taking part in a flame war. Despite the rocky start, I have grown to appreciate and respect her skills as a teacher and communicator. She can draw not only from her wealth of experience on the net, but has built an inter-Continental network of friends who can provide her with different perspectives on a variety of topics.

I can wholeheartedly recommend *Collector's Guide to Online Auctions* to anyone who wants to take part in the auctions on the Internet, or who just wants to be aware of what they are and how they work. Nancy's book is filled with good stories about how the Internet culture has grown, yet doesn't lose focus on helping you become proficient at online auctions.

James C. Armstrong, Jr.
Senior Engineer, Netscape Communications
Author of several books on the UNIX operating system

☞Introduction — Do These Come in Red?

My mother has an impressive collection of fan vases. While her collection could fill a series of Collector Books' price guides, she lacked — and desperately wanted — a red one. She had burgundy, Mandarin, and pink, but she didn't have a Santa-Claus-candy-apple-fire-engine *red* one.

I swore I'd find her one before someone else did!

Have You Checked eBay?

The only hope I had for finding the red vase was to scour antique malls and promising yard sales. But I kept coming up empty. Sandy and I were at the pinnacle of our Beanie Baby® shopfest. During one of our drive-by Beanie hunts, I revealed my mission.

"Have you checked eBay?" she asked. I looked at her blankly, so as we devoured a shelf of newly stocked Beanies, Sandy told me it was an Internet auction site. She explained that people would list an item for sale in the hope that someone else would bid on it — and buy it. When the auction closed, the parties completed the transaction off line.

To my untrained ear, eBay sounded like a menacing and confusing process — surely not a hunting ground for a piece of delicate glassware.

I didn't know if anyone besides my mother collected fan vases, and doubted even more that the high-tech world of the Internet would yield something so obscure. Most people would probably think a fan vase was a vessel for the storage of fans. Why would anybody sell one on eBay?

Sandy urged me to check.

Seek and Ye May Find

Doubtful but willing, I launched Netscape and typed "www.ebay.com" in the address line. I found a search page and read the advice to enter a specific description. I couldn't get more specific than "red fan vase." I entered those words, clicked the search button, and the browser churned.

A list of auctions containing the words "red," "fan," and "vase" appeared, but the words weren't always together or in that order. One auction offered a green Redwing Pottery fan vase. Another showed a cobalt blue vase with a red butterfly. A third listing described a fantastic red vase shaped like an onion. I checked every listing but nothing even closely matched what my mother had in mind.

"Keep trying," Sandy urged. "People list new stuff every minute." I continued my daily search of eBay only to discover that "red" had many meanings. The closest thing I found was a cranberry fan vase, and my mother already had several of those.

I kept trying. I didn't see a red fan vase, but I found many appealing ads. While some users described their items with plain text and no images, others looked like a page from a reference book. I passed many enjoyable hours surfing the listings, viewing the successful and not-so-successful presentations. And then one day, I hit the jackpot! I found a listing for a bright red fan vase.

Could it possibly be? I clicked. Holding my breath, I watched the digital photograph load pixel by pixel. I blinked. There it was! A Fenton dolphin-handled fan vase. And it was blood red. The auction description promised no chips, cracks, or other defects and praised it as a prized addition to anyone's collection. Such an understatement! The seller had set a reserve price, so I knew I must meet or exceed it to qualify as high bidder. One user had already bid, so I had to bid higher. I found the "Enter your bid" box and obeyed. Next, I typed in my user ID and password. At once, I became an official eBay user. My bid had registered — and I was immediately outbid.

Now What?

I reacted with horror. Did another user keep an around-the-clock vigil for this vase? My vase? My mother's desire? As dear as she is, I could not suspend time for the remaining four days in hopes of catching an auction sniper asleep at the keyboard. Then I realized that I could bid again. I hit the "Back" button on my browser and raised my ante. I now had the high bid, and it met the seller's reserve. Salvation!

My monitor speakers boomed "You've got mail." I feared the Fenton fanatic I bested was sending me hate mail. But it was from eBay, confirming my bid. The e-mail explained why the listing showed a figure lower than my bid.

"Your bid will be raised to your maximum bid if someone attempts to outbid you," it said. Now I would be the auction sniper and no vigil was necessary. I felt powerful.

Two days later, eBay sent me an outbid notice. The e-mail said there was still time and encouraged me to go back and bid again. I went right to the auction listing. The new bidder offered $55. "Surely my mother is worth it," I thought, and entered $75. I became the high bidder at $60. I was now on a shrewd cyber-high. I could snipe by proxy.

The Countdown

Determined to win, I watched the auction close. Ready at the mouse button, I waited in anticipation. I reloaded the screen and saw that there were three minutes left on the auction clock.

I slyly kept the site busy constantly reloading the page so nobody could elbow in a bid. At T-minus two minutes, I learned my trick didn't work. Aghast, I saw the bid raise to $62.50. Still the high bidder, I reloaded with panic. One minute left. No change. Then at thirty seconds my bid raised to $70. I frantically scrolled to the bid box, rapidly typed in $80, and clicked "Enter."

Nothing happened for twenty agonizingly long seconds. The screen stayed blank as the Netscape wheel icon turned. I felt manacled. Finally the confirmation screen loaded, and I was still the high bidder at $75. But my contender had bid again. If he bid once more, I was doomed.

With trepidation, I reloaded the auction screen and found the bidding closed. Sold, for seventy-five dollars. To me.

As I typed out an e-mail message to the seller to get her address and preferred method of payment, I was one happy woman.

Close to the Apple Tree

That first successful eBay purchase made an "eBeliever" out of me. I read the tutorial and advice pages for buyers and then read the notes for sellers. I checked out the eBay Café and chatted with a few users there. I couldn't get enough of my new hobby. It was so easy to find exactly what I wanted and buy it. I spent hours just browsing the site, looking at listing after listing of items I never thought anyone would sell or buy. And I watched many auctions close after last-minute bidding.

The apple doesn't fall far from the tree. The time I spent seeking that fan vase sparked my interest in glassware. Now I collect fan vases too. My mother prefers the clear glass of the Depression era, but I'm drawn to the bold opaque colors of Czech artistry. I've never seen Czech fan vases in antique shops but I have nearly twenty, all from Internet auctions.

Check the listings. I'm probably bidding on one now.

You Meet the Nicest People on a Modem

If you've already listed items for auction or entered bids, you've probably also heard from other collectors. The Internet is still an intriguing new place and people enjoy the easy communication it affords.

You'll soon discover that one common trait among collectors in cyberspace is their willingness to share information, especially with "newbies." And we're all newbies when we first venture into the auction cyberworld.

My friend Sandy used the Internet for collecting long before I did. As she shopped, many treasures came her way — a very special one in particular.

In 1994, a man named John offered a Jim Beam Man O' War decanter for sale. Sandy liked his online manner and checked his references. Feeling secure, she placed a bid. She ended up the high bidder and agreed to send a money order. While waiting to receive her payment, John "chatted" with her in e-mail, and they continued to stay in touch even after she received the decanter. Sandy learned that John was experienced in Internet deals, and he offered to become her online mentor. With his guidance, she grew adept at buying and trading collectibles on the Internet.

In 1995, eBay debuted and John took his treasures there. Sandy and John watched his auctions and together discovered which ones drew bids and what went unnoticed. Soon Sandy registered her own eBay account. She respected John's advice, not only on auction tactics, but also on dealing with people in e-mail. Ultimately, she successfully sold her entire Beanie Baby collection on eBay.

She and John continued to exchange e-mail, and they kept each other up-to-date on their collecting. In 1988, they decided to finally meet in person. With their respective mates in tow, they met at a mutually convenient location. The four spent a weekend filling in their online relationship. Now the best of friends, they continue to visit and send e-mail to each other almost daily.

"I've gotten a lot of things from online auctions and added many wonderful pieces to my collections," Sandy says, "but of all the things I've acquired from the Internet, the most treasured is my friendship with John."

I have "collected" many friends along my Internet travels as well. Many of their names appear on these pages.

About This Book

Thousands of people list items for auction every day. Most of the instructions they need are right at the auction site, in the form of an online tutorial. This is not a how-to book on the mechanics of entering an auction. There are many books on the market that have that information including my first book, *Collector's Guide to Buying, Selling, and Trading on the Internet* (Collector Books, 1999).

When I explore auction sites, I notice that many people don't fully use the capabilities of the auction sites. Some sellers don't include images, and others omit important information about the item for sale. Many don't realize that a well-formatted auction description will attract bidders. Worse yet, a few overdo it.

The purpose of this book is to aid you in using online auction sites to manage your collecting hobby and create auction listings that will bring success and profit to your Internet effort.

I organized this book in two parts. Part One contains the chapters in which I explain online auction sites and their use for collectors. I offer advice and hints for getting the most out of them based on real-life experiences in collecting cyberspace.

Part Two details six popular auction sites for collectors and explains their unique features. I also interviewed people who use each site regularly and include their personal anecdotes. Last, you'll find a detailed listing of more than fifty auction sites, along with their unique features and main interests. I hope you'll find this part helpful in deciding which online auction site is best for you.

Terms and Phrases Used in this Book

I use many terms in this book that pertain to collecting and collectibles, such as secondary market, limited-edition pieces, or "near-mint" condition. I detail these terms in *Collector's Guide to Buying, Selling, and Trading on the Internet.*

While you'll also find an explanation for them in this book's glossary, I hope both books will be your companions on your ride through collecting cyberspace.

I'll Take You There

I still love antique hunting with my family, as there's no substitute for those hours of companionship and fun. A bonus is that I frequently pick up interesting or choice items for a song at a yard sale. I then list them for auction on the Internet, not only for the extra cash, but also for the online auction experience.

I enjoy setting up my mini-photo studio, positioning and lighting the shots for the best angles. With a graphics program, I add borders to the images to make the item look irresistible. After a simple upload of the photo to my Web directory, I tweak my auction description template to add the right information. Once I enter the auction, I have three to seven days to watch collectors discover a treasure they can't live without and see the bids accumulate. This is part of the fun and success I hope to teach you!

Discovering treasures and outbidding the competition is an art I've grown good at. While I don't always win, I definitely make the fight memorable. There is no better way to manage collecting than getting in on the online auction excitement — and fun!

I invite you, the collector, to be part of it with me.

Part 1
About Online Auctions

Chapter 1 — From Gavel to Mouse-Click

Many years ago, my clever Aunt Libby conspired with me to dispose of a Kewpie doll. She claimed the item, prized by her husband, had a demeanor that personified her mother-in-law. She wanted it out of her bedroom forever — and knew just the brat for the job. In a smoothly choreographed movement, the ceramic carnival token met an unfortunate demise at the hands of twelve-year-old Nancy, who "accidentally" let it plummet from shoulder height onto a quarry tile floor. "Oops!"

Nowadays, Libby could arrange for a clandestine Kewpienapping and have me dispose of the item, for a smart profit, at an online auction site. I cringe when I see what carnival Kewpies fetch these days. They've become a hot item for collectors, who know just where to hunt for them — on the Internet!

Collectors turn to the Internet, and more specifically to online auction sites, by the hundreds. To be a smart online auction user and eventually a seasoned participant, it helps to understand the allure of auctions for both buyers and sellers. As a buyer, accurately worded auction descriptions will appeal to you. Sellers must know how to present their listings to interest bidders without misleading them.

This chapter covers the history of auctions, why we're drawn to them, and the effect they've had on collectors, collectible dealers, and the hobby of collecting:

- The auction – an ancient practice
- The auction appeal
- How it all started
- The impact of online auctions on the collectibles industry
- Managing your collection with Internet auctions

I focus here on Internet, or "online" auction sites used for buying and selling collectibles. You can find no better place for managing your collecting than the Internet, and online auction sites are rich havens for collectors.

☛The Auction — An Ancient Practice

Auctions aren't new. They've been around since the earliest recorded time. It isn't clear whether these ancient auctions involved designer togas or mint-year denarius proof sets — collect them all! — or if the auctioned items represented wealth. I'll place bets on the latter.

The first documented bidding was around 500 BC, when Greek historian Herodotus wrote about watching a Babylonian auction. Later in history, the Romans used auctions to liquidate items seized from their opponents in battle. The Roman Empire once sold at auction, but the successful bidder was overthrown and beheaded.

While a last minute outbid on eBay can be frustrating at best, Internet bidders are slightly more civil these days.

You don't need to be an auction historian to bid and sell online. It definitely helps to have some live auction experience but it's not necessary. Others may have more experience and savvy than you will at first, but if you do your homework, you'll be an audacious contender in no time. Just remember when you click that "Enter bid" button — auctions aren't new.

The Root Word

The word *auction* originates from the Latin root *auctus*, meaning "to increase." As the term implies, an auction involves potential buyers offering to pay an amount higher than the previous person's offer. This process is called *bidding*.

An item put up for auction really has no value when the bidding starts. When you bid, you're making an offer. To buy the piece, you must be the person offering the highest amount when the auction runs out. Therefore, the final bid determines the value.

So *This* is an Auction

Before I went online, I had never attended an auction in my life. I feared that I'd bid too high or speak at the wrong time. While I know that live auctions — those taking place in person — have a defined structure and rules, something about the concept made them seem like a place for the very impulsive, the very rich, or the very nuts.

With this said, I must now reveal that I spend more time on the Web than I do anywhere else. I have used, and learned to love, auction sites on the Internet. Right now, I have active user ID's at eBay, Up4Sale, Live Auction Online, Auctions.com (formerly Auction Universe), CityAuction, and Amazon.com. I probably have other accounts I've forgotten about.

Today I have 347 positive feedback comments on eBay. By the time this book goes to press, I'll have edited that number daily, even as I'm checking the galley proofs.

"My name is Nancy. I'm an online auction e-addict."

Different But Not New

Online auction sites introduced many people to auctions, not just online auctions, but also the traditional kind:

"Do I hear ten? Ten! Do I hear fifteen? Fifteen! Sold!"

Before the Internet, Dutch auctions and reserve prices were familiar terms to a relatively small culture; eBay didn't invent these terms.

While auctions and the auction vocabulary existed for many centuries, some folks didn't have the nerve to participate in the fast-paced auction activity. The frenzy and the "going, going, gone" staccato intimidated people. I can relate.

Collectibles Online Before eBay

Previous to the days of Internet message boards, collector forums, and live chat, collectors communicated via something called an "e-mail list." It started with two or three people sending messages back and forth with the "copy to" feature and, as word got out, the e-mail list grew to accommodate others.

The messages would vary. Someone was looking for a particular Precious Moments figurine and sought anyone with an extra to sell or trade. Another person introduced (and described) Crandall the Crab Louse, a fictitious Beanie Baby. Or, someone heard a rumor and wanted everyone's input. Messages flew back and forth with reckless abandon until there was no way to tell who was talking about what anymore. But, it was fun.

Then we discovered "The Net — Part One."

Usenet Newsgroups

Usenet, sometimes called "netnews," is the older, other half of the Internet. This was the first place to send, or "post," messages that other collectors would see. The simple process involved entering the text of your post and hitting "return." We didn't have to add names to lists like we did with e-mail. There was no way to tell who'd see the messages, though, since anyone who could type and had Internet access could visit a newsgroup.

I remember seeing the warning message before I'd enter a post:

"This message will be seen by hundreds of thousands of people all over the world. Do you want to continue?"

Note: A flame war is a barrage of completely off-topic insults thrown around on an Internet discussion forum. Stay out of them unless you have a ready supply of comebacks. Some people have lists of snappy responses to use as the need arises, but it's best to stay clear of flame wars. Nobody wins.

With an audience that size, of course I want to continue. You bet!

We posted prized collectible items for sale or trade, or tidbits of information about a certain antique. Others shared collecting experiences that hundreds of users could read and learn from. It was easier than ever to share information with people all over the world. It was also easy to start something called a "flame war" with total strangers. Most of us learned to watch what we said.

Just Us Geeks

Most early "computer people" worked with computers for a living and collected on the side. In that early crowd, being a computer geek was "in" and collecting was "pointless." It was far more exciting to find someone with his or her own UNIX computer we could dial into and "talk" to other users with a rudimentary chat program.

Online chat allows you to "talk" to people anywhere in the world by way of your computer. The conversation appears on your monitor. You simply type your comment in a text line and hit "Return," or click on a special "Enter" button. Your dialog appends to your name and shows up in queue along with everyone else's comments, as in this example:

> Mindy: Hi Gary! Glad you could join us tonight.
> Gary: Hey Mindy, what's new?
> Andy: Howdy Gary!
> Gary: Hi Andy. Did you ever get rid of that cold?
> Mindy: Andy and I were just talking about a new antique mall he found.

Chat rooms are all over the Internet. AOL provides many. You'll also find them at Web portals, on collector Web sites, and at almost any Web forum that also offers Internet bulletin boards.

Early chat rooms were fun if you liked spending hours talking about modem pools and ISDN with cyber-heads. Whenever I did, I always had a nagging feeling I should be doing something else — like shopping.

The collectible hunters and antique specialists had yet to discover cyberspace. When I explained to friends and family that I talked to people on a computer, they looked at me funny. It was a cozy network back then but I still felt like a geek.

America Online

Soon folks discovered how much fun it is to talk to people on a computer. As more of them connected to the Internet, cyber-communication took off with startling momentum. It happened so fast that it seemed like I woke up one morning and everyone had an e-mail address, even my veterinarian.

America Online, or AOL, coaxed many people out of computer phobias. Now we had chat rooms with novice users. The sessions I monitored back then went something like this:

> MeGaBUNZ: Cool.
> FLY510803: What's cool?
> MeGaBUNZ: This chat
> FLY510803: What's chat?
> MeGaBUNZ: Right HERE, where you are.
> FLY510803: On my computer? Cool!
> MeGaBUNZ: Wanna get a private room?
> FLY510803: Why? We're the only ones talking.

Maybe the movie "The Net" enticed people to the Internet, but I think that finding information about anything on a computer screen was the most appealing aspect. We can even shop there.

As collectors grew comfortable with the Internet and learned its capabilities, they invited their e-mail friends into chat rooms. Novice users soon joined in, giving birth to a whole new collecting network. Hundreds of collectors still use these information channels.

AOL was among the first Internet Service Providers to offer structured discussion forums where people could share information about collectibles. Today, hundreds of Web portals cater to collectors.

A Cyber-Trend Emerges

The first commercial Web sites were non-interactive and accessed mainly by other businesses. People used them to obtain information about the company, such as:

- Business address
- Phone number
- Product lists
- How to contact customer service
- E-mail addresses

But then programs like Java appeared and Web sites started talking back. Now users could order products online, with e-mail confirmation. No salesperson will call!

As people grew comfortable with the Internet, Web site developers got creative. First we had secured sites, where buyers could safely enter a credit card number and know their digits were safe and from cyber-pirates.

Then we discovered we could buy items on the Internet *and* affect how much we paid for them. Now we can bid on collectibles and antiques at home, at work, at a cyber-café, or anywhere we have access to a computer and an Internet Service Provider.

Don't Look Now, But You're Bidding

The same ease-of-use that put information right in our laps drew us to online auctions. You don't have to worry about parking in a ditch and dodging crazed participants as they barter for goods in a converted barn. On the Internet, there are no crowds, no auctioneer, and no worrying that you might accidentally bid and oblige yourself to pay for a life-sized cutout of PeeWee Herman. When you bid online, nobody's yelling in your ear. You know exactly when, and how, to bid.

Online auctions differ fundamentally from traditional ones:

- They run for several days.
- A computer records bids.
- For close calls, the auction program knows who bid first.
- Everyone has the same chance to win, regardless of how loud you can yell.

- You can ask the seller questions while the auction is running.
- There's less margin for human error.

As with off-line auctions, the person with the final high bid can buy the item, provided the amount meets or exceeds any reserve price set by the seller.

When you launch your browser and call up your favorite auction site, it's just you, your computer, and the desire to own something another person sells.

These days, you're a geek if you don't know what eBay is.

☛The Auction Appeal

Once seen as the last resort for liquidating property, auctions had negative connotations. Many of us remember the episode of Little House on the Prairie, where Charles, played by Michael Landon, had to auction his farm and treasured tools to pay off Oleson's Mercantile. His friends and neighbors rescued him by telling outsiders the auction was canceled, then buying his property back for a dollar.

Obviously, nobody set a reserve price.

In the past several decades, we've seen a plethora of items sold at auctions, such as:

- Estate liquidation items
- Repossessed property
- Antiques
- Automobiles
- Real estate
- Jewelry
- Fine art

We collect because it's human nature to surround ourselves with things we enjoy. We bid at auctions because our primitive roots draw us to competition — and sometimes for ownership of other people's stuff.

Everyone loves a bargain, especially online shoppers. Property that's promoted and exposed to a multitude of interested buyers usually commands top dollar. Sellers, on the other hand, can proffer goods on the Internet within their own time frame.

Buyers Set the Price

Human nature, more than economics, has a lot to do with the appeal of online auctions. There's that gotta-have-it syndrome, which I'll warn you about in Chapter 3. When buyers sense competition for an item they want, the appeal increases and they keep bidding. Smart bidders drop out of the auction when someone else drives the price out of line.

Supply and Demand

Collectibles and antiques are popular online trade, especially if the items bought and sold are current hot sellers and hard to find in stores. Remember how crazy people went over Beanie Babies? For awhile they topped eBay and Auctions.com listings by such a wide margin that everyone feared another Great Depression if the bottom fell out.

But Tickle Me Elmo and Furby to the rescue! Then came more McDonald's Teenie Beanie Babies and later yet, Pokémon. And there'll be something else after that. There's no better place than online auction sites to drive the demand for popular items skyward. As collectible dealers and antique malls "go cyber," our shopping district gets bigger and bigger.

It's Private

In the exuberant words of one of my Internet collecting friends, "With online auctions, I can overspend in the privacy of my own home."

Privacy is one appealing aspect of the Internet. When you turn on your computer, nobody says, "Just where do you think you're going dressed like *that?*" At checkout time, there's no fishing in your pocket to write a check only to discover you're out of them. You won't run into a neighbor reminding you of your leaky water heater as he tallies how much you're spending on Pocket Dragons.

Bidding online limits our inhibitions. Many people find competing with others too aggressive in person, but easy behind a computer monitor.

It's never fun to operate outside your comfort level, but it's worse to miss a prized addition to your collection because someone intimidated you. That's easy to avoid on the Internet.

Let the Buyer be Wild!

It's more convenient to buy a collectible item while seated at a computer than it is to go out and shop for one. The buyer bids, is outbid, then bids a little higher, and perhaps wins the auction.

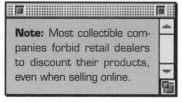

Note: Most collectible companies forbid retail dealers to discount their products, even when selling online.

She might pay more than retail for the piece but that's OK — the convenience is worth the extra cost. Or maybe she paid less than retail. Either way, the buyer gets the item, and the seller earns some extra cash in the process.

Michael Trenteseau, an online Boyd's Bears dealer, says, "after seeing what things go for on eBay, I'm less likely to pay retail for something if I know I can get it online from a private seller for less."

One Woman's Trash?

When Donna needed to thin out her collection of vintage Fiestaware, she decided to sell the pieces online. She bought a digital camera, registered at eBay, read the site tutorial, and explored Fiestaware auctions to see how other collectors listed the tableware for sale.

From her collection, she picked a casserole dish, or "nappy," with a cobalt blue lid. She acquired the dish at an antique show in 1980 for $25, and decided it was time to pass it along.

Inspecting it carefully, she noticed a few small chips in the bowl. She photographed the item from the front and rear, and then, remembering how auction listings detailed imperfections, took a close-up shot of the area with the chips. She formatted her auction description, viewed it in her browser to be sure it looked great, included the photos, and started the auction with a reserve price of $20.

"I went to bed smiling," she said.

The next morning she was staggered to find the high bid at $427, and 27 e-mail messages in her inbox. Stunned, she read the e-mail. This particular dish, she learned, wasn't supposed to include a lid. It was very scarce and only made for a short time. The rarest part of the item — the lid — was in mint condition.

With over thirty bids, the auction closed five days later at $997.00.

"Had I sold the item at a yard sale," she laughs, "I would have taken $20."

Not only did Donna pocket some easy money, but she also learned much more about Fiestaware through e-mail with other collectors. I'm sure this happens constantly. On the Internet, you reach well over a million potential customers, all for an insertion fee of around 25¢ — or less.

Cyber-Bargains

Buyers benefit too. What might be worth its weight in Roman bullion to you might be worth its weight in corrupted floppy disks to the seller, and you might not have bidding competition.

You can snag bargains. Many listings start at an enticing $5, and bids normally raise to the item's current value — sometimes much higher.

You need to remember a few things before you bid:

- **Shop around the Internet.** You might find the item listed lower at another site, or in another listing.
- **Determine the current market price.** Check secondary price guides, there are many online.
- **Don't bid over the market price.** A shill bidder might be raising the bid.
- **Read the auction description carefully.** An item might bid low because of a flaw.

Chapter 3 covers several important things a potential bidder needs to check before he or she places a bid.

Spirited bidders become competitive and bid the price over the current value. Smart cyber-shoppers surf the auction sites to make sure they're not missing a better deal somewhere else.

☛How It All Started

Barely a day passes without someone announcing a new Internet auction site. Everyone wants a piece of the action. Some of the specialized sites, like WineBid.com, attract buyers and sellers of a specific commodity. Others are huge cyber-flea markets, offering anything from garage sale junk to sewing machines to exhausted car batteries. Ambitious new sites pop up regularly, promising something new and different to set them apart from the rest.

By now, almost everyone who uses the Internet for collecting has a favorite online auction site. Some collectors thrive in the high-traffic atmosphere of eBay and Amazon.com, where endless offerings appear daily. Other collectors prefer a smaller, more distinct auction community.

Some people visit the auction sites only when they've decided to purchase special pieces, while others monitor auctions daily to check for trends or bargains. Either way, online auction sites are now the status quo for collecting on the Internet.

All you need is a computer, an ISP, and the willingness to register at the site and educate yourself about the online auction process.

The e is Lower Case

The first and most well-known online auction site was eBay. As explained on their Web site, Pierre Omidyar started eBay when his wife wanted a place on the Web to interact with other Pez dispenser collectors. Pierre agreed, and launched eBay on Labor Day, 1995.

Based in the San Francisco area, one can guess that the "e" stands for "electronic" and "Bay" refers to the San Francisco Bay area. eBay rapidly became the leading Internet "auction bay," making headlines with their initial public offering of stock in September 1998.

The first time I checked eBay listings, I envied anyone who knew more about using the site than I did. I was determined to change that. The tutorial on eBay is a great place to learn about bidding and selling online. As my quest for that red fan vase will attest, though, there's no substitute for practical experience.

Choosing a Favorite

Although I swear by it, eBay isn't the only online auction site and it may not be right for everyone. Explore the Internet to find what you want. Check the endless supply of auction site lists available on the Internet by using a search engine like www.yahoo.com or www.lycos.com. Enter a text string such as this:

```
auction sites collectors
```

You'll see many links to auction sites for collectors. Folks who specialize in collecting compile lists of online auction sites as a free Web resource for collectors. Their Web page might also include collectible reference books available from online bookstores like Borders.com or Amazon.com. Advertising funds some of these sites, and others receive commission if their links result in sales.

Software companies, like www.ricksplanet.com, offer auction programs and maintain lists of online auction sites, too. There's no shortage of online auction support on the Internet.

When you find a site with plenty of links to online auctions, bookmark it! You can return to the list later to examine the sites one at a time.

Learning Time Varies

My first timid eBay bid left me flabbergasted because someone immediately outbid me. Since I hadn't read the site tutorial nor had I ever bid online, I thought someone eager to place a bid higher than mine just happened to be at his or her computer waiting for a contender. Of course, this wasn't true; proxy bidding outbid me.

My first auction listing for a Hallmark Kiddie Car Classic closed with no bids. Not certain yet what a reserve price was but advised to set one, I entered the most I'd like to get for the item, not the least I'd accept. My reserve price was definitely not in line with the market.

Bulletin Boards and Chat Rooms

In *Collector's Guide to Buying, Selling, and Trading on the Internet*, I introduce collectors to places on the Web where they can meet other collectors. Some collectible companies, like Harbour Lights and Gene Dolls, wisely add collector forums to their sites. This encourages interest in the product by allowing collectors to share their enthusiasm and knowledge with each other.

Note: You'll read more about Web portals in Chapter 7.

You can also find independently run collector exchanges with the same features for communicating with others who share your passion.

Some are collector portals, like www.worldcollectorsnet.com. Here you'll find message boards and information pages for collectors of more product lines than I can list here, and the number would be out of date by the time this book goes to press. They add new ones all the time.

Collectible aficionados run some of those sites. They offer the site as part of their collectible dealership or because they're so hooked on a particular collectible that they devote a Web site, and lots of time, to promoting the line.

Almost all of them have one thing in common — rules about how and where collectors can sell items at the site. Some online collector forums don't allow selling at all, so collectors need a selling venue.

Let's Meet at the Auction!

Collectors can and do use online auctions to buy and sell items on the secondary market. Those seeking the same types of items get acquainted quickly because it's easy to communicate on the Internet. Some collectors gather at a smaller auction site to list items and bid, so they can stay among their trusted cyber-friends. Others take advantage of the high traffic at the major online auction sites.

While people sell everything on eBay, beanbag plush collectors flock to Auctions.com. Meanwhile, many auctions for eclectic items appear each month on Up4Sale.

You just have to surf.

☞Impact on the Collectibles Industry

Major online auction sites have more categories for collectibles than for anything else. Computers and car parts run a close second, but we're in the lead!

When listing an auction, the seller must list the item in a specific category. The choices are 85% collectibles: antiques, coins, stamps, sports memorabilia, advertising novelties, bean bag plush, popular toys, and a plethora of items defined as collectibles because of their secondary market value.

The categories that eBay, Amazon.com, Yahoo.com, and Auctions.com offer for collectibles and antiques far outnumber those for any other commodity. People collect just about anything, and the constant passing of time creates "new antiques." Supplies are unlimited!

I bought well over three hundred antiques and collectibles from online auctions. The only non-collectible items I purchased were a pair of ice hockey goalie pads for my son, and a pair of in-line skates for myself that I "accidentally" learned I should have let someone else buy. While I can acquire almost anything I need on eBay — except a new elbow — I'm there to hunt collectibles and little else.

Small Business Benefits

Online auctions allow businesses to expand their customer base. Some collectible and antique shops employ people full-time just to manage Internet auctions.

Collectible dealers benefit from online auctions in many ways. If they discontinue a line, they can quickly liquidate their stock by listing the items for auction. If a collectible line doesn't catch on in their area, they can use the Internet to reach places where sales might thrive. Instead of discounting, which most collectible companies forbid, they can sell the pieces at or above the retail price on the Internet. This also applies to antiques. That red fan vase may have sat on a store shelf unclaimed for many years, but listing it for auction on the Web opened the store to several customers willing to pay a premium for it.

The selling venue does more than just generate sales, however. Businesses can and do gain exposure from their auction listings.

"I couldn't buy the advertising I get from eBay," says Karen Gilbert, owner of Whimsical Wares (www.whimsicalwares.com) in Granada Hills, California. Karen started listing items on eBay in early 1998 but limits her auction sales to sec-ondary-market, rare, or unusual items. She doesn't list store merchandise, but by viewing her auctions, potential buyers find out about her shop.

Karen attributes a lot of her business to her Internet auction listings. She can tell from her Web page transaction reports that over a thousand visitors reach her Web site each week from the link she codes into her auction listings. When collectors read her Web pages, they realize she's an expert in her field.

"If people buy secondary-market items from me and like the way I treat them," she explains, "I stand a chance of becoming their dealer for open stock items and newly released pieces from their favorite collectible lines."

Karen lists 12-25 online auctions every week.

Independent Secondary Dealers

Bret Graves buys and sells secondary-market Harmony Kingdom items, exclusively online. He only sells live while room hopping or at the Swap 'n' Sell during Krause's International Collectible Expositions.

At the Swap 'n' Sell, Bret sets up a table among other sellers. Most of his customers know him from online exchanges on the collector bulletin boards. They've also seen his auction list-ings. Since the Internet crowd knows that Bret also collects Harmony Kingdom, they trust his knowledge of the pieces.

"Knowing your product and the compa-ny inside and out is also a plus when it comes to buying and selling," he says.

Like hundreds of other independent secondary-market collectible dealers, Bret uses Internet auction sites.

"My favorite is eBay," he claims, "because of the high traffic. But I have scanned listings at Up4Sale, and I occa-sionally use NoBidding.com."

Note: Room hopping hap-pens at a lot of collectible conventions. People post their hotel room numbers in the lobby and list the col-lectibles they're offering. Buyers can visit the rooms in hopes of a great deal. Last year we remembered to keep our voices down after 1:00 AM.

While he generates more business posting ads on Internet bulletin boards, Bret says he could not operate without online auctions. His sensible approach is probably why he's successful.

"Don't be greedy," Bret advises. "You may think you have the best products, but you'll be surprised by the number of people with the same products who are willing to sell them for less than you are. Keep an eye on the market and sales figures, and set your reserve prices accordingly. And most of all," he continues, "have fun!"

In-Home Operations

Dealers who operate out of their homes also benefit from online auctions.

"What amazes me most about selling collectibles online," says Cliff Baker, an Auctions.com user, "is that I'm doing business 24 hours a day, 7 days a week from a little mountain town in Oregon. My business isn't connected with or affected by the local economy or local conditions, yet it's directly affected by things like major floods, Hurricane Floyd, and the tornadoes in Oklahoma City. One little boy's collection was sucked out of his bedroom window, and we helped replace a few of the missing cars."

Cliff deals primarily in collectible sports cards, NASCAR items, and die cast farm toys. He lists numerous auctions each week on several different auction sites.

Charity Fundraising

At the first Harmony Kingdom collectors' convention, Martin Perry approached me for some advice.

I love saying that. Martin Perry is the Artistic Director for Harmony Kingdom and created the Harmony Garden series, featuring the Adventures of Lord Byron. It's not every day when a world famous artist asks *me* for advice.

Martin owned several hundred prototypes — the pieces made before they mass-produce an item — and found them useless sitting on shelves in his office. At the time, Harmony Kingdom prototypes, in the hands of lucky collectors, commanded as much as $4,000.

"Surely these could be sold, and the money donated to charity," Martin said. "I fear their value may drop, or worse yet, they'll be stolen." I understood. Several prototypes of suspicious origin had already found their way to the secondary market.

This was a few days after a series of deadly tornadoes devastated the Oklahoma City area, leaving many people homeless. I asked Martin to send me a few prototypes so I could list them on eBay to help the tornado victims.

Both Martin and Noel Wiggins, president of the Harmony Ball Company, distributors of Harmony Kingdom in the Americas, warmed to the idea and three intriguing prototypes arrived from England via UPS. Meanwhile, Noel assembled a committee — with me at the fundraising helm, to steer the project. We founded the Harmony Kingdom House of Peers, a council of independent collector clubs.

Note: We call ourselves "The HOP." Please — no jokes about the pancake house!

For the first HOP fundraiser, we auctioned a prototype to benefit the Feed The Children foundation in Oklahoma City. Noel wanted the auction to close on Memorial Day. For a five-day auction, I had to start it the preceding Wednesday.

The auction closed on May 31, 1999, at $4,085, with 40 bids recorded. Our second charity auction for a rare angel prototype earned $5,600 for the American Red Cross to help the victims of Hurricane Floyd. Many other independent collectors clubs use online auctions for their fundraising as well. Charity brings out the best in some people. These auctions typically bid high.

The Allure for Collectors

Online auctions make collecting easy. Even a long-term collector like my cousin Steve turned to eBay after vowing he'd never buy anything online. He disdained the idea of paying for something without seeing it first.

Those clear digital photos and detailed, eye-catching auction descriptions soon made a believer out of him, however.

If one buys from a catalog photo, after all, why not trust a clear digital image on the Internet and the ability to interact with the seller? Steve now boasts a respectable eBay feedback record and has added many new items to his coin and political memorabilia collections. He acquired these recent additions from online auctions.

Another friend insisted that the Internet was just for chat rooms and e-mail — until he found eBay and saw used photography equipment selling for more than he'd imagined. Days later he registered a user name and turned his old college darkroom equipment into an engagingly modern setup. Snagged by eBay's search and browse feature, he now also collects antique telephone equipment.

Making it Clear

When you find an interesting item at an antique mall, it's sometimes difficult to locate the seller if you have questions. Moreover, the seller may not even be the owner and could know very little about the piece other than the manufacturer and the price.

With advances in digital cameras, you can post a clear, sharp picture of an item with your auction description. You can zoom in on tags, monograms, or identifying hallmarks. You can also present it from several angles, even show the bottom if you think it's important.

While there's no substitute for physically seeing an item and interacting with the owner in person, the Internet is a close second. Plus, there are some advantages.

Auctions.com, eBay, Amazon.com, and Up4Sale all have hundreds of auctions running constantly. Collectors, retailers, and secondary-market dealers who study the market search listings and check closings for market values.

Thousands of users have active accounts on these sites. As Karen Gilbert discovered, there's no better way to attract customers than by listing an item for auction on one of the major sites.

Any Questions?

Online auctions include the seller's name and e-mail address. You can easily contact the person to find out more about the item. The seller is eager for a sale and usually answers your questions promptly and thoroughly. This rapport builds confidence between potential seller and buyer. Since the communication happens via e-mail, you can save the message and refer to it later.

Also, many avid collectors and dealers like to observe interesting auctions passively. They'll see you're the high bidder and may contact you with additional information, having no motive other than to share what they know. They're proud of their knowledge and experience and eagerly pass it along. And many, of course, acquired that knowledge by watching online auctions. What a great community!

Better Than a Thousand Words

It's nice to see an item in person, but with today's digital cameras and high-resolution monitors, a seller can replicate its likeness from all angles and zoom in on the nooks and crannies. By including digital photographs with listings, antique dealers can exhibit their rare and high quality items to literally millions of potential customers with minimal expense.

Like Donna, the seller should include close-ups of any imperfections. Not only is it an honorable approach to selling, but potential buyers sense this honesty. Unless they disqualify the item because of the imperfections, they'll bid with confidence. Plus, disclosing any flaws protects the seller if a dispute arises later.

The Secondary Market

When an item sells at either above or below the retail value, this is the *secondary market*.

There are many secondary price guides available for collectors both in print and online. No matter how the prices are compiled, no antique or collectible expert can claim to know the secondary market unless he or she studies Internet auction sites.

Because it's available everywhere, the Internet stabilizes the secondary market. At an online auction site, Little Gem Bears can't sell higher in one region than another since all contenders race the same clock, regardless of what their watch says.

But not all Internet transactions are auctions. There's no easy way to record and average transactions taking place via Internet bulletin boards or chat rooms. Collectible shops don't usually list their Internet-based sales on the Web so those can't figure in either.

Auction sites, however, offer the most complete collection of secondary prices paid for any class of collectibles, all in one place, from bids made by people all over the world. An average of these closing bids is, in essence, the current secondary market price for the item — and the values can be updated hourly.

"Since people who have computers are generally better off financially and have access to many sources of collectibles," says Michael Trenteseau, "successful online auction sites do reflect the overall market."

Michael maintains online secondary price guides for Boyd's Bears and Harmony Kingdom. He culls closing bids and lists the average price for each item having online auction activity in the current month. His lists help collectors and secondary-market dealers determine a reserve price when listing an item for auction.

Knowing current secondary market values is crucial for someone who frequently lists collectibles or antiques online, and you definitely need a secondary-market price guide garnered from auction activity.

Determining a Secondary Price

If you know the secondary price for an item, you know what to expect when you list the auction. If you have a good online secondary-market guide for the item, you've got it made. If not, you can calculate the value yourself.

You simply average recent auction closings to judge the secondary value of a collectible item, particularly one that often appears up for auction. And you can do this anytime.

Search for auctions that closed in the past 24 hours, or in the past week if you want a wider variance. Then average the closing bids. The number is a fair estimate of the current secondary-market value of the item.

Suppose you're looking for the secondary-market price for a retired "Versailles" model from the Just The Right Shoe collectible line. A completed auction search on eBay might bring up the following results:

Item Name	Closing bid
JUST THE RIGHT SHOE – VERSAILLES – NRFB	$36.05
Versailles Just The Right Shoe	$32.55
Just the Right Shoe/VERSAILLES (In BOX!)	$35.50
Just The Right Shoe "Versailles" RETIRED	$34.55

The average of all closing bids is $34.66, which is therefore an accurate secondary-market value for the item.

If you want a wider range, do this at several auction sites where the item recently closed and calculate one average price based on all recent auction closings for that item.

Let's say you found two auctions for the Versailles at Up4Sale that ended with these results:

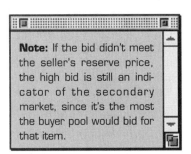

Note: If the bid didn't meet the seller's reserve price, the high bid is still an indicator of the secondary market, since it's the most the buyer pool would bid for that item.

Item Name	Closing bid
Just The Right Shoe – VERSAILLES L@@K!	$30.55
Versailles RETIRED Just The Right Shoe	$30.99

The average selling price on Up4Sale was $30.77. Using the average from eBay combined with Up4Sale, a very accurate secondary market value for this model is $33.37.

If you list the item for auction, a realistic reserve price would be $32. We'll talk more about reserve prices in Chapter 3.

> **Note:** This also tells you that you'd get more for the item on eBay, so you'd want to list it there. Surf the other online auction sites to check for hot sellers.

Managing Your Collection with Auctions

What exactly does *that* mean?

Managing your collection means acquiring items you want to collect and getting rid of any you no longer want. Some people buy doubles and sell one later for a profit. Others simply grow tired of collecting one thing and decide on another. Online auctions are great places to add items to your own or someone else's collection.

Got An Extra?

Maybe you couldn't find both of the new Boyd's Bears releases in your favorite shop, so you bought two in hopes of selling one. Maybe you snagged a valuable retired piece in a remote souvenir shop — have you checked Wall Drug lately?

Perhaps your Charming Tails dealer sold you a handful of the newest, hottest Puffkins and they clash with your Limoges.

Why look around for a buyer when you can list the items for auction online, where the buyers are searching for you?

Time to Let Go

Suppose your new apartment doesn't have as much room as your townhouse did. Maybe the items you collect suddenly need more room than they used to. Have you noticed the more popular a collectible gets, the bigger they make the pieces?

Or maybe you're just plain old tired of your barbed wire collection. Whatever the story, there's someone on the other end of cyber-mania who'd split the atom to take it off your hands. He or she is probably scouring the Internet right now.

It's generally time to let go of an item when you start thinking about its value more frequently than how much you enjoy having it.

Get the Ball Rolling!

I buy open-edition collectibles from my favorite dealer, but almost all my retired items and prized fan vases came from online auctions. I use eBay the most, but I find Amazon.com rich with great deals on collectible plush and antique jewelry. Up4Sale is perfect for buying reasonably priced Tiffany lamps.

Kewpies, by the way, can command over $1,250.

Online auctions are exciting, but they can also be confusing and frustrating if you don't learn how the site works, employ good strategies, and use the best site for you. Maybe you've been using eBay for a few months and want to try another site but you're not sure which one.

The chapters that follow will help you choose an action site to get the most from as you manage your collecting hobby.

Chapter 2 — Getting Started

Why not get the most out of collecting with the best selection of items? It's not only possible, but it's happening. When you connect to the Internet and call up a site like Amazon.com or Auctions.com, you're on the ultimate antique and/or collectible hunt. If you can't find an item at an online auction site somewhere on the Internet, it probably doesn't exist anywhere.

But you can't start a fire without a spark. Nor can you stoke one without kindling. And once it's burning, you must feed it.

When you get started with online auctions, you'll need your kindling and logs — or in this case your hardware, your reference guides, and your desire to buy and sell collectibles at auction. Then you'll need to watch auctions closely to know what's going on.

Along with your tools, it's important to pick the *right* online auction site — for you. Not every site appeals to every collector. Many collectors use more than one. This chapter will help you get started and determine if you should stay with one of the major sites, or try a smaller, specialized site:

- What you need to get started
- Picking the right auction site
- What you need to know about the site
- How to register
- Tracking your auction activity
- Using the sites

By the end of this chapter, you'll be ready to call up your favorite auction site, find the right help pages and listings, and prepare to bid and sell with confidence.

☞Tools of the Trade

It would be nice if you could just wake up one morning and say, "Today I'm going to start managing my collection with online auctions!"

If you've been online since the beanbag plush explosion, jump right in. However, some folks need a rudimentary review.

Forgive me if some of this seems profoundly basic, but it's my job to delineate the essentials for accessing the Internet. Even if you already know all of this, you might want to browse through it anyway.

Elements of Cyberland

Online auction sites reside on the World Wide Web, or more simply, the Web. The Web is one part of the Internet. To access the Internet, you'll need several important items:

- **A computer** – It's very difficult to access the Internet without one. Use a Pentium or something faster. You'll want pages to load rapidly during that last minute, split-second bidding. You definitely don't want to view auction listings that contain images using a 486 computer. Life's too short to deal with slow, outdated technology. Too many antiques and collectibles await you in cyber-land.

- **A modem** – Most computers come with them. This is what connects you to your Internet Service Provider (ISP) over a telephone line.
- **A cable modem** – You'll use this only if you connect to your ISP via cable TV lines.
- **A keyboard** – If your computer didn't come with one, it's time for a new computer. This is the board with all the letters and function keys.
- **A mouse** – You'll want one in good working shape so you can click on that "Enter your bid" button with ease.
- **A digital camera or scanner** – If you don't want to shell out for a digital camera, you can scan photographs. You'll definitely need one or the other since including photographs with your listings is imperative to Internet auction success.
- **A graphics program** – Corel Photo-Paint works great, Paint Shop Pro is perfect, and you can download others from the Internet on a trial basis. You'll need a graphics program you're comfortable using to finish up your auction photos.
- **An Internet Service Provider** – Also called an ISP. This is your cyber-transport to the World Wide Web and Internet auction sites.

Once you have the tools, then practice, practice, practice! You'll need to know how all of them work in order to be effective online. The following paragraphs cover them in detail.

Personal Computer

If you have a PC with a 486 chip, you're not going to get the most out of the Internet, and you're certainly not going to run fast enough for last-minute bidding. You need to upgrade to a computer with a minimum of a Pentium chip. If you purchase a computer with an Intel Pentium III chip, you can surf the Web and see the pages load on the screen with blazing speed.

On the Internet, fast is better. You'll want Web pages to appear quickly and not have image loading slow you down. Otherwise, you might miss the best auctions.

Once you've got your computer up and running and you know how Windows 95 or 98 operates, familiarize yourself with these Microsoft Windows programs:

- **Notepad** – This is where you'll enter text when you're formatting your auction description. To call up Notepad, click on the Start button, go up to Programs, and then over to Accessories. You'll find Notepad under Accessories.

  You can type text into Notepad just as you can in Microsoft Word, Page Maker, Ventura, or any other word processing program, only in plain text — no special formatting. This is perfect for auction descriptions that use Hypertext Markup Language (HTML). You'll read more about HTML further in this chapter.

- **Browser** – You can use Internet Explorer or Netscape. They vary somewhat in format and function, but it won't make a difference when you list your auctions or bid. Once you surf the Web a bit, you'll know which one you like better. It's definitely a personal choice.

- **Day/Time Properties** – This sets the clock. Double-click on the time of day marker at the bottom right of your Windows screen. This brings up a clock with a second hand. Set the clock to match the auction site, only in your time zone. You'll need to watch the minutes and seconds during last-minute bidding.

Modem

You know that screeching noise you hear when you pick up the telephone while someone's using the computer? That's the modem.

A standard dial-up modem converts digital information to analog signals (modulation), and then converts analog signals back to digital information (demodulation).

Digital information is what your computer produces. A modem allows your computer to communicate over the telephone lines by converting digital signals from your computer into signals your telephone system "understands."

Standard telephone lines carry analog signals. If you pick up your telephone receiver when your modem's in use and hear that weird, warbling noise, that's the sound of digital information converted to analog sound waves. This "carrier signal" from the modem actually carries information across the telephone lines.

When the telephone line sends analog signals back to your computer, the modem demodulates them, or converts them back into a format your computer can interpret.

Many newer computers have built-in modems. If yours doesn't, you'll probably use a modem that's about the size of a credit card and four times the thickness. Modems shrank over the years. My first one was large enough to serve as a base for my desk telephone and weighed several pounds.

Cable Modem

This type of modem connects your computer to the same coaxial cable used for your cable TV. You'll connect to the Internet by way of your cable company up to 50 times faster than with a dial-up modem.

If you're interested in accessing the Internet over cable lines, check with your local cable company for information about their service.

A cable connection is much faster than dial-up but costs more.

Keyboard

A keyboard is an input device for your computer. When you hit the symbol keys, it sends signals to your computer that translate into data. You'll use your keyboard mainly for entering text.

The computer keyboard has the keys arranged the same way as those on your old portable typewriter — or maybe on your father's old portable typewriter. Anyway, this standard arrangement is the Qwerty keyboard. If you look at the six upper-left letter keys, you'll know where this arrangement got its name. One of the earliest mechanical typewriters back in the 1870s had the keys configured that way, and now it's the standard.

Another keyboard arrangement is the Dvorak system. It positions the most common consonants on one side and the vowels on the other side, so typing alternates keystrokes back and forth between hands.

This is supposed to prevent carpal-tunnel syndrome, but you have to learn a whole new way of typing. I'll stick with good old Qwerty.

Mouse

This is another input device for your computer. A mouse allows you to use graphical user interfaces for making selections. Graphical user interfaces are those pop-up windows on the screen with the "click here" buttons. When you move your mouse arrow over one and "click there," something happens.

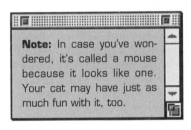

Note: In case you've wondered, it's called a mouse because it looks like one. Your cat may have just as much fun with it, too.

A rolling ball makes a cursor move around the screen. You select entries by pressing a button on the mouse. Controlled by moving across a surface, the ball rests inside and a little bit underneath the mouse.

Your mouse may not operate well on a flat desk, so use a mousepad. They're available just about everywhere. Some mail order companies will put anything you want on a mouse pad — even your driver's license picture.

You can control the speed of your mouse with the Mouse Control Program found within the Windows 95 or 98 Control Panel.

On most laptop computers, you'll either use a track ball, touch pad, or pressure sensor. Each serves the same functions as a mouse. Refer to your owner's manual for specific instructions.

Mouse Mess

If it feels like you and your mouse have a tug-of-war going, it's probably time to clean it. You'll use your mouse more than any other input device when bidding online, so you'll want it in fighting shape. Don't let your mouse control *you*.

Pop open the bottom, remove the rubber ball, and wipe out the inside with isopropyl alcohol (rubbing alcohol) on a cotton swab. Be sure to clean the little wheels that the ball contacts on the inside of the mouse.

Most computers come with a mouse. You can purchase some fancy ones separately that offer additional functions. Use whichever kind helps you register those bids.

Digital Cameras

A digital camera records photographic images in much the same way a traditional, or analog, camera does. An analog camera stores an image by using the incoming light to cause a chemical change in the camera film. A digital camera stores the incoming light in the form of a description of the image one line at a time.

Each color (or light frequency) the camera can read converts to a number. That number is stored as a digital (or binary) number consisting of 1's and O's. The image is broken down into a series of horizontal lines made up of picture elements, more commonly known as pixels. A binary number represents each pixel. The picture file is a series of numbers representing the color of each dot. When you open the picture file in a graphics program or send it to a printer, the picture redraws one pixel at a time.

Digital cameras rank by resolution, or by how many pixels are in a typical picture. The more pixels per inch, the more variations in color your pictures can have and the more life-like they'll appear.

Common resolutions for digital cameras start at 640 x 480. A better camera takes pictures at 1024 x 768. The more money you spend, the higher the resolution goes. Some digital cameras with a resolution of up to 1600 x 1200 sell for around $1,000.

Digital cameras store information in a number of ways, depending on which model you prefer.

Memory cards — Sometimes known as memory sticks, these store information in the PCMCIA (now known as the PC-Card) format. Others models use a proprietary memory card and you can only buy additional cards from a certain company. If you choose to go the memory card route, buy a camera that uses the industry standard cards. You can buy extra cards from many sources, often at a discount.

Some digital cameras store images in a non-removable memory card. They're convenient because you don't have to worry about having extra cards with you. The downside is that once you take your limit of pictures, you can't take any more until you download the pictures to your PC.

With this type of camera, you typically download images to your PC using either a serial cable or an infrared link. The infrared link is easy to use as long as you have a place to set the camera and the PC so they face each other and remain undisturbed while the transfer takes place.

I bought a camera like this to take pictures on vacation. It worked great — with one problem. The camera filled to capacity and the battery in my laptop was dead. There was no way to download the pictures from the camera to the PC. It became a choice of "what pictures should I delete to make room for others?"

Floppy disks — You can store fewer images on a diskette than you can with internal memory, but this has one obvious advantage. As long as you have plenty of floppies, you'll never run out of space to store new pictures.

Currently, Kodak, Olympus, Canon, and several other companies make digital cameras. I prefer the Sony Mavica because it uses a diskette. The diskette is your film; you slip it into the side of the camera, then pop it out and slip it into the disk drive on your computer. From there, you can copy it to your hard drive, finish up the image in a graphics program, and upload it to your Web directory.

Note: You'll read more about uploading images to the Web in Chapter 4.

Scanners

Not long ago, a scanner was the only practical way to convert a photograph into a digital image to use on your computer.

A scanner captures images from regular photographs or printed matter and converts them into digital format. The most common scanner is the flatbed type, where you lay the picture face down and close a cover on it.

Scanners usually come with software that lets you resize and otherwise modify the digital image. The device attaches to your computer with a cable.

While you'll get the clearest images with a digital camera, you can scan photographs for your auction descriptions. You can also place items directly on the scanner for a passable image. You'll have to experiment!

A Graphics Program

A graphics program is the software package that lets you alter digital images.

Your digital photographs or scans probably won't be right for an online auction listing without a few modifications. This is not a statement about your photographic skills — the file is usually too big and you'll need to crop out the background. I call this "finishing."

Note: You'll read more about finishing your photos and image file formats in Chapter 4.

A graphics program helps you get the image ready for the Web. For Paint Shop Pro, go to Cnet's www.winfiles.com and click on "Windows Shareware," then "Windows 95/98," and then "Multimedia and Graphics Tools." Select Graphics Editors from the Graphics Tools menu. You can download a version to test for 30 days, and you can order it online if you like it. I have had great results with Version 5.0.

Paint Shop Pro is also available from your favorite software dealer.

Internet Service Provider

I assume you have or are about to have the services of an Internet Service Provider (ISP) that offers Web access.

If you need to shop around for an ISP, watch your mailbox. You don't know this yet but when you bought your computer, they sent your home address to every computer mailing list in the world and told them you're an easy sell. I'm joking of course — in part. Many offers for free ISP trials will come your way. You'll see what I mean.

Most people who have Internet access at home use one of the more common ISPs, such as AOL, Netcom, or Microsoft Network. The major ISPs will send you an information packet and a start-up diskette if you call and request information about their services. You can also download their software right to your hard drive if you already have an active browser with an Internet connection on your computer. For a more complete listing of ISPs, go to thelist.internet.com.

Typically, ISPs provide unlimited usage at rates from $12 to $30 per month, depending on the plan you select. You might want to check with people who currently use one of them so you can decide which ISP is best for you.

If you can afford it (or if you have teenagers at home), it's usually a good idea to get a second phone line installed to use when you dial into your ISP. You may not think you'll spend a lot of time online, but once you start managing your collecting with online auctions, you'll use it more than you ever imagined.

A Little HTML Goes a Long Way

HTML, or Hypertext Markup Language, is the coding language for creating Web pages. You'll use HTML in your auction descriptions to avoid the boring plain-text default.

Appendix A contains an HTML tutorial to use when you prepare your auction listing. Keep that section handy!

If you do a lot of work on the Web, especially if you have your own home page, you might want to become proficient at HTML. There are many great reference books available. My personal favorite is *HTML — The Definitive Guide* by Chuck Musciano and Bill Kennedy (O'Reilly & Associates, Inc., 1997).

Online HTML Tutorials

Some Web page developers eagerly share their HTML knowledge by writing online tutorials to teach you the basics. If you need a refresher or want to see live Web examples, here are a few sites to explore:

Uniform Resource Locator	Site Name
www.pacinfo.com/help/tutorial.html	Pacinfo HTML Tutorial
www.cwru.edu/help/introHTML	Eric Meyer's HTML Tutorial
dtp-aus.com	The DTP/HTML Tutorials
www.angelfire.com/mi/grafix9/tutor.html	Nancy Hix's HTML Tutorial

www.geocities.com/Pipeline/1000/Help/ tutcontent.html	Pipeline HTML Tutorial
www.geocities.com/Baja/4361/index.html	HTML: A Guide for Beginners
www.ncsa.uiuc.edu/General/Internet/ WWW/HTMLPrimer.html	NCSA - A Beginner's Guide to HTML
pages.prodigy.com/pwphtmlhelp.html	Personal Web Pages HTML Tutorial
web.calstatela.edu/library/htmltutr.htm	HTML Basics
www.center.iupui.edu/tutorials/ html_basics.html	HTML Basics Tutorial
www.pongo.com	Pongo@Pongo.com
thecyberweb.com/HTML.html	Cyber Web's HTML Tutorial

Your Web page host — Angelfire, Tripod, GeoCities, etc. — should also have an online HTML tutorial.

Your High School English Books

I say this in all my books — how you write is how you represent yourself on the Internet. Since communication on the Web is about 95% writing, you need to hone the grammar skills Mrs. Beasley

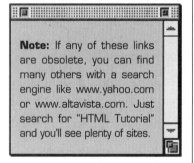

Note: If any of these links are obsolete, you can find many others with a search engine like www.yahoo.com or www.altavista.com. Just search for "HTML Tutorial" and you'll see plenty of sites.

taught you in fourth grade. Maybe she sensed the Internet and its popularity beyond 2000. On the other hand, maybe she didn't want you to sound illiterate.

It would suffice to say that you can never be too rich, have too much chocolate, or write auction descriptions too well.

Correct Spelling

Bidders want to read as much as possible about the item you're selling, especially if they consider laying down a good sum of money for it.

Well-worded auction descriptions attract buyers. Therefore, the text you use in your listing must get an "A" for "Accurate."

Some rules — or perhaps commandments — apply to the title or text in your auction description:

- **Never, ever spell any part of the item wrong.** How much can a seller possibly know about an item if he or she can't even spell it? Show you've done the required reading and spell Lladró, Riconada, and Harbour Lights correctly.

- **Never spell any words in the auction description incorrectly.** Here, too, spelling is important. The better you write, the more credibility you have. Maybe a potential buyer won't think "Wow! This seller sure is smart!" but he or she may sense that you know the product line well and bid on your auction.

- **Watch your grammar.** Again, a buyer will find you a lot more authentic if you express yourself clearly. A statement like this won't instill confidence in a potential bidder:

> This thing should of been in a muzeam but you can get it.

This sounds much better:

> This beautiful piece is museum quality — and it can be yours!

- **Don't overdo it.** OK, so you know big words. Remember, though, that you'll want bidders to understand your description. Most people have a working olfactory sense so don't pile it too high — if you know what I mean. You might turn them off with this:

> Mere descriptor fails physical property. Exalts the senses. Desist hesitation; contend immediately sans remorse.

This sounds far less retentive:

> This item is too lovely for words. Don't wait – bid with confidence!

You'll read more about wording your auction description in Chapter 4.

If your listing is more than a paragraph, compose it in Microsoft Word or another word processing program and use the spelling and grammar checking tools. That's what they're there for, and smart authors use them. Plus, it will be worth it when your item bids high because people trust your listing.

If your text is easy to read and understand, and accurately describes what you're selling at auction, bidders will choose your item over someone else's.

Well-written e-mail

Be nice. That's all it takes.

If you want to turn off a seller or discourage a buyer, send poorly punctuated e-mail full of spelling errors. If you want to send people screaming into the night, threaten them or be rude.

My friend Sally won an auction from an eBay user. When the auction ended, she sent cheerful e-mail saying how pleased she was about winning and asked the seller where to send payment. A stock response returned:

You owe me exactly $127.63. This includes my choice of shipping and a special handling fee I charge everyone. Payment must be made with a Postal Money Order. If you send a personal check or bank check I'll leave you negative feedback and hold your improper payment until you pay correctly. If you do not contact me within 24 hours, I will leave you negative feedback. If I don't get your payment in three business days, I will leave you negative feedback. If you don't leave me positive feedback the same day you get the item, I will leave you negative feedback.

Sally was horrified. She sent e-mail assuring prompt, correct payment and mailed a postal money order with her address. The item arrived several days later in acceptable condition, but Sally refused to be bullied into leaving positive feedback. She entered neutral feedback mentioning his demanding rhetoric, and hasn't heard from him since.

She was so turned off by his e-mail that she no longer bids on his auctions. Not many others do, either, as his feedback profile reveals.

Your e-mail communication with buyers or sellers is crucial to building a good reputation at online auction sites. Chapter 6 includes samples of e-mail messages to send after an auction closes, and you'll see other examples in Appendix C.

Now that you know more than you probably wanted to know about tools for the Internet, you could explore some of the Internet auction sites listed in Part 2 to see if you find them appealing. The following section will help you know what to look for.

☞ Just the Right Site

Remember that joke about the angels in Heaven keeping their voices down because they didn't want to disturb a certain group who thought they were the only ones up there? Well, eBay knows it's not the only auction site on the Internet, nor is it the only dynamic auction site on the Internet.

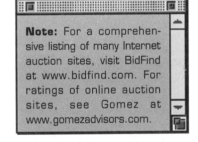

Note: For a comprehensive listing of many Internet auction sites, visit BidFind at www.bidfind.com. For ratings of online auction sites, see Gomez at www.gomezadvisors.com.

There are several online auction sites giving eBay a run for its money, but that isn't a bad reflection on eBay. It just means they have competition.

As you manage your collection, decide if you want to use a major site with guaranteed high traffic or a smaller, more specialized site just for collectors.

Web Site Traffic

In Web language, "traffic" is the volume of visitors to a particular page. Not how many different people access the page, but how often anyone visits the page. Each time the page loads in someone's browser, it's a "hit."

Some page counters increment with each page hit so you can tell how many users regularly visit. Many auction sites don't have counters, but this doesn't indicate low traffic. It could mean just the opposite.

A high-traffic site is one with tens of thousands of daily page hits. With all the loading and reloading of auction pages that goes on, a hit counter on a high-traffic online auction site could produce numbers large enough to run off your monitor screen. Don't judge a site by its page counter, especially if it's on the auction site's home page. Many users bypass that page and go right to their listings or to a search page via a browser bookmark.

A better judge of a high-traffic auction site is the number of active auction listings — with at least one bid — at any given time.

If a site has a lot of traffic, more potential bidders will see your auction listing. Also, there will be more auctions to visit. However, you may only want to target certain collectors. This is why you need to select which type of auction site is best for you.

La Crème de la Auction

Amazon.com, Auctions.com, Up4sale, and of course eBay have millions of users. These are some of the major auction sites on the Internet. They probably have the best prove out for users, but it's hard to compare the bottom-line figures. A 50% sales turnover is claimed by eBay, which is great, but other sites don't have the figures listed.

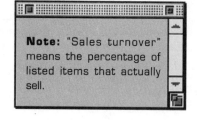

Note: "Sales turnover" means the percentage of listed items that actually sell.

While similar in concept, they vary in form and function, and it's hard to determine a success ratio among users.

Choosing an auction site is a matter of personal preference. Major auction sites have certain advantages over smaller sites.

Plenty of Servers

A Web server is a high-powered computer that holds the data for a Web site. To keep up with the high amount of selling and bidding activity, high-traffic online auction sites usually use more than one server.

The search engine for the site might be on one server, and auctions in popular categories might be on another. A site like eBay has many servers. As you browse from one part of the site to another, and through the various categories, your session moves from one server to another.

This enables the site to handle the traffic, and it's transparent to the user. You just cruise along as you would on any ride through the Internet.

The Crowd Roars

Amazon.com has over ten million users; eBay has easily as many, if not more. Auctions.com isn't far behind. All of these users can visit your listing and bid.

A large pool of bidders has many advantages, of course. The more descriptive you make your auction title, the more visitors your listing will have. This auction title will attract numerous bidders:

Planet Plush Wayne Gretzky Lion Bean Bag Toy

In addition to people looking for that particular item, your auction will come up in all of these searches:

- Lion
- Plush Lion
- Planet Plush
- Wayne Gretzky
- Beanbag toy

Your main audience is collectors of Planet Plush items, but with a larger pool, your listing appeals to many others as well.

Make Mine Rare

If you're selling an unusual item targeted for a narrow audience, you'll have the best luck at a high-traffic site. If you carefully word the auction title and include a photo and a thorough description, there's a much better chance the right group of collectors will notice and bid on your auction.

So Many Choices!

Collectibles. Not just collectibles, but Bears. Not just Bears, but Boyd's Bears. And not just Boyd's Bears, but Boyd's Bears in resin or plush.

On a major auction site, these category trees can be endless. As collectibles grow in popularity, the categories get more specific. A high-traffic auction site like eBay has thousands of item categories, and you can search each one.

No Hard Feelings

On a major auction site with tens of millions of registered users, you have a better chance of outbidding a stranger than a collecting friend. It's a lot easier to use those sneaky last-minute bidding strategies when you don't have to face the person you're besting in a chat room or worse, at a collectible show next week.

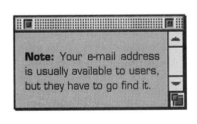

Note: Your e-mail address is usually available to users, but they have to go find it.

Using a clever site ID, you're anonymous in the cyber-crowd.

Smaller sites have certain advantages too.

The Minor Leagues

Most of what I call "smaller" auction sites are either newly started online auction sites, or those associated with a business. What makes them "small" is comparatively light traffic.

The Internet is still, by some standards, a very young medium. It changes constantly. What's obscure today makes headlines tomorrow. Definitely, don't rule out the smaller sites. After all, eBay was once a small site. You never know what option an up and coming Internet auction site has that's perfect for the way you want to operate.

Most of the smaller Internet auction sites I reviewed offer the same features and options that the main sites do, just to a smaller audience. Some have unique features.

Collectors and dealers use smaller auction sites for many reasons.

Lost in Space

If you're listing something very common, like Pokémon items or the latest holiday rage, your auction might get lost in a sea of other listings for the same item at a high-traffic site. You have a much better chance of selling your item for a higher price at a site that's not riddled with competition.

There are many collectors who find sites like eBay intimidating, and prefer the lesser known online auction sites. If the item you're listing is in high demand, you'll get plenty of bids — high ones.

It's Part of the Portal

Some folks enter the Web via a Web portal like Lycos or Yahoo. Many Web portals host online auctions. These are great for users who feel comfortable in their portal community.

At the collectible portals, people can list and bid at auctions, then meet in the portal chat rooms later. They can also list items for sale or trade on the message boards or in classified ads some sites offer. In addition, there's plenty of news and information about antiques and collectibles available.

You'll also find portals dedicated to online auction sites. You'll read more about Web portals and their auctions in Chapter 7.

An Exclusive Crowd

Let's meet at the auction! You don't have to worry about people you don't know listing auctions and bidding on items. You don't have to know everyone who bids on your auctions — most of the time you won't — but at a smaller site, there is less chance of fraudulent bidding, or shills. A new, unfamiliar user ID will stand out among the regulars.

Note: When someone uses another ID to bid up his or her auction, or asks someone to place a bid to nudge up the amount, this is shill bidding. It's illegal — don't do it.

To keep the items you collect within a specific group of people, use an auction site with less traffic. Some antique dealers only like to sell prized items to buyers they know will appreciate them.

Others want their valuable collectible "elusives" — items bringing top dollar anywhere — offered to a select pool of buyers. An auction site with fewer users and light traffic is perfect for this.

Fewer Categories — Shorter Searches

If you don't have that many categories to choose from, it won't take very long to find items you want to bid on. Some of the smaller sites don't even have sub-categories because they're not necessary. If the site is just for antiques, the main categories are specialized enough.

Auction Interactive 2000 (www.auction2000.net) demonstrates this type of listing. When you access the main page and click on "Auctions," you'll see five categories:

- Antiques
- Brittales
- Collectibles
- Jewelry/Gems
- Glassware

Click on any category for a complete table of active listings. It's that simple.

User Recognition

If the site has only a few hundred registered users, you'll recognize each other when you sell and bid. If you need to ask the seller a question, you'll be talking to someone you know.

There's always an element of risk when you send cash or collectible items through the mail. If you know the person on the receiving end, though, you don't have to worry as much.

☛What You Need to Know About the Site

To get the most out of managing your collection with Internet auctions, you'll want to know a few other things about a site before you sell or bid there. Although they're the same in principle — sellers list items and others bid — each site has subtle differences.

Not knowing everything about the site could cost you a high bid.

What Time Zone?

When you know an auction ends today at 19:55, you better make note of what time zone that's in. The eBay site runs on Pacific Time, but others are different. Be sure you know what clock you're watching so you don't run late.

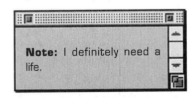

Note: I definitely need a life.

If you want your auction to be interesting, schedule it to close just as everyone's computer clock updates for Daylight Savings Time. It won't affect your auction clock but your bidders will get to see the clocks change in real time, right when it's happening.

What Does the Site Offer?

You can judge an online auction site several ways. Before choosing a site, decide which of these affect your use of the site:

- Search function
- Ease of use
- Navigation
- Options
- Features
- Item categories
- Auction networks
- Proxy bidding
- Fees
- Terms and conditions of the site
- Types of auctions offered

The paragraphs that follow explain the importance of each one.

Search Function

Most online auction sites have a built-in search function. The results of your search will list as a new page in your browser. You'll read more about how to use an online auction site search feature in Chapter 3.

Ease of Use

Internet auction sites like Yahoo, Amazon.com, and eBay are great if you're new to online auctions. You can click yourself through the site tutorials. Once you register, it's so easy to bid that it's scary.

Look for user functions that make navigating and using the site simple:

- **Browse** – This allows you to search auctions by category. Smaller sites let you view all active listings on one page.
- **Navigation bar** – Look for a row of page links at the top or bottom of the page. These help you jump around the site if you need to. A good site has a navigation bar on every page.
- **Search** – Enter a keyword, user ID,

Note: The Frequently Asked Question list, or FAQ, is an Internet standard. It's a list of questions asked so many times it's fair to assume you'll ask them too — so read the FAQ!

or auction number for select listings.
- **List your item** – All you do is fill in the blanks and hit "Enter."
- **Bid** – Just type an amount and "click here."
- **Site Help** – This is where you'll find answers to frequently asked questions (the FAQ) about the site.

Navigation

Hyperlinks, or "links," are trademarks of the Web. When you pass your mouse cursor over certain text — it's usually underlined or specially colored — the arrow changes into a little hand. This means you're on a link, or "hot spot." If you click the left mouse button, a new page appears in your browser (or in a new browser, depending on the page design). Links let you navigate the site.

You'll find links all over Internet auction sites. With one click, you're at the feedback page. Another click and you're contacting the seller. A third click and the auction description transmits, via e-mail, to a friend.

A well-constructed online auction site includes plenty of links so the site is easy to use. You don't waste time tracking down pages and missing auctions.

Options

Notice how many options the site offers so you can effectively manage your collection online. Here are a few you should look for:

- **Advanced searches** – Some sites allow you to search by key words in the auction title, or by seller, bidder, item category, and auction number. Most sites let you search closed items. A good search feature has plenty of criteria to select so you can narrow down the results.
- **Types of auctions** – You can choose from featured auctions, showcased auctions, Dutch auctions, English auctions, private auctions, or whatever kind of auction someone comes up with next.
- **Reserve price** – A few sites don't allow reserve prices; others won't let you list an auction without setting one.
- **Featured auctions** – For a few extra dollars, you can showcase your item on the home page of the auction site.
- **Fixed price auctions** – These are straight sales. The seller sets a price and the first bid wins.
- **User feedback** – This is the best invention since checking references via e-mail.

You may find other options you'll enjoy using. You'll read about several more in Part 2:

- First bid wins
- Image uploading and hosting

- Dynamic auction formats
- Personal paging
- Second chance listings

I discovered many unique features at the online auction sites I researched. I'm sure you will too.

Features

Most major sites let you use all features they offer, except featured listings that require a user to have a specific feedback rating.

Here are a few helpful online tools some major auction sites provide free:

- **Automatic messages** – This sends you e-mail if you've been outbid, if someone bids on your auction, or if your auction met reserve.
- **All in one user page** – Just type in your user ID and password, and the site returns a page listing all your current auction activity, such as auctions you bid on, auctions you listed, and your feedback comments.
- **Transaction-related feedback** – Allows user comments to link to the auction they resulted from.
- **Featured auctions and bold-faced titles** – For an additional fee, some sites place your auction prominently on their home page, or make sure it appears first on the list of search results. You can also set your auction title in bold-faced text so it stands out among the rest.
- **Accent icons** – A little icon you select appears by your listing when it comes up in searches. You can choose a birthday cake or holiday image, for example, at an additional fee.
- **Recommendations** – Based on bids you previously placed, the site e-mails you about auctions you might find interesting.
- **Account information** – View the status of your transactions showing account balance and payments.
- **User profiles** – Read what users say about themselves.
- **Personal shopper** – Enter item categories and the site sends you e-mail if any new listings might interest you.
- **Re-list capability** – If an item doesn't sell the first time, you can re-list it without missing a cyber-beat.
- **Edit your listing** – Before anyone bids, you can edit the auction description or certain other parts of the listing. After bids enter, you can add to the description.

Some sites have you pay for image hosting and escrow services. You'll read about those and many other auction site features further on in this book.

Item Categories

You can search for listings in item categories several ways:

- On the main search page. Select a category and every auction listed in that group returns in a list.
- At separate category search pages. Some sites have special pages to hunt for auctions by category
- By a category hyperlink that appears on whatever auction you're viewing.

If you limit your search to text strings, you may miss auctions with spelling errors or incorrect descriptions. One memorable listing for the Harmony Kingdom Treasure Jest® bovine piece called "Jersey Bells" became an anecdote among my fellow Harmony Kingdom collectors. One seller, obviously not familiar with the collectible line, listed:

Harmony Cows Trinket Box

The seller listed it in the Harmony Kingdom category but the name and description were incorrect. A text search for "Harmony Kingdom" would have missed it. Without a category search, we wouldn't have seen the listing.

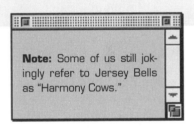

Note: Some of us still jokingly refer to Jersey Bells as "Harmony Cows."

Auction Networks

Sites like BidFind at www.bidfind.com and The Bidder Network Auction Site at www.bidder-network.com actually poll many different sites for listings that match your search criteria. This is an excellent way to be sure you don't miss auctions.

With one search, you'll see listings at many different auction sites all on one page.

Proxy Bidding

If you can't spend several days at your computer watching the auction in case someone outbids you, use a site that proxy bids for you. It's easy — all you need to do is enter the maximum amount you're willing to pay for the item and let the site do the rest.

When someone attempts to outbid you, the program automatically proxy bids for you up to your maximum bid. As long as your maximum bid is more than your current high bid, nobody knows the amount of your maximum bid until another user bids higher. If that happens, then he or she becomes the high bidder and you'll receive an outbid notice in e-mail.

Here is an example of how proxy bidding works:

1. The minimum bid is $5. You enter a maximum bid of $50.
2. You see that you are the current high bidder.
3. Your current bid is $5.

4. Another person bids $15.

5. Your bid automatically raises to $16 (or the next higher increment).

6. Someone else bids $28.

7. Your bid automatically raises to $29.

8. Another person bids $51.

9. You're no longer the high bidder and receive an outbid notice in e-mail.

10. You bid $52.

11. You're immediately outbid.

12. The high bidder's current offer is now $53.

13. You bid $60.

14. Your bid has exceeded the maximum bid of the current high bidder, so you are again the high bidder at $60.

The above routine goes on a lot during an auction, especially in the last hour before it closes. In case of a tie for the highest bid, the earlier bid wins. Proxy bidding typically won't work with Dutch auctions.

Listing Fees and Commission

Some sites charge a nominal, non-refundable fee to list an auction; other sites don't. You'll encounter listing fees at the high traffic sites for a number of reasons:

- They help discourage bogus listings.
- The site can regulate the number of listings by one seller.
- High-maintenance sites require the additional funding.

Listing fees vary. Some sites charge a flat rate, usually 10¢ to 25¢ per listing. High traffic sites base the fee on the minimum bid or reserve price.

A commission is the percentage the site charges you based on the closing high bid, as long as it meets or exceeds any reserve you set. Expect to pay around 2.5% of the price if it's under $25, and a slightly lower percentage the higher the bidding goes. If the auction isn't successful, you won't pay commission but you're still charged the listing fee.

Some online auction sites are totally free — no listing fees, no commission, and no charge for some of the additional features offered. The site might have only moderate traffic, but not necessarily.

You'll read more about listing fees and commissions in Part 2.

Terms and Conditions

All auction sites include the terms and conditions, or a user agreement, to detail their services. Sometimes this information appears on the registration page, or it's on a separate page.

Know the terms and conditions of any Internet auction site you use. Here are some of the items you'll see mentioned:

- **Registration eligibility** – You must be an adult who can form a legally binding contract.
- **Fees** – You must be able to pay any listing fees and commissions the site specifies.
- **Waiver of responsibility** – Most Internet auction sites are just venues for bidding and selling. They're not responsible for the accuracy of listings, bids, or user information.
- **Seller's responsibility** – You must not provide false information about the item for sale.
- **Bidder's responsibility** – You must not enter false bids and you must honor your high bids.
- **Accurate information** – The information you give the site about yourself (name, address, etc.) must be authentic.
- **No shills or other price manipulation** – Sellers must not bid on or influence any bidding on their listings.
- **No warranty** – No guarantee exists that the site will operate as it's supposed to. It may have to undergo maintenance resulting in downtime.
- **Breech of agreement** – The site can revoke your account if you violate any of the terms and conditions.
- **Limit of liability** – The site is not responsible if you lose profits on your sales or if you hurt yourself using a product you bought from a transaction at the site.
- **System integrity** – Don't use software that interferes with the system and don't allow anyone to use your account.
- **Feedback** – Only post feedback about users pertaining to transactions that took place on that auction site. Most sites don't care if you leave positive feedback for a user based on other Internet deals, but they forbid negative or neutral feedback left for that reason.
- **Not an agent** – There's no implied contract between you and the site.
- **Notices** – The site has three days to notify you of any action taken that affects your account.
- **Arbitration** – Any controversy or claim arising out of the terms and conditions settles by binding arbitration in accordance with the American Arbitration Association.
- **Applicable law** – Information about the governing body under which the site operates appears with the Terms and Conditions.
- **Patents** – If the site is covered by any patents, they list the patent numbers.

You'll see differences among the auction sites. Some agreements go on for several screens, and other sites just have a few paragraphs. They all say the same thing — play nice and follow the rules, or go away.

Types of Auctions

Not only can you manage your collecting with online auctions, but you can also select which type of auction to use. You can run a standard auction with no reserve price, list many items at once, or restrict access to your listing.

You'll read more about reserve price, Dutch, English, and private auctions in Chapter 3. Know the types of auctions a site offers before becoming a regular user.

Are You Eligible to Participate?

Not many online auction sites will exclude you from participating. As long as you're 18 or older and include all necessary information when you register, you can list items and bid. The only user restrictions I've seen are at very small, regional online auction sites where they want to transact in person. I'm sure there might be others.

Of course, you can have your site ID revoked at any Internet auction site if you violate the terms and conditions. No matter where you're bidding or selling, follow the rules!

☞Registering at the Site

Most sites let you browse listings as much as you want without a user ID, but in order to bid on an auction or sell anything, you must be a registered user.

Before you register, be sure to review the site's Terms and Conditions. If the site has a user agreement or something similar, read that also.

You only need to register once, and it's free at most sites. You're required to enter certain personal information that's maintained by the site in case someone needs to contact you. This information also puts the seller and buyer in contact when the auction closes.

Like many other registration processes on the Web, you might have to complete an optional online questionnaire. They usually include multiple-choice items you select with a mouse click.

A sample online auction registration screen is on the next page.

Although the registration process varies from one online auction site to another, you can expect to provide the same type of information at all of them:

- E-mail address
- Site ID you'd like to use
- Full name
- Company name (if applicable)
- Street address
- City
- State or province
- Zip or postal code
- Country

- Daytime and evening phone numbers
- Fax number
- A credit card number

Send a credit card number over the Internet? Please don't worry. It's very safe as long as the site uses SSL (Secure Sockets Layer) software when taking your personal information.

Register Here to Bid and List Items!

Required Information	
E-mail address	 Include your full e-mail name (name@email.com)
First and Last name	
Pick a User ID	
Street address	
City	
State	AL ▼
Zip or Postal Code	
Phone number	
Optional Information	
Age	
Education	High School ▼
Household Income	Under $25,000 ▼

Click here to Submit

Sample Registration Screen

Secured Sites

SSL ensures that your browser sends the information you enter in a secure, encrypted form that nobody can intercept. If the site lets you choose if you want to use SSL, definitely do, even if you aren't submitting a credit card number. It never hurts to protect your privacy.

Your browser may prompt you with a window when you enter or leave a secure SSL site. To double check, look for the little lock image in the very bottom frame of your browser. It's normally unlocked, but if you're on a page with SSL, the lock will be closed — or locked.

Here's what the lock icon looks like up close:

Unlocked   Locked

Check for the locked lock at any site that requires you to submit personal information, such as a credit card number. You definitely don't want this information in the wrong hands, and a secure site prevents that from happening.

Your User ID

At some auction sites, your e-mail address is your user ID, also called a site ID. Other sites let you pick your own unique site nickname after you register.

If your favorite site has you enter your user ID and password whenever you bid, pick a name that's easy to type.

Good User ID	Not-So-Good User ID
AFAM	**AntiquesFineArt&More**
ladybug10	**~%^lady_bug^%~**
Sassy1	**SassparillaMammaDooDahDay**

You may need to type your user ID fast during last-minute bidding.

Personal Information

You might have to complete an online questionnaire. The people running the site want to know a few things about you:

- How you heard about the site
- How you plan to use it
- Your gender
- Marital status
- Education
- Household income
- Other personal information

Note: Avoid using an underscore in your user ID. Since your user ID usually appears in hyperlink text, it's underlined. The underscore isn't visible in underlined text, and other users might think it's a space. The system ignores anything entered after the space. This is why a few comments in my user ID "marble" profile were actually meant for "marble_bob."

This section is usually optional. Be sure you're still at an SSL page before completing the online form and clicking "Enter." Check for the little lock!

Password

You need a password to participate. Some sites let you enter your own password, but others send you a temporary one in e-mail to use when confirming your registration. You can then change it to something else.

Activate Your Registration

If the site sends your password via e-mail, it will include the URL for a page

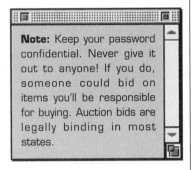

Note: Keep your password confidential. Never give it out to anyone! If you do, someone could bid on items you'll be responsible for buying. Auction bids are legally binding in most states.

where you'll confirm your registration. The figure below shows a typical registration activation screen. You'll enter your site ID and the password you received. Then you can change it.

Activate Your Registration:

Your Site ID	
Your temporary password	The one we sent you in e-mail
Pick a new password	
Enter password again	

Use your new password when you bid or list items. If you forget your password, click here.

Submit Registration

Sample Registration Activation Screen

Most sites display the terms and conditions agreement, and a button to click to indicate you understand and will adhere to the policies at that auction site. This process activates your user account.

☞Tracking Your Auction Activity

There are many reasons to track your activity on the Internet:

- Follow auctions you're bidding on so you don't outbid your wallet.
- Check your listings to monitor their progress.
- Review your closed auctions to be sure the transactions completed. Did the buyer pay? Did the item ship?
- Ensure that you left feedback for the other user.

This helps you manage your auction activity. If you're well organized and ethical in your dealings with others, it will show in your feedback ratings, and you won't overspend.

Search Your Activity

Some sites let you see all your activity on one page. More auction sites should adapt this useful feature. It could get cumbersome, though, if you list 100 auctions every month. For this reason, the search results typically list on several pages (depending on how often you buy and sell), and you'll browse through them with specially provided page links.

Other sites let you search by seller and buyer so you can track your activity. You can also check your billing information to see how much you paid in listing fees and site commission. You'll usually enter your site ID and password before the search retrieves that information.

Chapter 3 shows you how to search auctions by specific criteria.

Bookmarks

Some sites provide a link from every page right to your personal auction activity. It's a little harder to find on some sites, but you can make it easy by bookmarking the page. A bookmark is used to store the site URL with your browser so you can visit the page at any time with one click.

Both Netscape and Internet Explorer let you bookmark your favorite sites. When you find the page with your auction activity, select "Bookmarks" from the Netscape browser or "Favorites" from Internet Explorer. The browser lets you add the page URL to a list of sites you can easily return to later.

When you visit the page next time, you'll see updated information, possibly changed from the last time you saw it. On some sites, you'll search differently for bidding, selling, and feedback. Bookmark the pages with the results so you can check your auction activity.

☞Using the Sites

When you use an Internet auction site, you're responsible for following the rules. Most of them have the same general guidelines that follow the Terms and Conditions of the site:

- You must be an adult who can form a legally binding contract.
- You can't sell illegal or certain restricted items.

- You can't bid on your own auctions.
- You must sell the item to the high bidder or high bidder that met any reserve price you set.
- You must buy the item if you are the high bidder or high bidder that met any reserve price the seller set.
- You can't gather e-mail addresses from the site for advertising purposes, or "spam."
- You can't list bogus auctions. If the site administrator catches you trying to sell the space shuttle, they'll cancel the auction and maybe your site privileges with it.
- The buyer and seller must contact each other after the auction closes to complete the transaction.
- You must adhere to the terms and conditions of the site.

I Can't Keep All That Straight!

Sure you can. All Internet auction sites list the rules and the terms and conditions. If it's a well-designed site, there's a link to that information right from the home page.

The sites help you stay organized. Amazon.com, for instance, presents all of your auction activity on one page — the auctions you're bidding on, your current listings, closed auctions, and your feedback comments. The site even reminds you if you still need to post feedback for someone with whom you transacted.

E-mail Confirmation

Every Internet auction site I've used sends e-mail to confirm activity. Here are some typical e-mail messages you'll receive from the sites:

- **Listing confirmation** – This recounts an auction you just started and includes all the information you entered, including the auction title, the starting bid, your reserve price, and any features you selected.
- **Bid confirmation** – This confirms your bid, and includes the current bid and any maximum amount you specified.
- **Bid notice** – This tells you someone just bid on your auction, and how much he or she bid.
- **Outbid notice** – This lets you know if someone bid more than your maximum bid, and how much time remains on the auction clock.
- **End-of-auction notice** – If you're the seller, this includes the high bidder's site ID and the amount of the high bid. If your auction didn't meet your reserve price, the site invites you to re-list the auction. If you're the high bidder, you'll see the seller's site ID and the amount of the high bid. Bidders usually receive an end-of-auction notice only if the high bid met the reserve price.

Some users save this e-mail in case they need to refer to it later.

Your Responsibility as Seller

Selling at an online auction site carries responsibilities. If your auction receives one or more bids at or above your stated minimum or reserve price, you're obligated to complete the transaction with the highest bidder. You have a few other responsibilities:

- Describe the item accurately.
- List the features of the item.
- Set a minimum bid.
- Set the auction duration — usually 3, 5, or 7 days.
- State who pays charges associated with shipping.
- Specify payment methods accepted — personal check, bank check, credit card, etc.
- Contact the buyer when the auction closes.
- Operate within the site's terms and condition.

Those Rare Circumstances

Sometimes unforeseen things happen:

- The buyer refuses to pay for the item.
- You can't locate the buyer after the auction closes.

If you can't complete the transaction because the other person is unavailable or unwilling, you need to contact the site at the address on the Terms and Conditions page. They can refund your listing fee and commission.

You should give the buyer three business days to respond to an e-mail message before re-listing the item or offering it to the next highest bidder. We'll talk about posting negative feedback in Chapter 6.

Play Fair

It's tempting, but don't "bid siphon," or send e-mail to bidders in another open auction to offer a better item or price. Other sellers don't appreciate it, and most Internet auction sites forbid it.

Similarly, you can't enter bogus bids on your own auction, or shill bid. If you engage in fraudulent activity, you may lose your site privileges.

I include more information about bad practices to watch for in Chapter 3.

Note: If you need to end your auction early, some sites have you enter an outlandishly high bid on your own item to deter further bidding. Most sites, however, have an "end your auction early" feature. Be sure you know which method the auction site uses.

Your Responsibility as Bidder

Bidding is an agreement to purchase an item for your winning bid, as long as that amount meets or exceeds any reserve price set by the seller. You have certain responsibilities when you click on "Enter my bid."

- Be prepared to pay the amount you bid.
- Don't retract a bid, unless you've made a grave mistake with a decimal point. Re-enter your bid once you retract the incorrect one.
- Contact the buyer when the auction closes.
- Respond promptly to the seller's e-mail.
- Send payment in a timely manner, usually within seven days of the auction close.
- Mail payment in the manner the seller requested (money order, bank check, etc.)
- Operate within the site's terms and conditions.

Don't hesitate to ask the seller for online references if he or she has fewer than ten feedback comments.

On Second Thought...

Occasionally, things don't work out. The seller might add to the listing after you bid, making the item no longer desirable. In this case, you can retract the bid. Send e-mail to the seller explaining why.

At least one site will only retract bids at the request of the seller. Be sure you read the auction description and check the seller's feedback carefully before you bid. Also, watch those decimal points!

Bid Nice

Don't manipulate bids by playing games with bid retractions so you can bid lower once your competition reaches their maximum bid. Internet auction sites don't allow this anyway. Some sites block your participation in an auction once you've retracted a bid.

You may find yourself in competitive bidding with another collector you know. You must decide then if your desire for the item outweighs your friendship with the person. Some collectors agree not to outbid each other, but others thrive on competition and don't mind the challenge.

Now that you know your tools and your responsibilities as an Internet auction site participant, it's time to lace up your cyber-skates and get out on the virtual ice.

Chapter 3 — Let's All Go to the Auction!

As you surf around the Internet for that perfect auction site, you'll that find no matter how popular or obscure the site is, they all have the same basis — someone lists an item and others bid. The more you use auction sites, the more perceptive you'll be about what goes on there. You can determine the best time to list an auction and the most effective way to bid, and learn how to avoid trouble

You'll find hints and tips on how to bid smart and eventually get the most out of whatever site you use. Here's what we'll cover in this chapter:

- A successful auction
- Features all auction sites have
- Features unique to some sites
- Smart bidding
- Tips for checking out the seller
- What you need to watch out for

This chapter will familiarize you with the online auction site process. I recommend that you purchase an item from an auction site before you consider listing an auction. That's why I cover bidding first, and selling in the next chapter.

Your collection will multiply rapidly when you shop at online auction sites, especially if you know how the sites work.

Note: Want more information about using online auction sites? Check out the Online Auction Users Association at www.auctionusers.org.

☛A Successful Auction

There's no guarantee that every auction you list will meet your reserve price. When you're the prospective buyer, you can't always be the high bidder. However, if you know the best tips for listing auctions and bidding on others, you can successfully manage your collecting that way.

On an Internet auction site, a transaction between the seller and high bidder takes place after the auction closes. There is one exception. If the high bid is lower than any reserve price set by the seller, he or she is not obligated to sell the item.

An auction that closes with at least one bid, or one in which at least one bid met the reserve price (if one was set), is a successful auction. When I use the term "successful auction," it refers to one resulting in a transaction between the seller and a buyer.

I hope all your auctions are successful ones!

Types of Auctions

All online auction sites run differently. Standard operating procedures at one site might be options at another one. Most of the major auction sites let you decide how you want your auction to run by offering you several choices of auction types:

- Standard
- Reserve price
- Dutch
- English
- Open-ended
- Private
- Restricted
- First bid wins

This section covers each of them in detail.

Standard Auctions

Most online auction sites offer standard auctions. This is the bare-bones basic auction, where the seller lists an item and decides at what amount the bidding starts. The high bidder takes home the prize. There's one sale, no reserve, and no other special procedures except those typically performed by the auction site.

When the auction ends, the transaction is completed off-line.

Reserve Price Auctions

A reserve price represents the lowest price at which you're willing to sell the item. You can set the bidding to begin at a lower price (the minimum bid), and then set a higher reserve price. When you start the auction, only the minimum bid price is visible on the auction page. Bidders usually don't know the reserve price until the highest bid reaches that amount.

Some auction sites wait until the last hour of the auction to reveal if the bidding met the reserve price. Others don't reveal the high bidder's user ID until the auction meets or exceeds it.

Why Do Sites Allow That?

The whole purpose of taking part in an auction is to be the high bidder and pick up a bargain in the process. The high bid should be the selling price. Setting a reserve is sneaky, right?

Not really. Auctions with a high starting price usually don't attract as much bidding as auctions opening lower. Since bidders don't know the reserve amount, they can place early bids in hopes of meeting it, and then others will bid too. However, since there's only one winning bidder, who cares if the auction draws many bids?

The seller does. For some reason, bids attract more bids. When many people bid on the same auction, this tends to drive up the price. The seller is happy, the auction site gets a higher commission, and the high bidder has the thrill of winning.

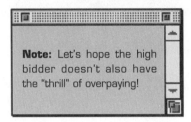

Note: Let's hope the high bidder doesn't also have the "thrill" of overpaying!

Benefits for the Buyer and Seller

A reserve auction definitely serves the best interest of the seller, not only to draw bids and a higher closing price, but for another reason — system failure protection.

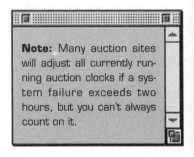

Note: Many auction sites will adjust all currently running auction clocks if a system failure exceeds two hours, but you can't always count on it.

If system problems occur and bidders can't access the site, the auction clock sometimes keeps running. If the bidding was low when the system failed, the item may sell at a price much lower than its value if the seller didn't set a reserve price.

Reserve price auctions can also protect the buyer.

- If you bid above your means, you aren't obligated to purchase the item if your bid didn't meet the reserve price.
- You'll know the item's value in the eyes of the seller.

Some auction sites don't allow reserve auctions, while others won't let you list an auction without a reserve price.

Drawbacks of Reserve Auctions

Sometimes the high bid doesn't meet the reserve price and therefore you don't sell the item. People who run the auction sites don't like this because it lowers their ratio of successful transactions per number of listings.

In the fall of 1999, eBay revealed numerous complaints about reserve price listings. Certain sellers set ridiculously high reserve prices to see what the item would bid up to, with no intention of actually selling it.

To discourage this, eBay now adds an additional charge to your listing fee if you set a reserve price. If the high bid meets the reserve, they refund the fee. Other auction sites may have adopted this policy by the time this book goes to press, but I hope not. It's unpopular among collectors who use reserve price auctions to protect their investments.

Dutch Auctions

If you have more than one of the same item to sell, you can list a Dutch auction. It doesn't matter if you have three or three hundred of them, as long as it's a multiple of the exact same item. This is thrifty; you can list multiple items and only pay one insertion fee.

How Do They Work?

It's very simple. The seller specifies the same starting bid for all items, and indicates how many of them are for sale. Buyers have the option of bidding at or above the starting bid for as many as they care to acquire. When the auction ends, the highest bidders purchase the goods at the lowest successful bid.

It pays to bid early because the earliest successful bids win. Suppose that five of the same figurines are for sale at $25 each. Ten people bid $25 for one figurine. The first five bidders can each purchase an item since they all offered the winning amount.

If anyone bid over $25 for a figurine, that person would be among the winners for the item. The other four who bid $25 before any others also would win. Each of the five figurines would sell for $25.

If all ten bids exceeded $25, then the five items sell to the high bidders at the lowest offer.

Here's an Example

Let's say that a seller has five of the same Lilliput Lane cottages for sale and starts a Dutch auction with the minimum bid for each one at $50. At the end of the auction, the following bidding has taken place:

User	Amount of bid	Date of bid	Time of bid
Lorenzo	$51	Aug 22	12:55:05
Bigfish	$52	Aug 22	12:55:06
Krugman	$55	Aug 22	12:56:27
MarkoPolo	$52	Aug 23	08:03:51
Franko33	$65	Aug 23	22:25:46
Smirka	$90	Aug 23	23:25:04
Hart2hart	$60	Aug 23	23:45:18
HeldOff	$55	Aug 24	04:03:55
Chowchow	$52	Aug 24	05:24:03
PeeWee	$100	Aug 24	05:24:25

This auction would result in the following sales:

Winner	Amount paid
Krugman	$55
Franko33	$55
Hart2hart	$55

Winner	Amount paid
Smirka	$55
PeeWee	$55

Since the low successful bid for the item was $55, each of the high bidders pays that amount for the item, even if their bids were higher.

Krugman and HeldOff tied for the low bid. Because Krugman bid before Held-Off, Krugman is one of the winners.

If the number of bids is less than the amount of items offered in the Dutch auction, then only those items sell to the winning bidders. The same logic applies as shown in the example.

If a bidder chooses to bid on more than one item, his or her offer must exceed the other bids in order to win the number of items included in the bid.

When you list a Dutch auction, the site determines the winners and the winning amount for you. You'll receive this information in e-mail after the auction ends.

English Auctions

I've only seen these available at a handful of online auction sites. With an English auction, you don't specify the number of days that you want your auction to run. The clock starts running when the first bid is entered.

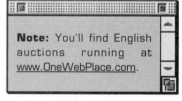

Note: You'll find English auctions running at www.OneWebPlace.com.

You'll list an English auction for a 3-day duration, just like any other item. If three days pass with no bids, the auction starts over for another three days. If after nine days no one has bid, the listing falls out of the system. English auctions are open-ended, meaning that the auction ends only if no one has bid for twenty-four hours.

Open-Ended Auctions

Some auction sites use open-ended auctions, where the bidding remains open as long as bids enter. For each bid placed within a specific block of time before closing, such as in the final hour, a certain amount of time is tacked onto the end of the auction. If the auction receives another bid within that time, the listing remains active for another stretch.

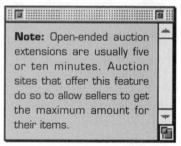

Note: Open-ended auction extensions are usually five or ten minutes. Auction sites that offer this feature do so to allow sellers to get the maximum amount for their items.

So Much for Sniping!

Open-ended auctions definitely hamper last-minute bidding. This can be advantageous for sellers because the price can keep increasing, but it might discourage bidders who will hence need to watch the auction "end" for an indefinite amount of time.

It's optional at some sites but at others, you can't disable it. If you don't like this practice, you may wish to use an online auction site that allows auctions to end at a specific time.

Private Auctions

This type of auction is gradually appearing at more and more online auction sites. Until recently, I thought sellers typically used them when they thought bidders might not want their identities known to others, such as when adult material is up for sale.

Private auctions have another use — sellers want to discourage better offers made to their bidders. Later in this chapter, you'll read more about bid siphoning and how it can take sales away from legitimate online auction sellers. Keeping bidder identities private prevents this type of auction site abuse.

At the end of the auction, only the buyer and seller receive notification, and the bidding history is not available to anyone.

How Do I Find Them?

If a private auction listing matches your search criteria, it will usually appear in the list of auctions returned by the site's search engine.

Restricted Access Auctions

Several auction sites restrict access to certain auctions. This category usually includes adult items and firearms. Any user with a valid credit card on file can access restricted listings. This is one way to ensure that the viewer is at least 18 years old.

It's certainly not my place to judge what you collect. If you list adult items or firearms on a site with restricted listings, only user ID's belonging to adults can view and bid on that listing. Be sure to enter the item in the appropriate category when you start the auction.

Where Are They?

If you want to see restricted auction listings, do a search for words you think would appear in such an auction. I'll forego listing examples. Some sites cancel auctions that contain such words; others don't. Take my word for it — if you're browsing the auction listings at work or with your kids around, stay away from restricted auctions.

First Bid Wins

Instead of waiting for an auction to close that may only draw one bid, some sites let you sell the item to the first bidder. The minimum price the seller sets is actually the price he or she expects for the item and doesn't care to see if the bidding goes any higher.

In this type of listing, the auction closes as soon as the first bid enters. The buyer and seller then handle the rest of the transaction off-line.

In Chapter 9, you'll read about Amazon.com auctions, where you can offer the first bidder a 10% discount on the final sale price if he or she remains high bidder when the auction closes. You'll read more about first bid privileges later in this chapter.

☞Features All Auction Sites Have

The sites want to make it easy for you. After all, if you like using the site you might become a regular. Moreover, your listings and bidding will draw other users. If the site charges listing fees and commission, they'll earn more. If advertisements fund the site, higher traffic means more visits to the sponsors' Web pages.

The more popular the site, the better for everyone involved. To encourage your participation, you'll find features designed to attract users:

- Site tutorials
- Search functions
- Choice of auction duration
- HTML enabled auction descriptions
- Bidding history
- E-mail notification
- Rules

The following paragraphs cover each feature in greater detail.

Tutorials

Some Internet auction site users have never read an HTML handbook, yet their auction descriptions are sharp and professional. This is due in part to a well-written site tutorial.

The auction site benefits from providing instructions for users. Sellers can learn to list auctions that include everything the buyer needs to know about the item. Since these listings attract bidders, the site earns more commission.

In addition, sellers who feel comfortable using the site will keep listing auctions, which means more fees paid to the site. Buyers bid confidently if the site seems well trafficked. Everyone benefits.

Where Do I Find It?

You'll usually find a link to the site tutorial right on the home page. You might see it called "How to use" or "How to sell and bid," or a curtly descriptive "Help."

You won't have to look hard for the tutorial on any of the major auction sites. The link is usually in clear view.

What Does It Cover?

Some auction sites have a series of links that take you to special pages where you can learn the basic site functions. Regardless of what the site labels it, all of these pages make up the tutorial. Here's what most Internet auction site tutorials contain:

For all users:
- Locating a person's e-mail address
- Checking user feedback
- Leaving feedback after a transaction completes
- Browsing the site
- Frequently Asked Questions (the FAQ)
- Using escrow services
- Preparing and adding photos to your auctions
- How to use the site's special features

For the buyer:
- Entering a bid
- Explanation of proxy bidding
- Last minute bidding hints
- Canceling a bid
- How and when to contact the seller

For the seller:
- Listing an auction
- Formatting the description with simple HTML code
- Modifying an active auction
- Canceling an auction
- The best time to list an item
- Setting a reserve price
- How and when to contact your high bidder

Some Internet auction site tutorials put others to shame. If you like everything about a site but find the tutorial lacking instructions, send e-mail to the site administrator. He or she may welcome your input, especially if it helps attract new users.

See Chapter 6 for information on how to contact the auction site administrator or the administrative staff.

Search Functions

Most Internet auction sites have powerful search tools that let you draw out specific auction listings.

You can perform precise searches in several ways:

- Key words in the title
- Certain words in the description
- Auction number
- Price range
- Seller's user ID
- Buyer's user ID
- Active auctions
- Closed auctions

You might search auctions a little differently at each site.

Most sites also let you search completed auctions with their "search completed auctions" option. It may also be "search finished auctions" or something similar. It does the same thing — it performs your search on auctions that have closed.

The Search Page

Here's how an Internet auction search page might appear:

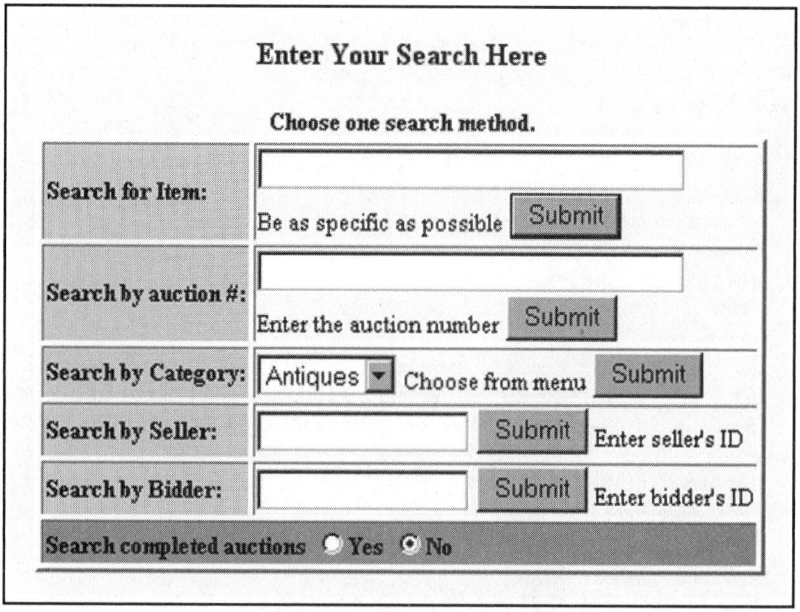

Enter Your Search Here

Choose one search method.

Search for Item:	[ ] Be as specific as possible [Submit]
Search by auction #:	[ ] Enter the auction number [Submit]
Search by Category:	Antiques ▾ Choose from menu [Submit]
Search by Seller:	[ ] [Submit] Enter seller's ID
Search by Bidder:	[ ] [Submit] Enter bidder's ID
Search completed auctions ○ Yes ◉ No	

Typical Auction Search Screen

When you browse a particular category, you'll see all of the listings in that category. The groupings, however, are usually very broad. If you're looking for a certain type of Czech vase and you search for the word "vase," you may see most listings in the art glass category. It would be quicker to narrow down your search by adding the word "Czech."

If you're following a particular seller's auctions, some sites let you enter the person's ID to view any current listings. If you know the number of the auction you want to view, you can go there directly by entering the number in the space provided.

Paring Down Your Search

If you want to limit your search results, enter the main search text in quotes and use a minus sign (-) in front of any terms that you don't want included. Here's an example:

"czech glass" –beads

This will return listings for Czech glass but ignore listings for Czech glass beads.

Search Results

Suppose you're seeking auctions for Bear Valley, a fictitious collectible line I created for use in this book. The search string "Bear Valley" might return a page of listings that looks something like this:

Your search returned the following results:

Item No.	Item Description	Bid Needed to Win	Bids	Auction Ends Central Time
2157110	Bear Valley FRIENDS FOREVER	$31.50	6	2/24/99 10:41:01 PM
2157115	Bear Valley "Bear With Me" **PIC**	$105.00	3	2/24/99 10:59:32 PM
2157127	Bear Valley Mother's Helper MIB!!	$35.00	4	2/24/99 11:27:25 PM
2157289	Bear Valley Rainbow Run NRFB	$20.00*	1	2/25/99 6:14:10 AM
2157343	Bear Valley CABIN FEVER **PIC**	$50.00	1	2/25/99 8:25:23 AM

*Reserve auction. Bid wins only if it meets or exceeds seller's reserve price.

Sample of Listings Returned by the Search

A typical page of listings shows the following information:

- Auction number
- Title of the auction
- Type of auction
- If the auction contains a picture
- If it's a reserve price auction
- Current bid price
- Starting and ending dates of the auction
- Time remaining in the auction

From your page of listings, you can click on the auctions one by one and decide which ones interest you.

Searching by User ID

Some online auction sites only allow you to track your own auction activity. At other sites, however, you can monitor other users as well.

This lets you conduct auction site "detective" work in situations like these:

- You can check for bidding patterns to determine if this person is an avid collector or possibly a shill.
- If you remember the user ID but not the name of the item involved, you can check that person's auction listings to refresh your memory.
- If a certain seller listed an item you want, you can go right to his or her auctions without wading through others.

The user ID search definitely helps save time.

And the Drawbacks...

Searches by user ID can be annoying if you're active in an online collector community. Everyone with access to the online auction site knows what you're bidding on, how much you've spent, and anything you're buying outside of your collecting interests. If this bothers you — and it might over time — you may want to consider using another user ID for auction activity you wish to keep private.

Note: If you have more than one user ID, they must never interact with each other in the same auction. This is shilling, which you'll read about further in this chapter.

On the Internet, you never know who's watching you.

Choice of Auction Duration

When listing an auction, the seller decides how long it will run. Common auction lengths are seven, five, or three days. Some auction sites run auctions for fourteen days or longer. Others last several hours or less.

I mention more about recommended auction durations for different types of collectibles in Chapter 4.

Note: Some auction sites now keep auctions open as long as there's active bidding.

HTML Enabled Descriptions

When you list an auction, you'll enter certain information, such as the title, item category, reserve price, and starting bid. The most involved part is the auction description. This is where you describe the features of the item to make it attractive to bidders.

Hypertext Markup Language, or HTML, is the coding language used to create pages on the World Wide Web. The auction-listing page appears as it does on the screen because of HTML code. When a page loads in someone's browser, he or she sees the result of all of the HTML code, including that which you enter in the description area.

Note: Some sites provide their own auction description formatting and thus don't allow HTML, as you'll read about in Part 2.

It's very handy to know at least the basics of HTML if you plan to do a lot of selling at Internet auction sites. The HTML tutorial in Appendix A contains all the HTML code you need to know to format auction descriptions that impress buyers and attract bids.

Images and Hyperlinks

Auction sites provide a space in the auction entry form to enter the URL to an image you're including with your listing. The photo usually appears in its own area under your description.

Using HTML tags, you can include pictures of the item and hyperlinks to other Web sites right in the description area of your auction. This is where you want the buyer focused.

Note: Never list an antique or collectible without a photo!

Bidding History

Some sites let you view the bidding history while the auction is active. Others only let you view the names of the bidders but not their bids. You can see the bid amounts once the auction closes.

Amazon.com lets you view the bidding history, with the amounts and user names, as soon as a bid meets or exceeds the reserve price. If the auction has no set reserve, you can view the history as soon as the second bid enters.

To get to the bidding history page, you'll usually find the link right on the auction listing. For an active auction, the bid amount usually doesn't appear, only the bidder's user ID.

Bidding History for Auction #435512957

Bidder	Bid Amount	Time of Bid
Sayshel	**	2/24/99 12:35:23 PM
Cobra430	**	2/24/99 11:34:08 AM
Moogie59	**	2/24/99 09:57:01 AM
FlyingVet	**	2/23/99 23:12:09 PM

**Bid amounts hidden until auction closes
or high bid meets reserve.**

Sample Bidding History for an Active Auction

If the auction is closed, the bid amounts appear. Some sites show them for active auctions once the high bid meets the reserve price. The figure below shows an example of bidding history for a closed auction.

Bidding History for Auction #435512957

Bidder	Bid Amount	Time of Bid
Sayshel	23.50	2/24/99 12:35:23 PM
Cobra430	22.00	2/24/99 11:34:08 AM
Moogie59	6.50	2/24/99 09:57:01 AM
FlyingVet	5.00	2/23/99 23:12:09 PM

Auction closed.

Sample Bidding History for a Closed Auction

Who Cares?

You will, for a number of reasons. You can track how often the same users bid. This gives you an idea of how eager someone is to get the piece and how likely they are to keep bidding down to the wire. Do you want to compete, and possibly overpay?

Here are a few more reasons:

- **Item interest** – Lots of bidding indicates enthusiasm. It's probably a great item.
- **Item value** – Many bids usually means the reserve and current prices are within the market value for the item.
- **Bogus bidding** – If the same aggressive bidder consistently bids on the person's other auctions, this could indicate shill bidding and you might want to avoid this seller.

Check the bidding history to familiarize yourself with how and when experienced participants place their bids. You can learn from their examples.

E-Mail Notification

All auction sites I've used communicate with you via e-mail. That makes sense, since e-mail is the main communication tool of the Internet. Here's when you'll hear from the auction site:

- When you register
- When you change any personal information on your account, like your e-mail address
- When you place a bid
- When you're outbid
- When an auction ends and you're the high bidder
- When the auction ends and the reserve wasn't met
- When you list an auction
- When someone bids on your auction
- When the high bidding meets your reserve price
- When the auction closes
- When you've violated the rules (inadvertently, of course!)

Not all sites contact you in all these cases. However, each message from the site helps you manage your auction activity.

Daily Auction Summary

Most sites send you a daily e-mail message summarizing your current site activity, those bids you've placed and items you've listed. You'll also hear from the site at billing time. They inform you if they billed your credit card, or oops, your charge wasn't approved and you need to send a check.

Rules

You can't live with them and you can't live without them. Actually, rules protect users. You don't want to participate at a poorly regulated site.

If you encounter a user with unethical practices that affect your transactions, the rules provide a basis for seeking recourse from the other person and assistance from the site administrators.

Site Restrictions

You can't do certain things at online auction sites. Most sites maintain strict policies to prevent users from conducting business that's unfair or annoying for other users. This includes:

- Bidding on your own auctions
- Simultaneously listing the item at another auction site
- Interaction between user IDs owned by the same person or organization
- Listing bogus auctions
- Charging the high bidder excessive fees
- Stating in the auction description that the item is illegal
- Requiring the winning bidder to purchase additional items
- Refusing to honor sales or bids
- Calling back a bid (some exceptions may apply)
- Canceling an auction (some exceptions here also)
- Absurdly high reserve prices
- Building lists of user IDs for sending spam
- Shills

Most online auction sites take no responsibility for the sale or delivery of merchandise. Though most have an e-mail address to which you can send site-violation reports, they rarely intervene if the buyer and seller don't agree.

Some online auction sites provide links to Internet third-party mediation services if anyone needs such resources to resolve an issue.

No Illegal Activity

This rule is universal to all Internet auction sites — don't break the law. Sellers must not list anything illegal to sell or possess. With antiques and collectibles, this might include certain types of ammunition, ivory, or animal skins from endangered species. It's illegal to sell stolen merchandise or controlled substances anywhere. Know the law!

Here are examples of illegal or restricted items:

- **Firearms** – Antique, sport, hunting, silencers, air guns
- **Unlawful weapons** – Brass knuckles, some types of mace dispensers
- **Pirated copies** – Music, software, videos
- **Law enforcement items** – Badges, uniforms, documents

- **Counterfeit items** – Collectibles, money, diplomas, IDs
- **Live animals** – Any type of living animals, including your kids
- **Endangered species and all human remains** – Skins, bones, tusks, and teeth
- **Illegal drugs or drug paraphernalia** – Controlled substances, hash pipes

When paying for an item, the buyer must remit valid and legitimate funds. Bidders must be persons of legal age who can enter binding agreements. Users cannot participate in any practice that would constitute swindle or fraud.

We all expect the seller to sell and the bidder to pay, but those are rules established by the site. Whether refusal to honor a high bid at an Internet auction site is illegal depends on individual state laws.

No Shills

When someone bids for the sole purpose of altering the high bid with no intent to purchase the item, this is shill bidding. It's illegal in all 50 states and many countries outside the U.S. You'll read more about shill bidding toward the end of this chapter.

☞Features Unique to Some Sites

As I mentioned in Chapter 1, up-and-coming Internet auction sites strive to offer features that set them apart from the rest. Other sites choose not to include certain features if the site powers-that-be don't find them effective or necessary.

To each his or her own. What you like about one site may not exist at another one. Have in mind the features you prefer when you explore an online auction site.

The following paragraphs include unique online auction features a few sites offer. You might find some of them useful.

Scheduled Start Time

This is a very handy tool, especially if you're limited in the amount of time you can spend at your computer.

At most sites, the auction clock starts the minute you hit that "enter auction" button. Suppose you want your auction to run for five days and end on a Friday evening. You'd normally need to be at your computer to start the auction the previous Sunday, at the exact time that you want the auction to close.

Auctions.com lets you schedule your auction to start at any time of day. You can enter the auction at noon and set it to start at 7 PM. That way you can enter a five-day auction at noon on Sunday that will end Friday night.

Can I Adjust the Starting Time Backward?

No, only forward. If it's 3 PM when you enter the auction and you schedule it to start at 10 AM, it will start at that time the next day.

First Bid Privileges

To entice people, some sites let you specify certain privileges for the first bidder on your auction. Amazon.com lets you offer that person 10% off the final bid amount if he or she eventually wins the auction.

Auctions.com has the ForSale program. The first person to "bid" secures the item at that price. You'll read more about straight-sales "auction" sites like NoBidding.com in Chapter 14.

Personal Paging

Here's the ultimate way to carry your online auctions with you wherever you go. Auction notifications can arrive on your personal pager, cellular phone, or a special paging unit.

The site will page you at certain times:

- When you're outbid
- When you've won an item
- When a bid enters on one of your listings
- When you've sold an item

The eBay paging feature is called "eBay a-go-go." You can purchase a paging unit right from them or enable the feature to interface with your own paging device.

I can't imagine being tethered to my Internet auctions that way, but the personal paging feature is certainly useful for those who earn a living online. It might also help if that special one-of-a-kind item *finally* comes up for auction and you don't want to miss out.

Mandatory Reserve Price

I've only seen this at one site. You must list a reserve price for every auction that's higher than the starting bid. As I mentioned before, setting a reserve with a lower minimum bid is a great way to entice potential buyers.

> **Note:** You may notice that some sites warn about reserve auctions being unpopular with bidders. Remember, though, that if the high bid doesn't meet the reserve price, no sale takes place and thus no commission for the site.

All-In-One Auction Managers

Auctions.com calls this feature "My Auctions.com" and Amazon.com offers a "Member Profile" page. They both serve the same purpose. You can track your auction activity on one Web page.

The following figure shows an example of my Amazon.com Member Profile page.

Amazon.com Customer Details Page

This is a convenient way to see all my auction activity at a glance. I can click on any link to keep track of what I'm doing at the site. I wish more auction sites offered this type of one-page tracking feature.

Transaction-Specific Feedback

Some sites won't allow you to enter feedback for another user unless you can link the comment to a successful auction. This prevents users from building up each other's comment file, which is possible with open feedback.

Some sites allow open feedback only for positive comments, but unless it's connected to a successful transaction, it doesn't count toward the person's final rating.

> **Note:** Open feedback means you can leave any type of feedback for any user. Auction sites that allow open feedback are getting more and more scarce, with good reason.

Other sites allow open feedback only for positive and neutral comments. At most auction sites, you can only enter negative feedback that relates to a particular auction. This prevents someone from tarnishing another user's report with multiple negative comments. This can irreparably damage his or her online auction reputation.

You'll read more about user feedback in Chapter 6.

☛Smart Bidding

When buying collectibles and antiques at an online auction site, it's important to know what you're bidding on and how much you want to pay for the item. This section contains tips to help you bid wisely. You'll find that most of the information you need to accomplish that is available right on the Internet.

You can make costly mistakes if you're not careful. You might also pay top dollar for less than perfect items. Smart bidders have a better chance of avoiding these situations.

Know What You Want

The endless supply of eBay handbooks on the market give essentially the same advice — know what you want before you bid. While this is sound advice for any online auction user, with collectibles and antiques it's a little more defined.

With collectibles, you want the piece in mint condition. The "minter" the better. Only if you can't find one in perfect condition should you settle for less.

With an antique, you want the piece to be authentic and in great shape. If someone restored parts of it, you want to know in advance.

Look for the best. Read the auction descriptions and contact the seller if you want clarification. Never settle for second best unless the item appeals to you so much that you'd sell your soul for it. Then be sure it's only a last resort. Remember that you'll have a much harder time reselling a collectible item that's not in mint condition. The same applies to antiques. Most folks don't want a smelly, wormy sofa no matter *whose* majesty once sat on it.

Study the Market

It's important to know the current secondary-market price for the item, or if it can still be purchased at retail. With antiques, be sure to have your value and price guides handy to know if the piece is a rare or common item.

Use a Search Engine to locate price guides. I include instructions for finding online secondary-market price guides in *Collector's Guide to Buying, Selling, and Trading on the Internet.* Many independent collectors compile secondary-market price lists for popular items by culling and averaging closing online auction bids. Take advantage of their research!

Know When to Stop Bidding

Try to resist the competitive end of online bidding. One common mistake is to go for the win instead of the purchase. If someone outbids you, keep telling yourself "yes I like it, but not for that much."

If you lose this one, so what! You just might get a better deal next time.

Avoid the Frenzy

You have the best chance of being the high bidder if you bid at the last minute. Many other users know this, though. For a popular auction, this often causes a bottleneck of bids as the auction clock winds down. Last-minute bidding frenzies drive the bidding up.

Speculation states that online auctions escalate the secondary-market prices for antiques and collectibles. From what I've seen, this is definitely possible.

People are competitive by nature and play to win. Remember, though, that this kind of game can be costly. The bids you

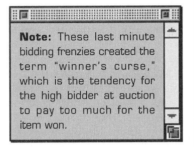

Note: These last minute bidding frenzies created the term "winner's curse," which is the tendency for the high bidder at auction to pay too much for the item won.

enter represent real money you have to pay if you end up high bidder. Try to use control. If the price goes up too high, let another bidder overpay.

Read the Description *Carefully*

When writing the auction description, an honest seller mentions any defects or imperfections. Potential bidders can accurately assess the item before bidding. Unfortunately, not everyone is as honest as we are.

Sneaky Sellers

To appear "honest," sneaky sellers will carefully word their way around the nicks and marks, hoping that bidders won't find out until it's too late. Sometimes the description is ambiguous because of clever wording.

For example, here's a sentence from a Fenton vase description:

There's an area under the base where the Fenton label appears.

Notice this doesn't actually say that the Fenton label is *there* — only that Fenton positions the label in that spot. This one just may be missing.

Most sites allow you to return items to the seller up to three days after they arrive, but some sneaky sellers hope you don't know that. They're hoping to dupe you into thinking you didn't read the fine print and now you're stuck.

When in doubt, send e-mail to the seller and ask questions. It also pays to know the seller's return policy. Some online auction sites have them as well.

Who Pays Shipping?

It's important to know this, especially if the item is large or very heavy. Shipping will be costly. You'll find that most sellers have the buyer pay shipping. If you want the seller to insure the item, he or she typically expects you to pay that cost also.

Very often, the seller doesn't know the actual shipping and insurance cost until the postal clerk weighs the item. Sometimes sellers must estimate the charges. Just be sure the estimation isn't outlandish.

You normally won't encounter sellers who ship COD. You can read my thoughts about shipping COD in Chapter 6.

Method of Payment

Some sellers don't accept personal checks; others do. You'll also encounter sellers who accept personal checks from bidders who have 25 or more positive feedbacks. If you've dealt with the seller before or you know the person, you can usually pay with a personal check. In any case, count on the seller holding your personal check until it clears the bank, usually ten business days.

If you plan to pay with a credit card, make sure before you bid that the seller accepts them. Many folks who list items are not set up to accept charge purchases.

Some sellers, on the other hand, will only accept credit cards. Read the description and if you have any questions, ask them in e-mail before you bid.

Check Out the Seller

I'm guessing that among the hundreds of thousands of users at major auction sites, you usually won't know every seller. Most online auction sites operate under the premise that all people are good and fair. It's great to assume honesty in everyone but unfortunately, it isn't always true. While successful Internet auctions definitely outnumber those that "go bad," you still need to protect yourself when dealing with people you don't know.

On the screen, you see just a user ID and the listing. In most cases that user ID is also hyperlink text to a page with the seller's e-mail and home page URL. That's a good place to start your hunt for information about the person. From there, you'll want to check other information sources at the site.

User Feedback

Before you bid, always view the seller's feedback, especially if you might bid a lot of money on an item. I usually read at least the fifty most current comments in a seller's feedback file to check out the person's transaction history.

If the seller has more than twenty feedbacks, you can usually bid with confidence, but definitely read them. A good seller has positive feedback with very few neutrals and no negatives. If the seller's feedback is over 200 and one or two negative comments appear, that's probably not cause for alarm.

If you see a negative comment, check the feedback of the person who entered it and read any follow-up comments. You may learn that the negative post was unwarranted. You'll read more about unfair negative feedback in Chapter 6.

> **Note:** Neutral feedback isn't always bad. Some sites enter a neutral feedback comment for you if you change your user ID or e-mail address. If a user cancels his or her site registration, feedback entered for anyone from that user ID may convert to neutral.

Check the transactions related to the feedback comments, if you can. The auction number usually appears by the comment as hyperlink text. Do they look like valid auctions?

Contact the Seller

If you're interested in bidding and the seller has less than ten feedback comments, send the person e-mail and ask about his or her online auction history. Most people are willing to cooperate if it means a potential sale.

Contacting the seller can add another benefit. It lets the seller know you're a buyer who's likely to pay fast for an item you want.

Here's an example of e-mail you can send a low-feedback seller to establish communication and put yourself at ease about bidding:

> Hi! I notice you have an antique fireplace bellows up for auction. I'd like to know more about the item. Are there any tears or holes in the leather? I'm also interested in how long you've been dealing antiques. Judging from your other auctions, you have some very nice pieces!

This lets the seller know you're interested in buying the item, so he or she will probably tell you anything you want to know. If you don't receive a reply or the answer leaves you with doubts about the person's honesty, don't bid.

If you see any negative comments for a low-feedback seller, you may want to avoid bidding on his or her auctions. Some folks get off to a bad start and later learn to use the site correctly. Let those sellers get experience with someone else.

Check References

In *Collector's Guide to Buying, Selling, and Trading on the Internet,* I advise you to ask a seller or trader for online references. At an auction site, it's a little easier because the person's feedback file is itself a handy list of references.

Some people leave positive feedback for marginal performance to avoid getting a negative comment in return. If you want to know how the seller operated in the past, send a short e-mail message to someone who left the person positive feedback. Here's an example:

> Hi! I'm thinking of bidding on an auction by eBay user "marble." I see you left him or her positive feedback last month. Do you still recommend marble as a seller?

He or she might tell you a little more if you make e-mail contact. A good report will put your mind at ease.

Other Auction Listings

Check other auctions the person has listed, both active and completed. Look at the photos. Are they similar in sharpness, intensity, hue, composition, and background? This would indicate that the person took his or her own photos and actually has the items. Watch out for borrowed images and bogus listings.

Also, beware of sellers listing many collectibles without packaging, boxes, or product enclosures. This could be stolen merchandise. Converse with the seller in e-mail to determine if he or she sounds like someone who will back online offerings.

Entering a Bid

Bidding is fun, as long as you remember that you must pay the amount you bid. There are two rules to remember when bidding online for antiques, collectibles, or anything else:

- Bid to buy, don't bid to win.
- Don't outbid your pocketbook

With that said, we can explore the specifics of online auction site bidding a little further.

The Bid-Entry Page

First things first. If the online auction site requires you to log in before you bid, you must enter your user ID and password on the log-in screen. You can then proceed to the auction page to bid.

The area of the page where you enter your bid will probably look similar to this:

Enter Your Bid for Auction #435512957 !!

Your User ID [   ]

Your Password [   ]

Current minimum bid: **$76.50**

Your maximum bid
(include decimal point, i.e. 51.50): [   ]

[Review and place your bid]

NOTICE: By bidding on this item, you implicitly agree to buy it if you are the high bidder when the auction closes. Shill bids are illegal. By placing a bid, you give this auction site permission to release your name, address and phone number to the seller of this item.

Sample Bid-Entry Page

Bid-entry forms may differ, depending on the auction site. You might not have to enter your user ID and password to bid if you previously logged in or the site knows you by a "cookie." If you encounter a site that does things differently, refer to its online instructions.

Maximum Bid

Your maximum bid is your self-imposed spending limit. You can usually raise this amount while the auction is active.

If you're the first bidder, the amount shown as your current bid will probably be lower than your maximum bid. The amount will match the minimum price set by the seller. The only exception is if your maximum bid meets the reserve price — then your current bid matches that, even if your maximum bid exceeds it.

Once you enter your bid, you can usually review it before confirming it with a mouse-click. This safeguards you in case you've made a grave error with the decimal point.

Your bid takes effect as soon as you confirm it. If you're the high bidder, the program returns a screen to notify you of this. Your user ID then appears on the auction page as the current high bidder.

If someone attempts to outbid you, the site proxy bids for you.

The Best Time to Bid

The best time to bid is right when you see the item. I recommend a low bid; you can increase it later. There are several advantages to bidding early:

- When you search for auctions you're currently bidding on, this item will come up even if someone outbid you. You'll remember that you're interested in the item.
- Your bid won't be as high if you bid early.
- In case of a tie, the first bidder wins.

Once you've made your first bid, don't bid again until there's an hour left on the auction. Otherwise, you and a contender might drive the price out of range. This will please the seller, but not your pocketbook.

Sniping

This is a coined term for placing a bid in the very last seconds before an auction closes. Snipers don't always win — they have to outbid the current high bidder.

The eBay site recommends that if you're the high bidder right before the auction ends, bid the absolute maximum you'd pay for the item and let proxy bidding do the rest. The only way a sniper can outbid you is if he or she wants to spend more for the item than you do.

If someone tries to snipe you out of the high bid, he or she must top your bid, but that amount is hidden — only you know it. Since this happens in the last couple of seconds, your contender probably won't have enough time to place another bid. Any successful attempt that doesn't outbid you will drive up your closing price.

How can you avoid having a sniper outbid you? You can't, unless you can snipe *better*.

Auctions to Avoid

Similar to precautions you take when trading items with people you don't know, you should watch for unsavory online auction activity.

Avoid bidding on anything absurd or outlandish, even if it's obviously a joke. You don't need to draw the attention of someone trying to sell the Eiffel Tower. Bidding on a joke auction may reveal to others that you're someone likely to place bogus bids. You definitely don't want this reputation. Remember that other users can track your bidding history.

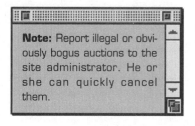

Note: Report illegal or obviously bogus auctions to the site administrator. He or she can quickly cancel them.

High Minimum Bid

Don't bid on items that start at the current market value unless the auction is about to close. Some sellers don't like to set reserve prices (and some sites don't allow them), so they start the bidding at the item's current value. These auctions typically don't draw many early bids.

Look for auctions that start with a low minimum and have a reserve price set near the current market value. Since you don't know the reserve price, check the secondary-price guides before you bid. This way you'll know when the bidding exceeds the item's actual value; then it's time to stop bidding.

Unclear Description

If the item description is unclear, the seller may not be familiar enough with the product to determine its quality and value.

Before you bid, read the description carefully. If something about it leaves you feeling uncertain about what you'd be bidding on, send e-mail to the seller and ask for a better description.

You can also research the item in a secondary-market guide or on a collector's Web site. Verify that the auction description specifies the appropriate collectible line. It may be a product knock-off.

As with any Internet transaction, if your instincts leave you feeling unsure or uncomfortable about the item for sale, don't bid. Given the amount of auction traffic on the Internet, a better opportunity is bound to come along.

Buyer Be Smart!

Here are a few more things to consider before bidding online:

- Can you get this item somewhere else, perhaps cheaper, off-line? There's no sense bidding on an item that's still available at retail from a dealer. It might bid over the retail price. Once you add shipping and insurance charges, you'll pay more than you should.
- Know the policies of the site. Who should you notify if there's a problem?
- The best payment for an item is made directly to the seller with a credit card. The credit card company will help you if there's a dispute.
- Save all of your e-mail correspondence, and include a note with your payment. You'll see examples of transmittal letters in Chapter 6 and e-mail templates in Appendix C.
- Pay the extra cost of insuring the item.
- Contact the auction site if you encounter any problems with a seller.
- Don't assume escrow services are part of the online auction process. Read Chapter 5 for more information about escrow before you consider using it.

I've participated in hundreds of online auctions with only a few mishaps. In every case, a person not familiar with how online auction sites operate caused the problem. Know how the site works before you participate. You may spare yourself some embarrassment.

I recommend that you bid and purchase an item or two from a site before you consider starting your own auction.

☛Be on the Lookout

According to eBay's Kevin Pursglove, eBay uses special software to detect suspicious bidding and boots out those who cheat. Many other sites, including most of the major ones, have similar ways to police users.

It's comforting to know the sites look out for us, but we can't rely on that alone. Carefully watch for suspicious activity and report it to the site immediately. Above all, don't participate in auctions where you see strange things going on.

This section describes some shady online auction site practices you need to watch for and avoid.

Bait and Switch

An occasional unscrupulous buyer might use your auction to unload a flawed or damaged item. It usually happens when selling manufactured collectibles because of their identical nature. Catie fell victim to one when she was still a new user at eBay.

"Following the suggestions of several experienced users," she said, "I scanned my item from several angles before sending it to the buyer. When his payment arrived, I carefully wrapped and packaged the item so it was secure during shipping." Catie then waited to hear from the buyer.

"A few days later," she said, "he said he wanted a refund." He told Catie the piece had a "rare flaw" that not many collectors knew about.

"When the item arrived," she continued, "I knew before I checked the scan that it wasn't the one I sent. The paint was different and I suspected it was fake." Luckily, Catie was able to have it verified. It was authentic, just not painted well.

"I refused to issue a refund and sent the piece back to the buyer. Then I found out from other collectors that he had a habit of buying imperfect items at a discount and using the bait and switch routine to get top quality pieces for his collection. I was not about to be taken advantage of that way!"

Catie now keeps photographic records of all items she sends to her online auction buyers. This is one safeguard against the occasional bait and switch artist. Many sellers inconspicuously mark pieces they sell at online auction. You'll read more about that in Chapter 6.

Odd Payment Requests

One seller I encountered in the collectible world would only accept Postal Money Orders. You can cash Postal Money Orders at any post office with a photo ID, but most financial institutions accept them too. It's very unusual for a seller to request payment with only one type of money order. Speculation said he was dodging the IRS.

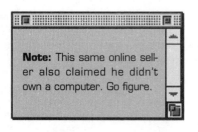

Note: This same online seller also claimed he didn't own a computer. Go figure.

Unfortunately, you may encounter other oddballs. One seller wants money sent via Western Union. Someone else asks you to send payment to one address and pick up your item at another. This is all very unusual. Unless this appeared in the auction description and you initially agreed to it, you should refuse to participate in any payment arrangement that wasn't stated in the auction listing.

If the seller specifies an unusual payment method in the description, this might be an auction to avoid unless you understand and agree with it. In that case, communicate with the seller before you bid.

Shills

When someone deliberately places bids to drive up the price of an item artificially, this is shill bidding. It's also called "bid padding" and it's illegal.

Bidding on your item (even from another account you own) for the sole purpose of inflating the final bid amount is forbidden, period.

Some sites let you have more than one user ID. If you have a business or club user ID, you may wish to keep that auction activity separate from your personal transactions. Avoid any interaction, such as bidding or feedback, between the accounts.

Bid Shielding

This practice was uncovered by eBay, and the story made local newspapers.

Bid shielding is where two people work in tandem. First, one enters a lowball bid. Then the other puts in an outrageously high bid that scares off all other bidders. At the last moment, the high bidder withdraws, leaving the lowball bidder the winner. Sellers must sacrifice the item for the low bid, as long as it met any reserve price.

If you see a high bid that's wildly out of line with the market, check the high bidder's record to see if he or she has withdrawn bids before.

Bid Siphoning

You may not know this but many thousands of non-participants watch auctions. You can access auction listings and check e-mail addresses at some sites without being a registered user.

Whether you like it or not, people know things about you by what you do on the Internet. You leave little clues wherever you interact in cyberspace. Once you bid on an item, you've let the world know that you're interested in buying it. You're fair game for online solicitation.

A sneaky seller might contact you and offer to sell you the same item for a lesser amount, off-line. This way he avoids paying listing fees and site commissions. This is bid siphoning, and he could lose his user ID for doing it — if he's even a registered user.

Note: Be sure to ask for and check online references for someone selling you something outside of the auction site!

Whether you want to accept the person's offer is up to you since the practice is legal. Keep in mind, though, that none of the protective features of the auction site will apply to the deal, and you can't leave transaction-related feedback for each other.

You need to be on the lookout for suspicious behavior, but most of your online auctions will be successful if you're prepared and know what to expect. Once you've made a few purchases and have some feedback to boast, you're ready to start your own auction.

Chapter 4 — Presenting Your Item

When a prospective buyer views a well-formatted auction description, he or she is more likely to bid on that one than on the same item listed with just plain text.

For successful online auctions, presentation is everything. Frills are cheap and easy on the Internet. If someone surfs the listings for just the right auction, the frills will impress, as long as they don't get in the way.

This chapter will help you have the best auction descriptions on the block, and offer hints and tips for putting the buyer at ease when he or she reads your description.

- Listing an item
- Creating a good auction title
- Writing your description
- Including a photograph
- Formatting your description
- How not to overdo it
- Starting your auction

Presentation is an important spoke in the online auction success wheel. If it were a toss-up between selling your item and losing potential bids, which would *you* choose?

☞How Do I List an Item?

Read the site's tutorial for the actual mechanics of listing an auction. Every site has a slightly different procedure. You'll see a sample auction-entry form at the end of this chapter. You should be familiar with that part of the site at any auction site you use. You'll find the process very simple when you're well prepared.

How does one "prepare" for listing an auction? Read on.

First, Have the Item

"Well of course I *have* the item. Why else would I list it?"

I'm glad you asked. I occasionally encounter sellers who list items they don't have. If the item sells online, they'll order

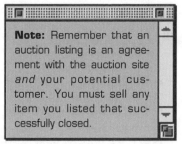

Note: Remember that an auction listing is an agreement with the auction site *and* your potential customer. You must sell any item you listed that successfully closed.

it after the auction closes. Those who practice this call it a *pre-sell*. Some sellers don't call it anything, and conveniently forget to mention in their auction descriptions that they don't actually have the item in hand.

But suppose the auction closes; payment arrives, and the seller then learns the item isn't available. He or she has to issue a refund to a disappointed buyer.

Pre-sells are risky business. You can end up with lots of justified negative feedback if you list items for auction that you can't ship right away. I definitely discourage pre-sells.

Buying and selling at online auctions is a great way to manage your collecting, but avoid taking unnecessary risks. Only list items in your immediate possession that you can ship to the high bidder once paid for.

When's the Best Time?

This is crucial. You probably won't get as much for that set of Limited Treasures Holiday Bears in June as you will in November when Santa's making his list and checking it twice. I hear he shops online now.

When it comes to timing your auction, keep a few things in mind to get the best results:

- **Is this item seasonal?** Those Charming Tails Squashville figurines are hot sellers in autumn but maybe not in the spring. Know any seasonal sales trends for the product line.
- **Will many folks want to watch this one?** If it's a hot collectible item or a special charity auction like the one I listed for Feed The Children, schedule it to end when people will be at their computers, like a holiday evening.
- **Is the Antique Road Show coming to town?** What a perfect time to list your antiques and classic collectibles!
- **What's happening this week?** List that autographed Sammy Sosa photo during his latest record-breaking run for seasonal homers. And those Salvino's Bammers Baseball Bears would probably sell well during the World Series. Use current events to your advantage.
- **How popular is the piece?** If it's that incredibly rare Harbour Lights Cape Hatteras lighthouse, it probably won't matter what time the auction closes, but you still want to be courteous to your audience. Make it easy for them to watch and participate by scheduling the auction to close at a reasonable time of day.

Any of these could mean the difference between an auction that doesn't make reserve and one that brings you a tidy sum.

Plan Your Closing Time

Auctions attract the most bidding just before the clock runs out. Make sure your auction ends in front of the largest possible audience.

Check other auctions for the same item. If there are many of them listed, plan for your auction to end the next day or later. Yours will bid higher without competition.

Since anyone in the world with Internet access can view your auction, it's impossible to pick the absolute drop-dead *best* time for it to close. But if you know that most of your potential bidders are in the United States, select a time when people are likely to be awake and at their computers. Not everyone can access the Internet at work, so don't assume that any time during business hours will suffice.

Shoot for the POAT (Prime Online Auction Time) hours. On weekends in the United States, this is any time between noon and 11:30 PM Eastern Standard Time (EST).

On weekdays, POAT is between 6 PM and 11:30 PM EST. If you plan your auction to close any time between these hours, you'll reach the largest possible audience no matter what U.S. time zone you're in. If you're at either end of the country, you may want to adjust the POAT hours accordingly. You can only pick one closing time for an auction, so plan it wisely.

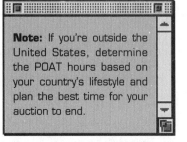

Note: If you're outside the United States, determine the POAT hours based on your country's lifestyle and plan the best time for your auction to end.

Remember — know which time zone runs the auction clock. Live Auction Online runs on Pacific Time, but Up4Sale uses Eastern Time. To determine the best auction-closing time, you'll need to do a few calculations, but it's worth it.

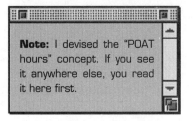

Note: I devised the "POAT hours" concept. If you see it anywhere else, you read it here first.

Everyone's schedule varies, but if you have your auction close during POAT hours, you'll get the most viewers and bids.

How Long Should My Auction Run?

This depends on what you're selling. If you plan to sell something wildly popular and thousands of other auctions feature the same item, choose a short duration, like three days.

A three-day auction quickly rises to the beginning of the listings where more potential bidders look. You'll attract impulse buyers. They bid on auctions about to close to avoid waiting days for the outcome.

Others bid on those listings to nudge the competition out at the last minute. A seven-day auction will be too far back on the list for these folks. There's a good chance nobody will even see the listing until the last day it's running.

However, if your item is rare or unique, you'll want it exposed to the bidding pool for a longer amount of time. In that case, a seven-day auction (or longer) is best.

Once you decide when and how long to run your auction, you can prepare the actual listing. It takes time at first but if you start at the beginning and follow through, you'll be a seasoned pro in no time.

☛The Auction Title

On the auction-entry form, the title is separate from the description area. A good auction title is important. It's the first thing potential bidders will see when your listing comes up in a search.

Keep a few things in mind when writing your auction title. It can make or break the success of your auction.

Space is an Issue

A typical title-entry line allows forty to forty-five characters. If you have my luck, that's usually about three characters less than you need. When you reach the character limit, you can't type any more.

Here's what the title-entry line might look like:

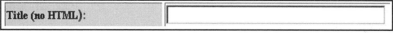

Title (no HTML):

Sample Title-Entry Area

If you've reached the character limit, your computer speakers will make that "you can't type anymore" sound if you attempt to hit any keys, and the cursor stops. You can only add another character if you remove one you already typed. That's when you might have to get creative.

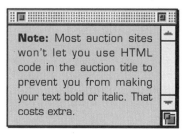

Note: Most auction sites won't let you use HTML code in the auction title to prevent you from making your text bold or italic. That costs extra.

Call It By Name!

Does your item have a name? If so, be sure you include it in the auction title. You definitely want to give your viewers the impression that you know what you're listing. You need to show them you're a confident, knowledge-able seller.

Here's a good auction title:

Hull Mirror Brown 6" Continental Mug

This tells the manufacturer (Hull), the style (Mirror), the item's color and size (Brown 6"), and what it is (Continental Mug).

If it's a collectible item from a current line, use the manufacturer and item name, as in this example:

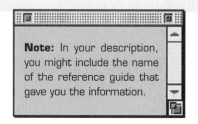

Note: In your description, you might include the name of the reference guide that gave you the information.

Precious Moments "Someone's Sleeping"

If your piece is a limited edition, include "LE" after the name. The more information you can squeeze into the title, the more likely people will read the description and bid.

Watch What You Abbreviate

Writing a good auction title is a lot like cramming a catchy phrase on a seven-character license plate. But on license plates, you can abbreviate. In your auction title, you don't want to abbreviate certain things, like the item name and style.

The reason is simple — search engines. If someone seeks a Royal Doulton Toby Jug, that's exactly what he or she will type into the search box. Search programs match characters, so this particular title won't list with the results:

> **Note:** Don't put the word "photo" in the auction title to indicate you've included one. This takes up too many characters needed for important information. Most sites put a little icon next to the listing if the seller entered the URL to an image. You'll read more about that further on.

R. Doulton TJ

Your Toby Jug may well be the best one on the auction block, but it's not going to get many bids if people don't know you have it listed. When in doubt, spell it out!

What *Can* I Shorten?

You can abbreviate anything that isn't the brand name or style of the item. It's fine to use an ampersand (&) in place of the word "and" to free up two characters as long as the word "and" spelled out is not part of the item name. Most search engines will look for the word as well as the character, but not always.

> **Note:** Avoid using special characters like an asterisk (*), tilde (~), or quotation marks in your auction title. Some of them interfere with searches.

Abbreviate descriptive phrases like MIP (mint in package), LE (limited edition), or any others that appear in the glossary at the end of this book.

☞Writing Your Description

The item description is the most important part of your auction. It can mean the difference between getting a lot for the piece, and not selling it at all. This is why I devote two appendices at the end of this book to help you format auction descriptions that look great and attract bids.

How they look isn't the only thing that's important, however. They must read well and contain enough information to inform, educate, and entice people into bidding on the item. Isn't that why you're listing it for sale?

Many people are still wary of sending a payment to someone they don't know. A well-worded and thorough description ensures their confidence in you. If you obviously know a lot about the piece, you'll come across as someone who appreciates and respects it. Collectors like to purchase items from people who know the product line.

Here's an example. Which of these descriptions appeals to you more? They describe the same piece:

Description 1:

I have no idea who made this thing is but it's a glass vase and it's a real pretty purple color. There's flowers on it. It's not very tall but bigger than other ones I have. It's OK. You might like it.

Description 2:

You're bidding on a very unusual piece of Mary Gregory art. Amethyst is not a common color among Mary Gregory items. This is an epergne type vase with a small tray above the base. The top, the center, and the stand have brass rimming. Fancy decoration adorns the tray and each side of the vase. One side has typical Mary Gregory trademark designs and the other three sides have flowers and leaves. The piece stands approximately 6¼" tall and the tray measures 3¾" square. The vase is in excellent condition with no chips or cracks. Lucky high bidder pays shipping and insurance. Seller prefers payment with a money order; otherwise, item will ship after personal check clears. If you have questions, please e-mail the seller.

Even if both included the same photograph, the seller in Description 2 knows the history and particulars of the piece. I can tell she did her homework and I trust her judgment because of the way she describes the item.

Description 1 left me wondering if the seller thought the item was a hideous eyesore and wanted someone to take it away — quickly. In that case, I sure don't want it!

We'll talk about formatting your auction description in HTML later. Meanwhile, give a lot of thought to how you write it. You need to include some important information.

Give Us the Facts

Know what you're selling. List an antique only when you can offer some information about it. Mention its era, the manufacturer or crafter, and the geographical region it comes from. Collector Books publishes many reference guides with descriptive information about antiques and classic collectibles. If you name a book title and page number where a prospective buyer can get more information, that's even better.

Watch Your Spelling!

If you want the respect of your potential buyers, call the item by its proper name and spell it correctly. In Chapter 2, I advise you to use care with your spelling and grammar. This is crucial when you list an auction, *especially* in the title.

Spelling an item or company name wrong can rub some nerves raw. Stay in good graces with your potential buyers and get the name right.

What's So Great About It?

Tell people why they should bid on your item. If it's a great item — and you wouldn't sell it otherwise — transfer plenty of information about it to your potential buyers. Entice them!

Include phrases like this, as they apply to what you're listing:

- Very limited edition. You don't see many of these for sale.
- Weathered nicks and dents add to its beauty, and attest that a hard-working Colonial family once used it.
- Here's a great item for someone seeking a true rarity.
- Bid with confidence on this handcrafted gem.
- These antique thimbles have prestige. Picture Betsy Ross wearing one as she sewed our first U.S. flag.

With persuasion like that, how can they resist bidding on your auction?

Remember Those Adjectives

Convince your buyers they can't live without this venerated masterpiece, and word it up a bit. If it's yellow, say it's a "rich, buttery" yellow. If the item's in mint condition, say it's "museum" or "collector" quality. If the piece shows its age, the wear and tear "adds character." It's easy once you get the hang of it.

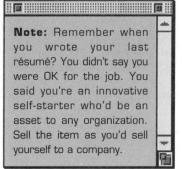

Note: Remember when you wrote your last résumé? You didn't say you were OK for the job. You said you're an innovative self-starter who'd be an asset to any organization. Sell the item as you'd sell yourself to a company.

Promise Me Something

Tell the buyers everything wonderful about both you and the item. Make them feel good about bidding. The possibilities are endless, as long as you're honest:

- Never used — still in original packing
- Museum quality
- Photo doesn't do it justice (although *yours* better)
- Taken out of box only to inspect
- One adult, non-smoking owner

- Modest reserve is below current market value
- Item still has that new "sheen"
- A lovely addition to your Little Gem Bears collection
- Will blend with any decor
- No chips, cracks, crazing, or other flaws
- Present owner is an antique chamber pot specialist

Obviously not all of these statements apply to every item you list. You'll know which ones do and I'm sure you can add a few "teasers" of your own. Don't leave this part out! Many people look for it.

Be Honest!

Sure, first I tell you to word it up a bit, and then I say "be honest."

There's a difference between eccentric, enthusiastic item descriptions and blatant lies. If you claim an item's in mint condition when it's actually flawed, that's a lie and the buyer has a right to be upset when a less-than-perfect product arrives on his or her doorstep. If the flaw is noticeable, like a huge chip out of a glass rim, your deception appears intentional and you may find yourself with some very damaging negative feedback.

Be truthful about what you're selling. People are apprehensive enough about buying things on the Internet sight-unseen. Don't make it worse. Most auction sites take complaints about false item descriptions very seriously. You could lose your user ID.

Your Expectations as the Seller

Just as your buyers have certain expectations of you, you'll want them to cooperate too. To help this along, include details in your auction description that prepare both you and the high bidder for the upcoming transaction.

Terms of Sale

Be clear about how you expect payment. If you mention this now, you'll have less chance of trouble later.

Your terms of sale should include:

- Who pays for shipping and insurance
- How soon you expect payment
- Payment method you prefer
- Are you willing to use an escrow service?
- Length of time you hold personal checks to clear the bank
- Expectations of the buyer
- What's your return policy?

It's a lot better to state this clearly in the auction description than to have disputes about it when the auction closes. I know of one case where a high bidder demanded that the seller use an escrow service, but the seller refused. She had over 600 positive feedbacks and accepted credit card purchases, which offer fraud protection.

Escrow clearly wasn't necessary. The discord erupted into an online flame war that spanned several collector bulletin boards. Each left the other negative feedback at the auction site. The seller had the site administrator block bids from that buyer on her future auctions.

To avoid this, the seller could have stated in her description that she doesn't use escrow services. The buyer should have asked about using escrow in e-mail before she bid.

> **Note:** You'll read more about escrow services in Chapter 5.

Disclaimers

Collector communities quickly blackball people with dishonest practices, usually with good reason. Watch out for your own interests. You have the right to protect yourself. Some sites let you cancel or refuse bids from anyone with a bad transaction record.

In the text of your auction description, discourage users with excessive negative or hidden feedback from bidding. Let them mend their ways at someone else's auction.

With a few standard disclaimers, you can protect yourself from a potentially bad situation. I use phrases like this in my auction descriptions:

> **Note:** You may be able to refuse bids from anyone you had problems with in the past. Contact the auction site administrator to arrange this. Be prepared to provide auction numbers where you had problems with the person so the site can verify your request.

- Seller reserves the right not to sell to anyone with excessive or recent negative feedback.
- Payment is due within ten days of auction close.
- Personal checks accepted if you have 25 or more positive feedbacks.
- Seller will not honor requests to end the auction early.
- Any items not paid for within ten days of close of auction will be re-listed.
- Seller prefers not to work through an escrow service. Excellent feedback record should suffice.

If you make your terms of sale known in advance, you'll have fewer problems later.

It's How You Say It

Be friendly. Try to come across as someone easy to work with. You don't want to put people off or make them afraid of you, or they won't bid on your auctions. Combine a good, personable style of writing with a touch of humor to put your buyers at ease. Then combine all the important information into a few easy to read paragraphs.

This sample title and auction description touches on all the right stuff:

Title:
Bear Valley "Gimme Some Love" MIB

Description:
Here's a unique item from the creator of the Bear Valley line. Rita Brodsky, the artistic designer for Bear Valley Unlimited, created "Gimme Some Love" solely for her daughter's use in her books about Collecting on the Internet. Now you can own it!

A Very Handsome Bear

This one-of-a-kind chocolate brown bear is soft and fuzzy from his head to his hand-stitched feet. He proudly sports a gold bow around his neck. What a perfect addition to your teddy bear gallery!

Item has had one adult non-smoking owner and will ship in its original shoebox. No rips, teeth marks, or other defects. Modest reserve to protect seller from site malfunction. You're bidding on the exact item shown in this photo.

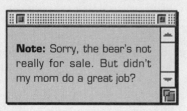

Note: Sorry, the bear's not really for sale. But didn't my mom do a great job?

Buyer pays shipping and insurance, seller reserves the right not to sell to anyone with excessive negative feedback. I do leave positive feedback for all successful transactions. Payment with money order. Personal checks accepted if you have a 25 or higher positive feedback rating. Check out my other auctions to save on shipping. Have fun bidding!

Now that you know what to include in the description, you can prepare to add a photograph. The better the listing looks, the more confidence your sellers will have in your ability to deliver quality merchandise.

☞Including a Photograph

If you're selling brand new, still-in-the-box computer equipment, you can probably get away without including a picture in your auction. A stock or catalog number might suffice rather than a photo of the outside of the packing carton.

Antiques and collectibles are much different. They draw interest from an eclectic and artistic standpoint. Collectors and dealers want to see them.

Auctions with photos close higher than listings with just a text description. *Always* include a photo with your auction. Even if you're selling the most common collectible in the line — the trademark edition everyone knows by heart — a well-composed photo will help sell it.

Photos lend an aura of authenticity to your auction because the buyer can actually see what he or she is bidding on. In addition, it's proof that you actually have the item. Remember — people will wonder about that.

Note: Always include a photograph of the *actual* item you're selling, not a picture you borrowed from a Web site or a scan from a catalog page. No two antiques are alike, and your buyer wants to see the exact item. It's especially important with collectibles because there are occasional color and style variations. The item's condition will interest potential buyers, too.

Image Files

Your photo must be in digital format before you can use it in your auction. The best file format for photographs is something called JPEG (pronounced "jay-peg"). JPEG stands for Joint Photographic Experts Group, the people who designed the file format. A JPEG file has the extension "jpeg" or "jpg," as in cobra.jpg.

Another common image format is GIF (pronounced "jiff"). GIF stands for Graphic Interchange Format. CompuServe developed it to establish a standard. Photographs can be GIF files but they aren't as clear as JPEG files because the manner of compression for the image is different. GIF files, on the other hand, are far better for non-photographic images such as arrows, drawings, animated icons, and those little "We Accept VISA" images. A GIF file has the three-letter extension "gif," as in arrow.gif.

Though other image formats exist, JPEG and GIF are the two most commonly used on the Web.

Going Digital

There are several ways to produce an image in a digital format:

• Use a digital camera.
• Scan a regular photograph.
• Place the item directly on the scanner and capture its image.

Once you have your digital image file, you'll need to put it on the Web. We'll cover that further on in this chapter.

Electronic Photo Services

If you don't have a digital camera and don't plan to buy one, an electronic photo service will let you send your film in to have the images transferred to digital format. One such service is PhotoNet (www.photonet.com). You can also try Kodak PhotoNet Online at www.kodak.com.

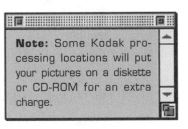

Note: Some Kodak processing locations will put your pictures on a diskette or CD-ROM for an extra charge.

When your film is developed, a technician uploads the images to an Internet site you can call up in your browser with a special password. From there you can save them to your hard drive and finish the images. Then you can upload them to your own Web site for use in your auction descriptions.

Smile for the Camera!

Using a digital camera gets the quickest and best results. In Chapter 2, I mention different types of digital cameras available. If you plan to use online auction sites to manage your collection, a digital camera is a wise investment. It eventually pays for itself if you list many items for auction. You'll use it a lot if you decide to present your collectibles on a Web page, too.

Suppose you just picked up the newest items in the collectible line or you discover a valuable antique at a yard sale. You'll want to get an image up on the Internet to share it with your friends on a Web page or in a bulletin board post. Digital cameras are the greatest invention since ... well, since the ones that use film.

Setting Up Shop

Designate a well-lighted area for taking photos. You don't need anything elaborate. Find some cloth to use as a background drape. I use a white tee shirt, or a variety of silk blouses that no longer fit. I'm sure you can find something similar lying around, especially if your kids grow as fast as mine do.

My "studio" consists of a secretary's document stand with a clip, an old dresser top, and a desk lamp with a bright bulb.

Choose a background with some contrast to the item's color. White or black usually works well. Clip the cloth to the front of your stand and drape it down over the front of the flat surface; then set the item directly on the drape. This produces a seamless background.

Here's where my auction photographs are born. Don't laugh — it works! And it's all you need.

My Very Functional Photo Studio

Your photo will look great. Once you shoot it you can finish it, or "prime it for auction." Re-size and crop the image and add a color border. Don't forget to copyright your photos. It's very easy — read on!

Cropping and Re-sizing the Photo

Most digital cameras produce images that are too large for auction description pages. The buyer doesn't need a poster-sized view of your Blue Goddess Gene Doll. Re-size the image so it takes up no more than one-third the width of your browser.

Of course, this will vary, since everyone has his or her browser set to a different size. However, one-third is a good reference point assuming you have your browser set on full screen. Unless it's necessary — if the item is huge, for example — less is more when it comes to the image. Just be sure the picture adequately portrays the item.

For photo finishing, I get the best results with Paint Shop Pro 5.0. In Chapter 2 under "A Graphics Program," I explain how you can download a copy of the program from www.winfiles.com that you can try free for 30 days.

Once the image is on my hard drive, I can crop and re-size it with minimal distortion in a few easy steps:

1. From the Paint Shop Pro File menu, select "Open."
2. Browse to the image file and double-click on it. The image will open in the Paint Shop Pro window.
3. From the tool bar on the left side of the screen, click on the crop tool. It looks like this:
4. Click inside the image and drag your cursor to draw a box around the item. Position the outline around the image buy pulling the little squares with your mouse to crop out any unnecessary background.
5. Place your mouse cursor inside the crop area and double-click. Only the area you selected will remain. If you need to start over, go to the top of the Paint Shop Pro window and press the Undo button, which looks like this:
6. Once you've cropped the image, check the size. Most images taken with a digital camera should be reduced by at least 50% to be practical for publication on the Web. To reduce the image, select "Resize" from the Image menu.
7. Select "Percentage of Original" and enter "50" in height and width.
8. Click on OK. Your image is now 50% smaller.
9. To save the file, go to the top of the Paint Shop Pro window and click on the Save button, which looks like this:
10. Now add a border.

Adding a Border

You don't need to have your picture surrounded by color but it adds so much and is easy to do, so you might as well. Just be sure the border color enhances your photo and goes with the color scheme you'll use when you format your item description.

Here's how to add a border in Paint Shop Pro 5.0:

Note: You can also download a helpful image re-sizing utility at www.davecentral.com/img-comp.html. DaveCentral Shareware has many interesting shareware programs you can explore.

1. Open the image file in the Paint Shop Pro window.
2. At the far right side of the Paint Shop Pro window, you'll see a tool button that looks like this:

3. Click once on the lower square. A color chart will appear.
4. Click on the color you want for the image border by clicking in the colored square in the chart, and then click on "OK."
5. Select "Add Borders" from the Image menu at the top of the Paint Shop Pro window. The "Add borders" dialog box appears.
6. If you want the border to be the same width an all sides, select "Symmetric." Then select a thickness in pixels for the border. If you don't want it to be symmetric, you can choose how thick you want the top, bottom, and sides by entering the appropriate number in the spaces provided.
7. Click on "OK." Your image now has a border.
8. Click on the Save button menu at the top of the Paint Shop Pro window. If you want an additional border, repeat the process and use a different color.

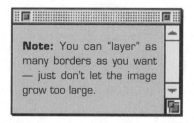

Note: You can "layer" as many borders as you want — just don't let the image grow too large.

Wasn't that easy? And your picture looks just great. You're almost ready to put it on the Web. But first, you'll want to be sure that nobody steals your work.

Copyright Your Photo

You may not care if someone reuses your photos, but they could easily fall into the wrong hands. With a swift right-click of his or her mouse button, a dishonest seller can steal your image and use it in a bogus auction. Since you did such a great job finishing up the photo, someone will eagerly bid and may end up a victim of auction fraud.

Also, another seller could use your own photo to compete with you. Don't let anyone steal your photos. Let each seller do his or her own auction preparation.

With a graphics program, insert copyright text where nobody can crop it out. Here's how you add text to a photograph in Paint Shop Pro 5.0:

1. Open the image file in the Paint Shop Pro window.
2. Go back to this tool button and click on the top square. That sets the text color.

3. You'll see the color box again. Select a color that shows up against your photograph but won't distract from the image. Light gray is usually subtle. That's a good color to use against a dark background. You may have to experiment. Click on "OK" once you've selected a text color.
4. From the tool bar on the left side of the screen, click on the text tool. It looks like this:

A

5. Position your mouse cursor inside the image, and left-click. This brings up the "Add Text" box.
6. At the top of the text box, you can select the font style, size, position (center, left, or right) and effects (underscore, etc.). Pick a size and style that's appropriate for your image.
7. At the bottom of the text box you'll see a field labeled "Enter text here." A standard copyright statement is the word "Copyright" and the copyright symbol (©) followed by the current year and your name. For example:

Copyright © 2000 Mindy Smith

8. Enter your copyright statement in the text area and click on "OK." The text will appear on your image.
9. Click on the Save button.
10. With your mouse cursor, position the text where it's readable and doesn't interfere with important details in your image. Make sure nobody can crop out the text and

Note: To get that copyright symbol, hold down the ALT key and type 0169 on the numeric keypad on the right side of your keyboard. Mac users, press option+g.

reuse the photo. Once you have the text where you want it, click the right mouse button and it locks in place. Here's an example:

Photograph with Copyright Information

As you can see, cropping out the text would cut our bear in half.

If you're satisfied with your finished picture, save it to a directory on your hard drive so you can retrieve it later when you upload your image to the Web. Just select "Save as" from the File menu.

Scanners

The price of scanners has dropped dramatically over the last few years.

Note: Remember — use the "Undo" button to reverse any action you perform on the image if you don't like the results. You can undo all commands in reverse order since you last saved the file.

Scanners that would have cost over $1,000 a few years ago now sell for $200. You might find them in cereal boxes before too long. Seriously, the price of scanners has dropped to the point where almost anyone can afford one. If you do enough selling at online auction sites, you'll want to consider buying a scanner.

There are two types of scanners. One is a specialized piece of equipment made to scan photographic slides. The second is the flatbed scanner, which is the most popular. Flatbed scanners have three types of interfaces.

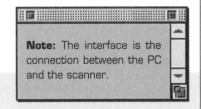

Note: The interface is the connection between the PC and the scanner.

- **Parallel port** – By far the slowest
- **Universal serial bus (USB)** – Moderate speed
- **Small computer system interface (SCSI)** – Definitely the fastest

Scanners that use the SCSI interface are fastest but also the most expensive. The USB and parallel port models are the least expensive.

If you plan to use your scanner to capture images for use on the Web, a good middle ground is a scanner that uses the USB interface. USB is the latest innovation in the computer world and many new devices will be able to use this interface. If you don't already own a scanner and are thinking of buying one, make sure

Note: I said least expensive, not cheapest. All three scanners will do a good job. The main difference is in how much time you want to wait for the scanner to complete its duties.

your PC has a USB port before you buy a USB scanner. Most new PCs have them. If yours doesn't, you have three options:

- Spend the extra money and buy a scanner that uses the SCSI interface. Most of these come with their own interface card. This is the fastest scanner and you'll probably love it.
- Buy an after-market USB interface card. You'll install this inside your PC just like an internal modem or any other peripheral card. The problem is that not all companies that make these cards keep up with the standards. I know of more than one person who bought a USB scanner and then had to buy a USB interface card. He later found that the card didn't work with his scanner. If you choose to go this route, be sure you have a money-back guarantee.
- Select a scanner that uses the parallel port, which is also the printer port. You'll disconnect your printer from the PC, connect the scanner cable to the parallel port, and then plug the printer cable into the rear of the scanner.

I use a Hewlett Packard 4100CSE USB scanner. Since it uses the USB port, we can use it on our laptops, any of our desktops, or we can take it to a friend's house and use it there. It is very lightweight, easy to use, and completely portable.

Scanning a Picture

The basic procedure to scan a photo is the same no matter what type of scanner you have. The biggest differences come in the software that controls the scanner. I kept the procedure as generic as possible so it works with just about any scanner on the market.

Here's how you'll scan a photo:

Note: If you have scanner problems, refer to the manuals that came with your scanner software. If you didn't receive any software manuals, refer to the Help function in your scanner software. As a last resort, pay a visit to the scanner manufacturer's Web site, if one exists. Hewlett Packard has a great Web site at www.hp.com.

1. Open the scanner cover and place the photo face down on the glass scanner bed. Most models have rulers running across the top and down one side. Position the photo so that one of its corners is at the corner of the two rulers, if your scanner has them.

2. Carefully lower the cover, trying not to move the photo.

3. Start the scanner software if you haven't already. Select "Scan" or "Start New Scan" from the appropriate menu or button. This starts the warm-up period of the scanner lamp. When it has warmed up, you'll see it scan the entire bed of the scanner. This is the preliminary scan. Some scanners will only scan whatever you put on the glass bed of the scanner.

4. Check the software settings. You'll want to use the best setting for color photos. This happens when you adjust the resolution. For photos you'll use on the Web, limit them to around 75 dots per inch (dpi). If you go any higher, the photo will be too large. If it takes too long to load, no one will want to see your auction.

5. Select the area you want to scan. Move the mouse cursor over the scanned image. If it turns into a crosshairs, or a plus sign, you're ready to continue. If not, look in the menus for an item such as "Select area to be scanned." When you have the crosshairs, move the cursor to the upper left area that you want scanned.

6. Hold the left mouse button down and drag a selection area around the part you want to save.

7. Once you've selected this, click on the "Scan" button, or look for a menu item that says "Final Scan."

The device will scan the area you selected and you'll see it on your monitor. To save the image, click on the "Save Scan" button or select that option from a menu item.

You'll see a dialog box where you can type a file name for the new image and select a directory in which to save the file. The scanner software usually lets you save the picture in several formats. Always use JPEG for photographs.

Once you've saved the file, you can open the photo in Paint Shop Pro and finish it.

Scanning the Item

Scanning the actual collectible is not very practical but it does work sometimes. The procedures are the same as for scanning a photo except you won't be able to close the cover on the scanner.

Since you want the image to look nice, you need to be careful how you scan the item. For example, if you're scanning an item with two or more pieces that fit together, put a rubber band or a piece of tape around the item to prevent the pieces from falling away from each other.

When you are ready to scan the item, open the cover to the scanner and gently place it on the glass, somewhere near the top. Carefully close the scanner cover. Since you don't want the picture to appear washed out by the light leaking in from the sides, place a towel or a blanket over the scanner.

Now follow the steps for scanning a photograph. You may have to experiment a few times before you get the results you want.

Putting the Picture on the Web

To allow the rest of the world to see your lovely photograph, you have to move it from your computer to a place where others can access it. It needs its own address on the World Wide Web. This address is the Uniform Resource Locator, or URL.

Once it has an address on the Web, you can link to it on other Web pages, such as Internet bulletin board posts or on your home page. You're also ready to use it in your auction.

Finding Your Image's URL

Suppose you're already using the image on a Web page but you don't remember the image's Web address. You need to know the URL of the image to use it in your auction description. Here's how you can find out what it is.

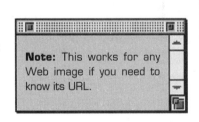

Note: This works for any Web image if you need to know its URL.

Internet Explorer and AOL users:

- Place your mouse cursor over the image and right-click on it. You'll see a menu.
- Select "Properties" from the menu.
- The Properties box appears. You'll see the Address (URL) of the image.
- Highlight the entire URL (including http).
- Right-click on the highlighted URL, select "Copy," and then paste it into Notepad or another word-processing program. Now you have the URL of the image.

Netscape users:
- Place your mouse cursor over the image and right-click. You'll see a menu.
- Select "Copy Image Location" from the menu, then close the menu box.
- Right-click inside Notepad or another word-processing program and then choose "Paste."
- The URL of your photo writes in the text file.

Now you know the image's unique address on the Web. If you don't have the image on the Web yet, the next section will help you get it there.

Hosting Your Image

When you put a picture on the Web to use temporarily, such as for an auction, this is *image hosting*. If you have a home page on the Web, you can use that area as your image host. Upload your picture to the directory in which you keep your Web page picture files, and make note of the directory path to the image. This will form the image's URL. For example:

http://www.angelfire.com/il/marble9/images/bear.jpg

This is the unique URL to an image on the Web.

What — No Home Page?

Free directory space is available all over the Internet. Most ISPs offer it to their users. Check with your ISP to find out how much Web space you have and how to access it.

In addition, many places on the Web offer free home pages and Web directories. There's a long list of them in *Collector's Guide to Buying, Selling, and Trading on the Internet* along with instructions on how to make your own Web page.

Here are some of my personal favorites:

Uniform Resource Locator	Site Name
www.angelfire.com	**Angelfire**
www.tripod.com	**Tripod**
www.geocities.com	**GeoCities**
www.homepage.com	**HomePage.com**

These sites have built-in, easy-to-use file-uploading capabilities. The figure on page 115 shows an example of how a file upload utility appears on the Web.

Click the button to browse your hard drive. When you find the image file, double click on it. Then click on "upload" and the file copies to your Web directory.

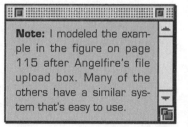

Note: I modeled the example in the figure on page 115 after Angelfire's file upload box. Many of the others have a similar system that's easy to use.

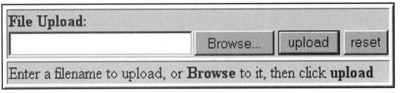

File Upload:

| | Browse... | upload | reset |

Enter a filename to upload, or **Browse** to it, then click **upload**

Sample File Uploading Screen

Angelfire lets you organize your directory by placing all of your uploaded .gif and .jpg files into a directory called "images." Other sites have a similar structure.

Here's what the URL to one of my image files on Angelfire looks like:

http://www.angelfire.com/il/marble9/images/bear.jpg

When you enter the image URL shown above in the address line of your browser, you'll see the picture on your screen because I uploaded it to Angelfire. I can use the image on my Angelfire Web pages and in my auction descriptions. Appendix A shows you how that's done.

Most home page sites work the same way.

Note: Free home page sites prefer that you use uploaded images on your Web pages, not just for your auctions. Build a Web page with pictures of collectible items you've bought and sold at auction. Add some descriptive information and post the URL on a collectibles online bulletin board. Your collecting friends will love the information resource!

The Birth of Routine

Sure, there are a few steps involved in getting a picture up on the Web, but you'll move faster each time. I can have a photo ready for my auction in less than five minutes. Here's the whole process in fast-forward:

1. Position the background drape.
2. Set the item on it.
3. Turn on the lamp.
4. Slide a blank diskette into the camera.
5. Turn the camera on.
6. Take the lens cap off (I have trouble here sometimes).
7. Frame the shot in the viewfinder.
8. Snap! Click! Shoot it from a few different angles.
9. Remove the diskette and insert it into the computer.
10. Bring up Paint Shop Pro.
11. Open the first image.
12. Save the image in my "auctionpix" directory on the computer.

13. Crop, resize, and add borders to suit.
14. Add my copyright information: Copyright © 2000 Nancy Hix
15. Save the image.
16. Repeat Steps 11 through 15 for any other images on the diskette.
17. Log into Angelfire.
18. Upload the images.
19. I'm done.

Wasn't that easy? You can prepare several pictures at a time this way so they're ready to use later.

Image Hosts on the Web

An image host stores your picture and makes it accessible to anyone using the Internet.

A hosting site usually charges a small fee to host your image file. You might want to check out a few of these. Most of them specialize in hosting auction images.

Uniform Resource Locator	Site Name
www.photopoint.com	Photo Point
www.imagesrus.net	Images "R" Us
www.picturebay.com	Picturebay Image Hosting
www.auctionwatch.com	Image Hosting at AuctionWatch
www.imagehosting.com	ImageHosting.com
www.weppiheka.com	WeppiHeka
www.pixbay.com	PixBay
www.imagehost.com	ImageHost
www.pongo.com	Pongo
www.traderjax.com	TraderJax
www.myitem.com	MyItem
www.pixhost.com	PixHost
www.bay-town.com	Bay-Town Auction Tools
www.webdigger.com	Web Digger Auction Image Hosting

There are many more out there. Chapter 14 includes information about Web sites that offer image hosting and many other online auction programs.

Auction Sites with Image Hosting

Many auction sites, like Up4Sale.com, offer an image-uploading feature. You can upload an image from your hard drive and the site hosts it for you, either as an auction service included in the listing fee or for an additional charge. Check your favorite auction site to see if it includes this function.

☞Formatting Your Description

This is where you'll need to refer to Appendix A and Appendix B at the end of this book. Everything you need to know about formatting your description appears there.

Appendix A: HTML Tutorial — Provides some basic HTML tags that allow you change the color, font, and size of your descriptive text.

Appendix B: Auction Description Templates — Includes examples of auction descriptions coded in simple HTML.

If you like one of the templates I included, type it into Notepad and customize it with your item's information.

Decide on a Style

Design your auction description in a way that enhances the item you're selling. Many folks who list items for auction eventually develop their own trademark style of presentation.

This book includes examples of two different auction description styles, table and handbill. You'll see more examples of each style in Appendix B.

Table

A table style auction description includes all of the information, including the photo, inside a table.

Table capabilities in HTML allow endless types of formatting on the Web. For Web pages, tables add color and style to an otherwise dull text layout. For your auction descriptions, tables are perfect.

Here's what you can do with them:

- Use different color backgrounds in table cells.
- Present text in columns.
- Set chiseled borders around blocks of text.
- Add heading text that spans columns.
- Insert images in table cells that span rows.
- Align images and text inside table cells.

The top figure on the next page shows an example of a table-style auction description.

Handbill

The handbill style looks a lot like its name, a handbill or an advertising flyer. The information appears as it would on a leaflet or newspaper ad. You can do a lot with this type of description, since it's less restrictive than a table. You won't be able to change the background color to enhance the appearance of the description, but with a clever layout that won't be necessary.

The bottom figure on the next page is an example of a handbill-style auction description.

Bear Valley "Gimme Some Love" Exclusive!

Here's a unique item from the creator of the Bear Valley line. Rita Brodsky, the artistic designer for Bear Valley Unlimited, created "Gimme Some Love" solely for her daughter's use in her books about Collecting on the Internet. Now you can own it!

This one-of-a-kind chocolate brown bear is soft and fuzzy from his head to his hand-stitched feet. He proudly sports a gold bow around his neck. What a perfect addition to your teddy bear gallery!

Item will ship in its original shoebox. One adult non-smoking owner. No rips, teeth marks, or other defects. Modest reserve to protect seller from site malfunction. You're bidding on the exact item shown in this photo.

North American bids only please. Buyer pays shipping and insurance, seller reserves the right not to sell to anyone with excessive negative feedback. I do leave positive feedback for all successful transactions. Payment with money order. **Personal checks accepted if you have a 25 or higher positive feedback rating.** Check out my _other auctions_ to save on shipping. Have fun bidding!

Sample Table-Style Auction Description

Bear Valley "Gimme Some Love" Exclusive!

Here's a unique item from the creator of the Bear Valley line. Rita Brodsky, the artistic designer for Bear Valley Unlimited, created "Gimme Some Love" solely for her daughter's use in her books about Collecting on the Internet. Now you can own it!

This one-of-a-kind chocolate brown bear is soft and fuzzy from his head to his hand-stitched feet. He proudly sports a gold bow around his neck. What a perfect addition to your teddy bear gallery!

Item will ship in its original shoebox. One adult non-smoking owner. No rips, teeth marks, or other defects. Modest reserve to protect seller from site malfunction. You're bidding on the exact item shown in this photo.

North American bids only please. Buyer pays shipping and insurance, seller reserves the right not to sell to anyone with excessive negative feedback. I do leave positive feedback for all successful transactions. Payment with money order. **Personal checks accepted if you have a 25 or higher positive feedback rating.** Check out my _other auctions_ to save on shipping. Have fun bidding!

Sample Handbill-Style Auction Description

The border that appears around the handbill example will not appear on your screen. Each format has many advantages, and with practice, you might develop something completely different to suit your own style.

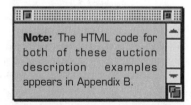

Note: The HTML code for both of these auction description examples appears in Appendix B.

Check Your Results

You can view the results of your auction description in your browser as you create it. Just save the file with an .html or .htm extension. Here's how you open the file in your browser:

With Internet Explorer

1. From the "File" menu on your browser window tool bar, select "Open."
2. Browse to the .html or .htm file you saved on your hard drive.
3. Double click on the file name and it appears in the pop-up window on your browser screen.
4. Click on "OK."
5. The formatted file will appear in your browser.

With Netscape

1. From the "File" menu on your browser window tool bar, select "Open Page."
2. Where you see "Open location or file in:" select Navigator.
3. Click on "Choose File."
4. Browse to the .html or .htm file you saved on your hard drive.
5. Double click on the file name, and it will appear in the open page window on your browser screen.
6. Click on "Open."
7. The formatted file will appear in your browser.

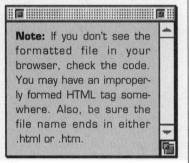

Note: If you don't see the formatted file in your browser, check the code. You may have an improperly formed HTML tag somewhere. Also, be sure the file name ends in either .html or .htm.

The Auction Description Field

This figure demonstrates the area, or "field," on the auction entry form where you'll enter your HTML auction description code.

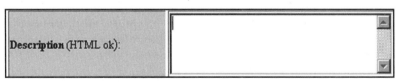

Description (HTML ok):

Sample Auction Description Text Entry Area

The small vertical line you see in the description area is a blinking cursor that tells you where your typing must begin. The text-entry area behaves like any word processor. You can move the cursor to any existing text. Just position your mouse arrow in another part of the entry area where you have text, and left-click. You can then enter more text from where you placed the cursor.

You can also replace text by highlighting it with your mouse and typing the new text right over it.

Although the text-entry area looks small, it expands to fit whatever you type there. The field doesn't get any bigger, but once your text exceeds it, a scroll bar appears at the right side. If you drag the scroll bar up and down with your mouse, you can view all your text.

Here's an example of the text entry form with a scroll bar:

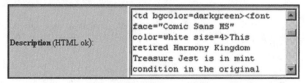

Sample Auction Description Entry with Scrolling Text

Up4Sale is the only online auction site I know of that limits you to 400 characters and doesn't allow HTML in the auction description. They have their own formatting method that looks professional once the listing activates. I didn't encounter any character limits in the auction description area at any other site I researched. Maybe the text for my descriptions hasn't exceeded the limits of any site.

When you're formatting the description, choose colors, fonts, and images that go well with the photograph you include. This adds comfort and distinction to your listing that the potential bidder may not readily notice – but will sense.

Show Me Some Style

No matter how nicely you worded your description, it won't sell your item if nobody can read it, or if nobody wants to read it. With all the auctions to choose from, you could easily deter a buyer if he or she has to work hard to read important details about your item.

You need to use care in certain areas.

Don't Use ALL UPPER CASE!

Please PLEASE don't enter your auction description in all upper case. If you type that way, break the habit now. Don't send e-mail that way, don't post on bulletin boards that way, don't type in chat rooms that way, and whatever you do, don't write your auction descriptions that way.

Sure, it's easier if you're a novice typist, but it's very hard to read. See for yourself which block of text reads better:

Example 1:

BUYER PAYS POSTAGE AND INSURANCE, AND SELLER RESERVES THE RIGHT NOT TO SELL TO ANYONE WITH EXCESSIVE NEGATIVE FEEDBACK. PAYMENT WITH MONEY ORDER SHIPS RIGHT AWAY. PAYMENT WITH PERSONAL CHECK SHIPS AFTER 10 BUSINESS DAYS.

Example 2:

> Buyer pays postage and insurance, and seller reserves the right not to sell to anyone with excessive negative feedback. Payment with money order or bank check ships right away. Payment with personal check ships after 10 business days.

Our eyes are used to reading standard upper and lower case text. You want your potential buyers to read your auction description. Make it easy on their eyes.

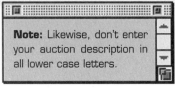

Note: Likewise, don't enter your auction description in all lower case letters.

The Fonts

The HTML tutorial in Appendix A shows you how to alter your text font. Be sure you use a common font that's likely to be available on everyone's PC. If not, the font will revert to plain old ordinary text.

Limit your use of gaudy typefaces. Those gothic and wedding-invitation typefaces might be fun to use, but the idea here is to encourage people to read your description and bid on your item. This type of text may be more distracting than appealing:

> *Buyer pays postage and insurance. Seller reserves the right not to sell to anyone with excessive negative feedback. Payment with money order or bank check ships right away. Payment with personal check ships after 10 business days.*

If you want a serif typeface (letters with short stemming lines, as used in textbooks), don't set a font. Most browsers default to Times New Roman, which is a serif typeface. Instead, change the size of the font or make it bold so certain essential points stand out. You'll find examples in Appendix B.

If you want a sans-serif typeface (letters with no stemming lines), use Arial, Helvetica, or Verdana. You can specify all three in your HTML font tag so if the first one isn't available, the browser uses the next one. You'll learn how to do that in Appendix A.

If you want a whimsical typeface that's very easy on the eyes, use Comic Sans MS. I'm sure you'll recognize Comic Sans. It's that typeface that looks like the neat printing in comic book dialogue balloons. The figures on page 118 use Comic Sans font. Microsoft created it and it's all over the Web these days. I used it in some of the auction description examples in Appendix B.

Diacritics

Also called accent marks, some languages require them over or through letters to indicate a variation in pronunciation, like in the word Lladró. The collectibles industry is rich with words that use diacritics. Definitely, use them if they're part of the item name or style.

Both Netscape and Internet Explorer recognize most diacritics, but to create them you need special escape sequences or complicated font programs.

Forget that! When you see the special character on a Web page or in an online document, highlight it with your mouse, then copy and paste it into Notepad or your word-processing program. You can also use the Character Map included with Windows 95/98/NT. From the Start menu, select Programs, then Accessories, then Character Map for all types of letters and symbols.

Note: You can't copy text that's part of an image.

☛Don't Overdo It

Annoying ads don't sell products. The same applies to auction descriptions that are too bright, too loud, to busy, and too ... bleeech.

On a major auction site, your bidder has a lot of browsing to do. If he or she spends more time reading your description, I hope it's because your description is interesting and informative. Don't make anyone wait too long for the page to load.

The Internet has enough of its own naptimes — those days when every site you visit takes forever to load. Do what you can to speed up the page-loading process and entice viewers.

The Colors

The Internet has more in common with television than it has with paper publications. You can get away with certain things in print because light shines toward it, not you. With a CRT, or cathode-ray tube like your monitor has, the light comes from behind the source right into your face. This is why long hours in front of a monitor strain your eyes more than reading a book does.

Keep this in mind when you're designing auction descriptions or any Web page. Too many different patterns and bright colors on one screen may cause people to lose interest — with good reason.

Avoid Complements

No, not the good kind. Compliments are nice! But colors opposite each other on the spectrum — complementary colors — appear to bounce or vibrate when placed side by side.

If you choose a background color for table cells in your auction description, be sure your font color doesn't complement the background. Avoid using these complementary colors side by side on any Web page:

- Red and green
- Orange and purple
- Yellow and blue

This includes all variations or hues of these colors. When you view the description in your browser, stare at it for a few seconds to see if the colors seem to "wiggle." If they do, choose less psychedelic colors. You want to create an artistically pleasing auction description, not nauseate people.

If your background is a dark color, use beige, gray, or white text. Bold colors work fine on light or pastel backgrounds. Avoid combining bright shades.

Photo Too Big

You might code the best-looking auction description in on the Net — animation, large detailed photos, bullet icons, and fancy backgrounds — but if the page takes too long to load, you'll lose your bidders. They may surf elsewhere.

Why All That Background?

Who wants to wait for a photograph to load that's 99% background? With your graphics program, trim as much as you can without disturbing the subject of the photo. As long as it's in focus and shows accurate color and detail, the photo doesn't need to be very large at all.

How to Annoy a Buyer

My father has an effective defense against annoying TV commercials. He mutes the volume. Some auction listings make me wish I could mute my monitor. Instead, I hit the "back" button and view another listing.

What you may think gives your auction a nice touch could have the same effect the singing carpet man does on dear old Dad. Here are some things to keep in mind:

- Heavy metal rock will not sell your antique or collectible. Keep the background music for your home page.
- Never use a blurry photograph. Practice focusing your camera, or use the "sharpen" feature included with your graphics program.
- Don't set a patterned background for the entire auction page. This makes the auction site text hard to read. They usually clash with the site images anyway.
- Keep that goofy Internet shorthand (U for "you," LMK for "let me know") where it belongs — in the chat room. How you write is how you represent yourself.

You want to inform, educate, and entice potential bids. You don't want to induce headaches.

Good Selling Practices

To save time, you might be tempted to list ten of the same "unique" items in ten different concurrently running auctions. When you do this, you're competing with yourself. List your auctions a little more sporadically to let your items shine in their own spotlight. They'll probably bid higher.

☛Start Your Auction

By now you have the tools you need to present your collectible item for auction with tasteful pizzazz. Let's get that auction running!

Listing Checklist

Before you put your item up for auction, here's a rundown of what you need:

* Have the description completed and opened in Notepad or another plain text word-processing program.
* Choose an item category for your product from the selection.
* Know the item's current market value.
* Decide on a reserve price for the auction. If it's a low-valued item, you probably don't need one.
* Have a GIF or JPEG image file (digital photograph) of the piece.
* Have the image file stored in a Web directory and know its URL.
* Know how to complete the auction-entry screen at the site you're using.

If the auction site has listing fees, be sure you've activated your account and have enough credit to cover them. If you have a credit-card number on file or you've pre-paid your account with a check, you're all set.

The Description Text

By now you have your auction description coded in HTML and you've opened it in your browser to make sure it looks the way you expect. The text is open in Notepad and you know how to copy it into the description area.

Look it over one more time:

* Is your auction title correct?
* Do you explain the item in a way that encourages bids?
* Did you spell everything correctly?
* Are your terms of sale and return policy defined?
* Is the photo positioned properly?
* Do your hyperlinks work?
* Can you read the text against the background color you're using?
* Is the text a reasonable size? Paragraphs in huge text don't read well. Only use large text for short phrases.

If everything's there, then it's time to launch your listing.

Pick a Category

Most auction sites offer category levels, especially in the varied world of collectibles. Be sure you list your item in the most specific category possible.

Here's a pared-down example from eBay's vast category choices:

Coins & Stams ->	Coins ->	Non-US ->	Mint, Proof Sets
	Stamps ->	US ->	Commemorative
	Philately ->		Currency
			Certificates

If you're listing non-US mint coin proof set, you can select the most definitive category for your item.

Name Your Price

Decide where you want the bidding to begin and know your reserve. In *Collector's Guide to Buying, Selling, and Trading on the Internet,* I list many places on the Internet where you can get secondary market price information for antiques and collectibles.

List Your Item

User ID: [ ]	**Password:** [ ]
Title (no HTML):	[ ]
Category (Select from list):	[Antiques ▼]
Description (HTML ok):	[ ]
Image URL (include http://):	[ ]
Type of auction (Select from list):	[Reserve ▼]
Duration:	[3-day ▼]
Minimum bid:	[ ]
Reserve price (If reserve auction):	[ ]
Featured auction?	○ Yes ◉ No

[Click here to review your listing]

Typical Auction Entry Screen

Be sure your reserve price is in line with the current market, and start the bidding at 10% of your reserve price, or higher. This allows a fair margin to entice some early bids.

Follow the Bouncing Ball

Once you're satisfied with the description, it's time to start the auction. Leave your Notepad window up so you can copy the text when you get to the description-entry area.

Call up the online auction site and access the auction-entry screen. Enter your user ID and password wherever the site asks for them.

Most auction-entry programs are similar. Some of them contain less information and others may ask for information that isn't included here. If so, refer to the site tutorial.

See a typical auction entry screen in the figure on page 125.

The Image URL Field

The Web address, or URL, of your image goes in this space. When you enter a Web address there, some auction sites add that little picture icon by your listing to let folks know there's an image that goes along with the auction.

Note: Some sellers use the image entry area to add those little "We take VISA" icons. If you do that, be sure your auction description contains a picture of the piece you're selling!

But suppose you code the description so the picture appears right in with the auction description. You don't want to repeat the same picture just to put something in the "image URL" field. That slows the loading time for the page. However, you need something in that field to get the little "image included" icon by your listing. People look for titles with the picture image and view those auctions first. Some folks don't even view auctions unless that little icon shows up by the title.

If you don't need to add another picture to your auction, use this space to add some cute little icon you grabbed from another site and copied to your directory. It can be an animated icon, a flower, a smiley-face, or whatever you want. Just make sure you have the correct URL and it's a pleasant picture. Use one that's tiny and doesn't take long to load.

Here's the Step by Step

This is a good list to read before you actually start an auction. This might seem like a lot of work just to list an item for auction, but it does get easier after you do it a few times.

Here goes:

- **Enter a title** – Use the name of both the item and the collectible line in your title. This will ensure that bidders see your auction when they do a text search. Remember, you're limited to the number of characters you can put in your title and you can't use HTML tags. Choose your words wisely.

Good Title
Harmony Kingdom Jewels of the Wild MIB

Not-so-Good Title
Buy my pretty hummingbirds

- **Pick a category** – Highlight or use a pull-down menu to select your item's category. Since some auction sites have sub-categories, try to narrow down the category as much as possible. If your collectible line has its own grouping, great. This will make it easier for your buyers to find your auction with a category search. If there isn't a category for your item, find something close. You'll want your item to come up when buyers search for items by category.
- **Copy and paste your description** – Click over to your Notepad screen. From the Edit menu, click on "Select all." Go back to the Edit menu and select "Copy." Go back to your browser and click inside the box where you enter the item description. Go to the Edit menu on your browser and select "Paste." Your description will load into the text entry area. Proofread the text after you load it into the description-entry area to ensure that everything copied over.
- **Add the picture URL** – There's usually a field for the image URL. Enter it into this space and don't forget to include http:// unless the site clearly indicates you don't need it. It might be assumed.
- **Enter the type of auction you're running** – Unless you're selling an inexpensive item, I recommend you enter a reserve auction to protect your investment. Don't use Dutch auctions unless you have a multiple of the same item and clearly understand how they work. There's usually no need to use a private auction unless your collectible item is the type I'd rather not mention.
- **Enter the duration of the auction** – Decide how long you want the auction to run. Since most bidding happens at the end, use a three-day auction for popular items.
- **Enter your minimum bid** – The bidding starts at this amount. Start your auctions with a low minimum. This attracts buyers.
- **Enter your reserve price** – Make sure it's close to the item's current market value so people don't stop bidding before the auction hits the reserve price. They're under no obligation to purchase the item if the high bid is lower than your reserve price.
- **Decide if you want a featured or showcase auction** – If you want your auction to attract attention, make it featured or showcase. The additional fee appears on the auction entry form. If you want to list a regular auction, leave those fields blank or choose "N/A" if that option exists.

- **Review the auction** – Proofread the entire form to ensure it's correct. Most auction sites let you review your auction before you start it running. If the site doesn't have this feature, go back and check the form one more time.
- **All set?** Click the "Enter" button.
- **View the auction** – You'll usually have the option to preview your listing. Review it carefully. Does it look right? Is the title OK? Did you select the right category? Are the minimum bid and reserve price correct? Did you format your description right and do your pictures show up? If not ...
- **Edit if necessary** – Hit the Back button on your browser and return to the auction-entry page if you need to correct anything. You might have to re-enter your user ID and password because some browsers erase them when you hit your Back button. When you're done, preview the auction again to be sure it's correct this time.
- **Hit the start button and let the bidding begin!**

Once you start the auction, the program takes you right to the auction page or to a link for it. Go check it out!

Now What?

Now that your auction is running, you need to think about what you'll do when the auction closes. The next two chapters offer advice to both buyers and sellers at online auction sites for completing the transaction off-line.

Chapter 5 — Verification and Escrow Services

Since the auction site bows out of the transaction once the auction closes, the seller may agree to handle the sale through a verification and authentication service, or an escrow service if the buyer requests it. Before you decide to involve a third party in your transaction, though, you need to know exactly what to expect and how your request to use a service might affect your online auction transactions.

Here's what we'll cover in this chapter:

- Verification services
- What's an escrow service?
- Who benefits from using escrow?
- Web-based escrow services
- Do you really need escrow?
- Disadvantages of using escrow
- What you'll pay for the service

Verification and authentication services can safeguard your investment while affording you peace of mind during the transaction.

Escrow services can safeguard folks who purchase extravagant items at auction, like computers, furs, jewelry, and even high-end collectibles like rare stamps or coins. It's particularly useful if you've never dealt with the seller before and you have no way to verify his or her previous transactions with others.

If you're a long-term collector of a particular line and participate in online auctions, however, you'll see certain names reappearing that bid on and list the rarest, most expensive pieces. Sellers who list the top-end items usually stand out in a collecting community. You may even know the person from a collector's convention or exposition. If you buy or sell to one of them, you probably won't need escrow no matter how high the bidding goes, especially if the person has a good record of successful transactions.

Escrow services are popular with some online auction users but definitely not with others. This chapter will help you decide for yourself how you feel about an escrow service handling your transaction.

☞Verification Services

Before I go too far into this chapter, I must differentiate between an *escrow service* and a *verification service*. An escrow service handles payments; a verification and authentication service specializes in examining a collectible item or antique using special criteria before it changes hands during a transaction.

The seller sends the item to the service, where it's unpacked and examined by a specialist. When you hear word from the service that the item is valid, you can send payment to the seller. The service forwards the item to you after the seller receives your payment.

Someone who is a well-known and trusted expert in a certain collectible line or type of antique might offer this service, for a fee. When a rare item or variation is involved — particularly one that's often misidentified or counterfeited — third-party verification can be an invaluable service.

An expert can let you know if the seller described the item accurately. You can have a few different services performed.

Grading

This determines the physical condition of an item. Given the frequent misuse of the term "mint," a verification service can distinguish mint from "poor quality" and the categories in between. The actual grading system depends on the item. For example, trading cards grade from A1 to F1. Coins grade from Poor to Perfect Uncirculated.

Collectibles have grading systems too, including mint, mint in package, collector quality, near mint, slightly imperfect, damaged, or fake. An expert can verify the quality and/or authenticity of the item before forwarding it to the buyer.

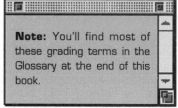

Note: You'll find most of these grading terms in the Glossary at the end of this book.

Authentication

Authentication relies on the expertise of whoever performs the service. Someone with the right training can easily detect counterfeits from subtle details. If you need an item authenticated before you agree to purchase it, rely on someone you know or an expert with references.

Sometimes a specialist can authenticate a collectible item that's part of a line, especially if there are known fakes on the market, but not always. Marking or signing an item as authentic may require the services of a company representative.

Appraisals

An appraiser estimates an item's value using a variety of methods, including examining the item with a trained eye, or estimating the value based on recent sales for the same or similar pieces. An appraised value is usually accurate only at the time of appraisal and for a short time afterward.

Variation Authentication

Anyone who collects items that are part of a collectible line probably knows all about variations. Early releases may be painted differently than later versions. Sometimes the company changes the mold or design midway through production so the item is easier to produce.

Only someone very familiar with the line, like a seasoned collector who owns the variation, can authenticate a genuine variation. This is an important service if there are unofficially altered versions turning up on the market.

Clearinghouse Services

Some collectors perform clearinghouse services by listing antiques or collectibles for sale on a Web site. The buyer sends the money to the clearinghouse, which then tells the owner of the item to ship it to the buyer. When the buyer receives it in satisfactory condition, the clearinghouse sends payment to the owner of the piece, minus a service fee.

This differs from escrow in that the buyer is actually viewing a classified ad on a Web page — not bidding at auction.

The escrow services I mention in this chapter are non-specialized services devoted to transferring goods and payment between a buyer and a seller. When escrow is used, the transaction itself becomes the main attraction, not the valuable antique or collectible item being transferred.

Where Do I Find a Verification Service?

Collector's Universe offers links to their grading services. You can reach the main site at www.collectors.com.

Check the "Help" or "Buyer Services" pages at most online auction sites. If the site doesn't provide the service, you'll usually find links to sites with more information.

Note: Chapter 14 contains more information about the Collector's Universe auction site.

You can also search for "Verification Service" or "Authentication and Grading" with any Internet search engine.

Here are a few services I found links for at several online auction sites:

Uniform Resource Locator	Company Name
www.isa-appraisers.org	International Society of Appraisers
www.beckettgrading.com	Beckett Grading Services
www.sgccard.com	Sportscard Guaranty Card Grading
certifiedsports.com	Certified Sports Authentication, Inc.
www.psacard.com	Professional Sports Authenticator
www.pcgs.com	Professional Coin Grading Service
www.realbeans.com	Real Beans

Before you use any private verification or authentication service, ask for the e-mail addresses of people who have used the site. Ask these experienced users what they thought of the service.

Note: I have not personally used any of these sites. By listing them here, I'm shortening your search time — not endorsing the services. Research any online verification and authentication service you consider using.

☞What's an Escrow Service?

An escrow service is a third party that holds money for an online transaction until the buyer agrees to release the funds to the seller. You can find many Internet-based escrow services if you use a search engine. Some auction sites include links to them.

A few auction sites provide escrow for an additional fee. Most, however, form an agreement with a private service and get a commission from referrals.

The escrow transaction takes place via US mail or a carrier the service specifies. The buyer's payment remains in an escrow account until he or she tells the service to release it to the seller.

> **Note:** Using an escrow service is *not* a regular part of the auction. It's a service typically separate from the auction site, and costs extra.

Because of the high sales turnaround, many online escrow services cater to Internet auction users. Since it involves extra effort and payment delay for the seller, you won't find many experienced online auction sellers too eager to use escrow — with good reason.

How It Works

Instead of sending payment directly to the seller, the buyer sends it to the escrow service.

The seller's part of the transaction runs one of two ways, depending on what the service requires:

1. The seller waits for the escrow service to indicate they received the buyer's payment. Then the seller sends the item directly to the buyer.
2. The seller sends the item to the service, which then forwards the package to the buyer after inspecting and re-packing the piece.

In both cases, once the buyer indicates that he or she is satisfied with the item, the escrow service drafts a check to the seller for the amount the buyer and seller agreed upon when the auction closed (minus any fees, if the seller is paying or sharing them). The buyer does not pay the seller directly.

Who Initiates Escrow?

After both parties agree to use escrow, the buyer contacts the service and establishes an account. The service usually assigns a tracking number to the transaction that both parties must reference when sending the service anything related to the transaction, such as payment, parcels, or e-mail.

Some services let you check the status of your transaction online.

Who's Protected?

The services claim to protect both the buyer and seller during an online transaction by acting as a neutral third party that handles the transaction.

Here's the implied benefit:

• The buyer can inspect the item before paying.
• The seller won't endure fraudulent payments.

The escrow service holds payment until the buyer approves or declines the merchandise, or until a specified inspection period ends. The service sends payment to the seller after the buyer gives the OK, or if the inspection period expires — whichever comes first.

The Inspection Period

The buyer usually has two days to inspect the item after it arrives. This prevents the buyer from delaying payment to the seller. If the escrow service doesn't hear from the buyer within the allotted time, they send the payment to the seller and consider the transaction successfully completed.

What if I Don't Like the Piece?

As the buyer, you may decide you don't want the item after inspecting it. You must then notify the service of your intent to return the item. They will instruct you to pack and return it directly to the seller, who in turn notifies the escrow service when it's received in satisfactory condition. The service then sends the buyer a refund, minus the service fee.

The buyer pays shipping and insurance for the returned item.

Do you feel these extra steps are necessary? That's up to you to decide. Remember that the seller isn't getting much in the way of protection, only the buyer.

Fraudulent Payments

While the services claim they protect the seller against fraudulent payments, I haven't seen much evidence of that. What exactly is a "fraudulent payment?"

No smart seller will ship an item before a personal check sent as payment clears the bank. Some online auction sellers are set up to accept credit card purchases, which the financial institution approves before the goods ship. Once the charge is approved, the seller isn't responsible if it ends up being a lost or stolen card. Nobody should send cash through the mail, so there's little worry about counterfeit money.

What exactly is the seller protected from when using escrow?

Escrow services don't offer any safeguard that sellers can't do on their own.

> **Note:** We'll cover fraud protection further in this chapter.

Only fraud protection benefits the seller, and not all escrow services offer that.

If the service's sole purpose is to hold payment in escrow until the buyer receives the item, the seller doesn't benefit at all.

For All Intents and Purposes

In a traditional party-to-party online transaction, the buyer is at more risk than the seller because he or she must send payment before actually seeing the item. Escrow services boast that their service evens the risk.

But who protects the seller if the service botches the transaction? None of the escrow services I researched allows you to post public online feedback for them. How does the seller know the service has an untarnished record?

As I see it, escrow is only for the buyer's peace of mind. If you find a seller willing to go through with it, leave extra-special super-positive feedback when the sale completes because he or she agreed to use escrow for your benefit alone. Sellers at most online auction sites are not obligated to use it.

Ask Before You Bid

In their auction descriptions, sellers don't usually mention willingness to use escrow. Why should they, if their feedback record is in the hundreds? If you feel strongly about using escrow, ask the seller in e-mail before you bid on the item. Escrow is not a requirement simply because the buyer wants to use it. Only auction sites that exclusively handle high-end, costly items like fine art and jewelry where closing bids are tens of thousands of dollars have mandatory escrow, and under those circumstances, I'd want to use it too.

For auctions that deal with antiques and collectibles of a more modest value, some sellers prefer you to rely on their feedback, and will offer online references to avoid the delays associated with escrow. If you still prefer to use an escrow service, be decent about it — pick up the tab.

Remember two things you're doing when requesting an experienced, high-feedback seller to use escrow:

- Subjecting the seller to payment delays
- Clearly stating that you don't trust the seller

If you plan to bid on the seller's items in the future, it might be better to deal directly, especially if he or she accepts credit card payments.

An auction site seller in good standing has the right to expect payment without third-party intervention and should not receive negative feedback for refusing, especially if his or her positive rating as a seller is over 100. This shows a steady trend of successful transactions.

The Anatomy of an Escrow Transaction

Suppose you're the buyer, and your seller has agreed to use an escrow service. Every escrow service varies in the way they operate, but for the most part you can expect to follow a similar procedure with any of them.

Here are the steps involved if you're the buyer and you want to use escrow:

1. Access the online escrow service's Web site and register the transaction. You'll need to enter your name and e-mail address, and that of the seller. You should also know the amount of the transaction.
2. The escrow service assigns you a transaction number. The service then e-mails the transaction number to both you and the seller. You'll use this number on all correspondence with the escrow service and the seller.
3. Next, you'll send payment to the address the escrow service provides. This payment includes the escrow service fee, which is usually non-refundable.
4. The service lets the seller know when the funds arrived. The seller ships the item to the service (or directly to you, depending on what the service requests) within a certain period, usually 24 hours. The seller must insure and track the item.
5. The service unpacks and inspects the item, then forwards it to you, or you receive it directly from the seller. Either way, the inspection period begins when you sign for the item.
6. If you accept the item, you'll notify the service by e-mail and they release the payment to the seller. If your inspection period expires and you don't contact the service, they automatically forward the funds to the seller.
7. If you don't want the item, you'll ship it back to the seller, who notifies the service when it's received. The service then sends payment, minus the service fee, back to the buyer.

Who's Liable for Damage or Loss?

A well-run escrow service provides shipping insurance, but some don't. In most cases, the seller must insure the package on its way to the service, and the buyer must insure the package if he or she decides to return it to the seller.

The service should cover any loss resulting from a carrier they use to send the item to the buyer. If you're considering an escrow service, ask in advance about liability. You may not find a telephone number on their Web site, so read the "fine print" carefully.

☛The Benefits of Online Escrow

An Internet search for escrow services returns plenty of links, so it must be a successful business. That doesn't mean the service is always necessary.

Let's take a closer look at who gets what out of it. Then we can determine the real benefactors.

For the Seller

As I mentioned before, online escrow services that don't offer fraud protection are of absolutely no benefit to a person who sells antiques and collectibles at an Internet auction site. No benefit. None. Zero.

I hope that's clear.

For the Buyer

The buyer's benefits are more implied than real.

The service boasts that you're sending payment to their company, instead of to a stranger. But who's receiving your payment at the escrow service? A stranger, of course. When you send money to an auction seller, at least you know his or her name and address. You can check seller feedback and talk to others who did business with the person. Some escrow services will not give references and you'll address payment to the service, not to an actual person.

Credit Card Payments

Escrow services will accept credit card payments. Many independent sellers at online auction sites aren't set up to take credit cards. Paying an escrow service with a credit card is easier than sending a check to the seller. Most credit card purchases ship the next day. Not in this case, however.

While you're giving your credit card number to the strangers at the escrow service, the seller is packing up the item to send to the same place. It's going to take time for the item to arrive at the service. Then someone has to open the package, inspect the item, re-pack it, and send it on its several-day journey to your house. You're definitely waiting longer than if you'd pay a private seller with a money order. And you're paying for the delay.

Note: Some escrow services have the seller send the item directly to the buyer. Upon inspection, the buyer tells the service to release payment to the seller. This does hasten the transaction, but it also lessens the need for the service.

When you use an escrow service, you know you'll get something in return for your money. That's a nice assurance, but you'll have the same odds from a seller with over 100 positive feedback comments and online references you can contact.

So, what are the benefits of using an escrow service?

For the Auction Site

If the auction site mentions the escrow service on their pages, they typically get a referral fee whenever someone uses the service for a transaction stemming from that auction site. That's one reason auction sites mention and provide links to them.

They really don't care if you use them. Yes, they want the transactions to work out — that helps their reputation. But once the auction closes successfully, that's usually their bogey, not what happens later. Many sites want to know about fraudulent users so they can flush them out of the system, but they offer little else in the way of safeguarding transactions for you.

Most auction sites refund your listing fee if the person doesn't buy the item, but you'd need that service regardless of using escrow. The auction site can revoke the site ID of a proven dishonest user but again, that doesn't involve escrow. Private escrow services are separate from the online auction site business. Even online auction sites that run their own escrow services usually charge extra for them.

Some auction sites make it look like escrow is part of the online auction process. If I haven't made this clear enough, I'll state it again: At 99% of online auction sites, escrow is *not* part of the auction transaction. It's a separate arrangement altogether.

The auction site puts a link to the escrow service and appears to endorse it because they make more money that way.

For the Escrow Service

Bingo! The escrow service benefits the service most. By preying on a newcomer's fear of doing business on the Internet, the escrow service is essentially charging to perform a service that anyone who uses an online auction site or an Internet collector exchange can do just fine unassisted.

I hope you've figured that out by now.

My Disclaimer

My obvious feeling is that escrow services do little more than make money for themselves. However, there are many well-run escrow services in operation. Those who use them will usually get exactly what they pay for — a third party handling their transaction. I'm not condemning any business that runs well and upholds the standards set by the Better Business Bureau or any other regulating agency. And I certainly don't frown on a business that makes honest money.

If you want to use escrow, many fine services in operation will gladly handle your business with integrity. I just want you to know in advance who benefits the most from it.

☞Escrow on the Web

Several private escrow services on the Internet specialize in auction transactions. Most of them also extend to any type of buying, selling, or trading for parties that know each other only from contact on the Internet.

You can check these out for yourself:

Uniform Resource Locator	Company Name
www.iescrow.com	i-Escrow
www.tradedirect.com	Trade-direct
www.int-escrow-serc.com	D&M Internet Escrow Service
www.buyersguardian.com	Buyer's Guardian Escrow Service
www.tradesafe.com	TradeSafe
www.secureexchange.com	Secure Exchange
www.safebuyer.com	Safe Buyer

Before you use any private escrow service, ask for the e-mail addresses of people who have used the site before. Ask these experienced users what they thought of the service. If the service won't provide names for reference, pick another service that will.

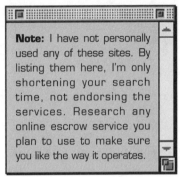

Note: I have not personally used any of these sites. By listing them here, I'm only shortening your search time, not endorsing the services. Research any online escrow service you plan to use to make sure you like the way it operates.

What They Expect of You

In order to operate in the best interest of both parties, the escrow service expects buyers and sellers to follow certain procedures in order to guarantee that the transaction eventually completes.

Buyer's Duties

As the buyer during an escrow transaction, you'll be responsible for a few things:

- Contacting the escrow service to initiate the transaction
- Sending payment to the escrow service within a predetermined time
- Inspecting the item after receiving it
- Notifying the escrow service within your inspection period if you accept or reject the item
- Packing and shipping the item back to the seller, if necessary

You must also agree to all terms and conditions of the escrow service.

Seller's Duties

The seller has certain responsibilities as well:

- Shipping the item to the service (or to the buyer, as the service specifies)
- Insuring the package
- Reporting the tracking number and date of dispatch to the service
- Accepting the item if the seller returns it

Typically, the seller has no margin of dispute if the buyer returns the item within the specified time.

Cancelled Transactions

Some escrow services will refund your fee if the transaction is canceled before they act. Either party can usually cancel the transaction at certain times:

- Before the seller has shipped the merchandise, by a request from either the buyer or seller.
- After the seller shipped the item, and before the examination period ends, by a request from the buyer. Also by a request from the seller, but only if the buyer agrees.

The buyer usually can't cancel a transaction after the examination period ends. The service, however, can cancel under certain circumstances:

- If they don't receive payment from the buyer
- If the seller doesn't send the shipping or tracking number by the date the service specifies
- Any other reason the service feels is appropriate

Remember that the service will, at times, have both the item and the payment in-hand. This definitely puts them in "trump card" position with both parties.

☞Do You Really Need It?

Using escrow is not mandatory, and nobody should talk you into using it if your feedback file reflects good practice.

You don't need to use escrow if the seller has a merchant account and accepts credit card payments. If it's used at all, escrow is for private parties doing business together and hopefully, only for the first transaction between those two parties.

Most sellers would rather not use escrow because it adds another layer to the transaction. They would rather get your check or money order and send you the goods. Buyers who insist on using escrow will not be favorites among sellers.

If you're not dealing with an item of significant value and the seller's feedback checks out, you should be OK sending him or her a money order or, better yet, paying with a credit card. If you would like to establish a lasting relationship with a certain seller, don't mention escrow.

It's Like COD, Except...

The buyer doesn't pay for an item sent via COD (cash on delivery) until the package arrives.

With escrow, the service receives the payment before the package ships. There's also that inspection period, during which the buyer must inform the service if he or she accepts the item. If it's undesirable, the buyer must send it back to the seller and wait for a refund. Escrow involves more work for the buyer than COD does.

Escrow also lessens the risk that you'll encounter a "lazy buyer," one who uses the time between agreeing to the purchase and the package arriving to decide if he or she really does want the piece. If the buyer refuses the COD item, the seller endures the shipping fee, insurance, and plenty of lost time and aggravation.

In Chapter 6, I advise collectible sellers to avoid using COD for several reasons, the foremost being the payment delay involved. It's far easier to provide online references or direct the wary buyer to your feedback file for reassurance that you're an honest seller.

Both escrow and COD mean essentially the same thing — the buyer doesn't trust the seller. But there are better, less expensive ways to ease your apprehension. Ask for and check references. At online auction sites, you can read the seller's feedback file.

Whatever you do, don't tell the seller you want to use escrow "in the best interest of both of you." There's no truth to that whatsoever.

When You Might Need It

I've made hundreds of online auction purchases and sales and I never once used escrow. The type of situations where it's warranted are, hopefully, few and far between. Most are avoidable if you "do your homework" before you bid. However, a few situations could arise that might make third-party involvement viable.

Hidden Feedback and Warnings

Some auction sites let you conceal your feedback. Users may do this if they don't want others to view negative comments others left for them. You'll read more about this in Chapter 6.

Suppose a seller has hidden feedback, but you bid on his or her listing anyway because you really wanted the item. Then the auction ends, you're the high bidder, and suddenly your inbox is full of e-mail from people warning you about the seller.

At this point, it would be unethical (and illegal in some states) to back out of the purchase. You knew about the hidden feedback before you bid, but it didn't deter you. Now you're faced with the possibility of sending payment to someone with a questionable online auction reputation.

In this situation, you might consider using an escrow service to handle the transaction. Unfortunately, since you didn't mutually agree to use escrow before the auction ended, the seller has the right to refuse. If that happens, you must decide if you want to risk sending payment, or backing out and possibly getting negative feedback from the seller, which he or she can do if you back out of a successfully closed auction.

New Seller, No References

I advise anyone who plans to list items for auction to bid and buy a few items first, to garner some feedback before selling. Even if feedback only relates to buying, it helps indicate good character.

Suppose the person's first listing, however, is for an item that closes at an amount higher than you feel comfortable sending to someone who doesn't have seller feedback. You might consider using an escrow service, especially if the person can't offer online references.

If you're sending several hundred dollars or more, it might be worth it to endure the fee and hassles of escrow. The seller may gladly agree. Your positive feedback when the transaction completes may lessen the need for escrow. Even in this case, before you bid, be sure to e-mail the seller to find out if he or she is willing to use escrow.

Big-Ticket Items

A few collectibles and certainly many types of antiques can close for hundreds, even thousands of dollars at online auction. Unless you're dealing with someone you know from past transactions or a reputable dealer, using escrow to handle the transaction isn't a bad idea at all.

Just be sure to research whatever service you use to be sure you're comfortable with their method of operation. Check with others who had good results from the service.

Fraud Protection Guarantee

Some escrow services take responsibility for the item if it's lost or damaged when both parties deny responsibility. There's usually an additional fee for fraud protection — typically a percentage of the purchase price.

Here are some situations where this type of insurance would apply. The first two apply to scenarios where the seller sends the item directly to the buyer.

- The buyer receives eight trading cards instead of the expected ten, but the seller claims he sent ten.
- The buyer claims the piece is unsigned, but the seller insists she sent an autographed figurine.
- The buyer examines the product and then decides to return it. When the seller receives the package, the box is empty.
- The buyer returns the item. The seller receives it and finds a lesser-valued product in its place. The buyer claims to have returned the original item.

In each case, someone is lying but nobody knows who. An escrow service that offers fraud protection will pay for the loss.

Read the fine print for restrictions, fees, or limitations.

☞The Down Side of Escrow

Perhaps it's obvious from the tone of this chapter that I'm no rabid fan of online escrow services for transactions involving moderately valued collectibles. Escrow is fine when you're buying a house or investing millions in the crown jewels of Atlantis, but probably not when dealing in beanbag plush or porcelain figurines. An online auction site isn't exactly Sotheby's.

Only under the specific circumstances I mentioned previously do I agree that using online escrow is necessary or justified. I'd never advise an experienced seller to offer it in the text of an auction description. Nobody should ever be that desperate for bids.

If I could change one thing about auction sites, it would be removal of links to escrow services from their site pages and replacement with statements relinquishing the sites' responsibility if you decide to use an escrow service. Let the escrow services advertise themselves.

But business arrangements abound. It's my responsibility, therefore, to advise you that escrow isn't necessary if you cultivate good Internet trading practices as you buy and sell collectibles online. In some respects, escrow services can detract from private Internet commerce. Here's why.

Fear and Loathing on the Internet

Links and endorsements for online escrow services send the wrong message to new Internet auction users:

You need to be afraid.

People may not realize the service is a moneymaking venture, *not* a safeguard based on fraudulent transactions at that site. If this were true, the auction sites wouldn't have the high traffic they do. Ominous messages won't make people comfortable using Internet resources and auction sites for managing collections.

In *Collector's Guide to Buying, Selling, and Trading on the Internet,* I devote an entire chapter to talking to strangers, people you know only from the Internet. I advise collectors to check references, follow their instincts, and proceed with caution, but nowhere do I advocate paranoia.

Some folks come to the Internet ready and willing to get the most out of it. Others dip their toes into the Internet puddles cautiously, but relax and "learn the ropes" after their first few successful transactions. That's exactly as it should be.

Advice from a "Seasoned" Seller

Kelly Bloom, who owns and operates the Internet-based Caravan Spice & Trading Company (www.caravanspice.com) in Fayetteville, North Carolina, also sells collectibles on eBay. As this book goes to press, her positive feedback rating on eBay is well over 650, a number that could easily double by 2001. She lists up to twenty items every week, sometimes more.

Kelly accepts several credit cards and prefers that method of payment. She knows that buyers want their merchandise as quickly as possible and with a credit card purchase, she can ship the next business day. Plus, it's a safeguard.

"Credit card purchases not only protect the customer," Kelly explains, "but they protect me as well. In the case of a properly-reported stolen card, the financial institution eats the loss, not the merchant that accepted the approved credit card transaction."

When asked to use escrow, Kelly tells buyers it's not necessary because a credit card transaction is faster, more efficient, and safer.

"I don't like auction escrow," she continues, "because it cultivates fear of Internet commerce. Someone *that* leery of Internet transactions shouldn't be online."

The sooner you get used to dealing directly with people on the Internet, the more confident you'll be with the process. Whether you're trading items with another collector you meet in a chat room or buying something you won at auction, it's far better to develop your own strategies than depend on a third party for hand-holding.

Credit Card Disputes

As a buyer, your credit card company will assist with merchant disputes. If you need to return the item for any reason, they will, in most cases, reverse the transaction for you.

If you paid for your escrow transaction with a credit card, however, you typically can't recoup a loss through them if you find the item counterfeit, damaged, or otherwise undesirable, unless the escrow service specifically offers this protection.

At least one online escrow service I researched makes very clear their release from liability once the transaction completes, credit card purchase or not. Your credit card company may not be able to help you either since you purchased a *service* from the escrow provider — not the item itself. You can't dispute a service once it's been properly rendered.

The piece involved in the transaction came from the seller. Guess where the escrow service sends you to settle a post-transaction dispute? Right back to the seller. And didn't you use the service to avoid that direct contact in the first place?

But by then, the service may claim to have fulfilled their responsibility. They forwarded the item and the payment to the correct party according to their service agreement. Once that's completed, you have no recourse with them. If you couldn't examine the item until after the inspection period expired and then found a problem, you'd be out of luck unless the seller agreed to reverse the transaction.

Handle With Care — Twice

As I mentioned previously, some escrow services instruct the seller to send the item to their location for inspection before forwarding it on to the buyer.

How do you know the escrow service will re-pack it properly? I'm guessing the previous owner of the item, the seller, knows a lot more about the item than whoever handles it at the escrow service. Especially when it comes to unique and fragile antiques. Since many sellers are also collectors, I prefer that someone with experience handling the item do the packing, and let me unpack it.

Also, if the buyer and seller are both on the east coast and the escrow service is based in Arizona, this means the piece will travel much farther in unknown hands than it would if the transaction is handled party-to-party. I'd be concerned. Even if the escrow service will cover the item to its full current market value, if it's rare and it's ruined, it's gone forever.

☛It's a Business — They Charge

Not every escrow service charges the same way, and most of them don't care who pays their fee.

One auction site escrow service charges an annual fee for membership, then handles transactions upon request of the buyer and seller involved. Most of the privately run escrow services charge separately for each transaction.

Who Pays?

The escrow service normally deducts the fee from the amount the buyer sends, but most escrow services allow either the buyer or seller, or both, to pay escrow fees. You can negotiate that in e-mail before you contact the escrow service.

For online auction transactions that involve collectibles, the buyer should definitely pay the fee if he or she requests escrow. If the escrow service forwards the item to the buyer after inspection, they'll deduct shipping charges from the buyer's payment as well.

Standard Rates

The fee will be a percentage of the purchase price you negotiate with the seller. Here's a typical payment schedule for an escrow service:

Purchase Price	Escrow Service Fee
$0 – 100	$10.00
$101 – 400	$15.00
$401 – 1,000	$20.00
$1,001 – 1,500	$25.00
$1,501 – 2,000	$30.00
$2,001 – 2,500	$35.00
$2,501 – 3,000	$50.00
$3,001 - over	Contact them

For transactions over $3,000, you'll normally have to negotiate the fee with the escrow service.

Overall, the escrow concept is wholesome, but I advise you to become comfortable enough with the online auction process to handle your transactions unassisted.

The next chapter will help you remain in good favor with others as you manage your collecting with online auctions.

Chapter 6 — User Maintenance

Once the auction closes, it's time for those involved in the bright lights and chorus of the auction stage to put away the grease paint and get in touch. The transaction comes off the Internet and moves into real life. This is where the person's user ID becomes an actual name, and you get to reveal your personality, with something other than creative HTML, to the bidder who devoted hours to winning your auction.

The buyer is probably just as eager to do the same, especially if some fancy last minute bidding went into winning that auction.

Good communication and follow-through means good feedback comments later. You also want to do everything you can to make the transaction as easy as possible for yourself and for the other person.

Here's what we'll cover in this chapter:

- The auction closed — now what?
- Communicating with your buyer
- Communicating with the seller
- Who sends what when
- Packing the item to ship
- Leaving feedback
- Communicating with the auction site
- Keeping records

You'll learn what you need to do once the auction closes, whether you're the high bidder or the person who listed the auction.

☞The Auction Closed — Now What?

If you're the seller, you should contact the buyer as soon as you can after the auction ends. Some sellers wait and send e-mail after all auctions closing on the same day finish, which is fine if they don't span too much time during the day. It's not always easy to sit by the computer waiting for your auctions to close so you can open communication with the buyer, but timely communication is always good online auction practice.

When someone races to bid at the last minute, he or she probably wants to hear from you right after the auction closes. Start the communication process soon to finish the transaction. Even if the bidder wasn't watching the auction's final seconds, he or she will appreciate hearing from you quickly.

Your payment might arrive much faster if you contact the buyer right away.

Bidders can also initiate contact with the seller after the auction closes. Some sellers want to pack the item to ship as soon as your payment arrives, so sending your address is helpful. Hearing from the buyer also puts the seller at ease because that means the payment is definitely on the way.

Sending E-mail

This is the first step to getting up close and personal with your co-participant.

Unless the buyer and seller made contact during the auction, the e-mail you send after the auction closes is the initial one-on-one contact. There is no better time to make a good first impression than during this phase of the transaction.

This section covers the information you need to include in your e-mail messages to help the transaction run as smoothly as the online auction did.

> **Note:** Examples of many different e-mail messages to send during auction transactions appear in Appendix C.

Include the Auction Number

Always include the auction number in the subject line of your e-mail messages. That way, both you and the other party know exactly which transaction the e-mail refers to. The auction number will carry over into any responses you get. This makes tracking easier.

It serves another purpose, too. If you need to hunt for a message later, you can find it by browsing e-mail subjects. You won't have to open all of your old mail to find the right one.

Another important reason to include a reference to the auction in the e-mail subject line is the spam and junk mail people receive every day; they delete messages from users they can't readily identify. Others fear computer viruses sent in e-mail from unknown accounts. You don't want your auction e-mail deleted by mistake!

Message to the High Bidder

When you send e-mail to your high bidder, remember that this person is about to buy something from you and may feel a bit apprehensive. Be polite and friendly and include everything the buyer needs in order to prepare and mail out the payment.

Here's an example of what I send to my high bidders:

> Hi! Congrats on being the high bidder on auction #435512957 for the set of eight Peaceables Plush collectibles. That was some fancy last minute bidding you did! I hope you enjoy the items.
>
> Your high bid was $65. Please add $6.50 for shipping and insurance for a total of $71.50. Since you have an excellent feedback rating, a personal check is fine. Please send payment to:
>
> Nancy Hix
> 1234 Auction Drive
> Bidville, IL 57432
>
> Be sure to include the auction number and item name (or a copy of this e-mail) with your payment so I can leave feedback for you and ship your items

out to their new owner! Let me know when you've sent payment so I can watch for it. Thanks!

-Nancy

A message like this includes all necessary information and adds a nice personal touch. This could help the buyer feel more confident about sending payment to a stranger.

Message to the Seller

Here's an excerpt from an e-mail message I received the night before I started this chapter:

Hi! Wow, I'm so happy I won your auction! You won't believe this but I snuck out of bed while my wife was sleeping to bid on your Charming Tails 1998 ICE event piece. She's wanted it forever so it will make a great birthday present for her! She's a third grade teacher and she brings Charming Tails pieces to school for the kids to write stories about. My name's Tom. Please let me know where to send payment.

What a nice message!

I answered him with the same information I send to all my high bidders and thanked him for contacting me right away. The only reason I didn't offer to gift-wrap the item is that I knew he'd want to inspect it when it arrived. Otherwise, I surely would have.

The transaction completed with no problems, and Tom and I left each other positive feedback.

Transmittal Letters

Always include a note when you send payment or ship an item. Two types of notes help you and the other party keep track of the transaction:

- **Shipping Note** – This helps the buyer recall the auction. Include your name, address, and a telephone number or e-mail address so the buyer can contact you, if necessary. Also, include the auction number and your user ID so he or she can run right to the keyboard and enter positive feedback for you as soon as the excellently packaged item arrives.

- **Remittance Letter** – This is the note you send with your payment. I can't count how many times I've received an envelope with just a check in it, and it always happens when I'm expecting twenty other checks for the same amount. For all you know, the seller may have 200 auctions running at one time. Make it easy for him or her and indicate the item you're paying for. Include the auction number. Your shipment has a better chance of arriving promptly.

A sample remittance letter is on page 154, and a shipping note on page 157.

Save your transmittal letters in Microsoft Word or another word processing program. Then you can print out several blank forms and fill them in manually each time you need to send one.

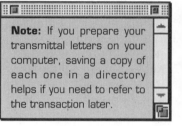

Note: If you prepare your transmittal letters on your computer, saving a copy of each one in a directory helps if you need to refer to the transaction later.

You can also complete the letter on your computer, print it, and then remove the information for that transaction so the letter template is ready for next time.

Who Sends What When?

Not long ago, I listed a mallard duck figurine on a popular auction site. When the auction ended, I contacted the high bidder and told her where to send the payment. She answered promptly and included her address. I assumed she sent her address in case I needed it to determine postage and get the item ready for shipping.

The same day her payment arrived, I received e-mail from her:

"I sent you the check!" she wrote. "Now where's my duck?"

She apparently thought I should send the item the same day she sent the payment. I explained to her that I needed to receive payment before I'd ship the item. Moreover, since she sent a personal check, I planned to wait ten business days for the check to clear the bank.

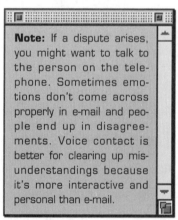

Note: If a dispute arises, you might want to talk to the person on the telephone. Sometimes emotions don't come across properly in e-mail and people end up in disagreements. Voice contact is better for clearing up misunderstandings because it's more interactive and personal than e-mail.

It's important to communicate clearly with people when buying and selling at online auction sites. Resolve any misconceptions before they have the potential to escalate to a full-blown disagreement that results in negative feedback.

Communicating With the Seller

Never send payment without an enclosure. You might assume that the seller can just get your name and address from the return envelope or the face of your check, but that's not always possible. If you send a check without a transmittal letter, it might delay your shipment.

If the seller lists ten or more auctions each week, he or she must track down the right auction to know which piece to send you. Auction sites occasionally close (or "go down") for maintenance and the seller can't reference the auction online. If you want your item quickly, make it easy for the seller. Include the information needed to get your item on its way.

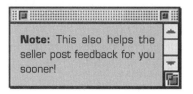

Note: This also helps the seller post feedback for you sooner!

When Should I Send the Payment?

Excellent question! Send the payment as soon as the seller tells you the amount that is due, and where you should send it. Some sellers wait as long as ten days for the payment to arrive before re-listing the item but I'll let you in on a secret: They like to be paid much sooner than that.

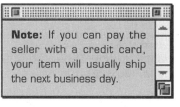

Note: If you can pay the seller with a credit card, your item will usually ship the next business day.

I send my auction payments out within one day, if I can. Sometimes I wait an extra day or two if another auction is closing and I expect to be the winning bidder; then I can make out my remittance letters and get money orders (or write checks) all at once. I try not to let more than three days pass before I send payment on a winning auction. It's too easy to let the transaction fall into a forgotten cyber-crack that way.

I recommend sending out your auction payments as soon as possible. You'll please the seller and receive your item faster.

Remittance Letter

The letter you send with your payment should include everything the seller needs to know to package and ship the item to you:

- Item name
- Auction number
- Amount of payment
- Payment date
- Your shipping address
- Your phone number or e-mail address
- Your auction site user ID

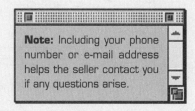

Note: Including your phone number or e-mail address helps the seller contact you if any questions arise.

Copy the name of the item from the auction title so the seller can reference it quickly.

All auction sites assign a number to each listing. Include this number and the date you're mailing the payment. Indicate the payment amount, including shipping charges. This helps the seller keep track of the transaction and send you the correct item. Then add your address, telephone number, and user ID.

Here's a sample remittance letter:

Payment is Enclosed!
The enclosed check/money order covers payment as we agreed upon for:
_____ Amount: _____

Auction number: _____
Today's date: _____

Shipping Information:
Please ship the package to:

Nancy Hix
1234 Auction Drive
Bidville, IL 57432

If there are any problems or you need more information, please call me at
1-800-555-1234 or send e-mail to **Marble90@aol.com.**

If You're Happy with our Transaction:
Please post positive comments for my user ID (**marble**), and I will do the same for you.

If You're NOT Happy with our Transaction:
Please let me know right away. I am an honest, experienced trader and will take whatever measures necessary to be sure we're all satisfied with the outcome.

Thanks!
(Signature)

Sample Remittance Letter

Auction sellers appreciate when the buyer includes all necessary information with payment. When you use auction transmittal letters, comments like "very professional" will appear in your feedback file, and you'll deserve it!

The Buyer Pays First

Online auction transactions are a different process from trading collectibles, where you both ship the same day. Unless the buyer and seller have done business with each other before, it's never a good idea for the seller to ship the item the same day the buyer sends payment.

The seller is selling, the buyer is buying, and it's no different from any other transaction where money exchanges for goods. Besides, if you're paying with a personal check, the payment isn't "received" until the check clears the bank. The seller needs to wait at least ten business days before shipping the item, as I did before sending the duck.

If the seller accepts credit card payments, he or she should ship one business day after the financial institution approves the charge. In every case, the buyer pays before the item ships.

Types of Payment

The seller's preferred method of payment should appear in the auction description. Contact the seller to propose alternative payment and get his or her agreement *before* you bid.

There are several ways to pay for an item won at an online auction:

- **Personal check** – Accepting personal checks makes the transaction easier for the buyer and the seller usually receives the payment sooner. As the seller, be sure to wait until the check clears the bank before shipping the item. This takes a minimum of ten business days.
- **Credit cards** – If the seller accepts charge purchases, this is an excellent way to pay since it protects both the buyer and the seller, as you read about in Chapter 5.
- **Bank check** – Most financial institutions issue checks in the amount you specify for a nominal fee. You pay for a bank check with cash or automatic account withdrawal.
- **Postal money order** – U.S. post offices issue these for a small fee and cash-only payment. You can redeem them at any post office if you produce the required identification.
- **Other money orders** – Most work just like a bank check. You specify the check's amount and pay cash along with a small fee. You can purchase money orders at many places: currency exchanges, grocery stores, department stores, and even convenience shops.

Discourage people from sending cash through the mail. There's no easy way to trace it if it's lost. Some international buyers, however, may not be able to pay any other way. If you receive a cash payment through the mail, include a receipt with the shipment. Retain a copy.

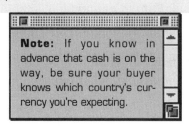

Note: If you know in advance that cash is on the way, be sure your buyer knows which country's currency you're expecting.

Sending Payment

Unless you arranged another form of payment in advance, follow the seller's directions. They're usually included in the auction description.

If the seller requested a money order, ask before you send a personal check. Tell the seller you understand that it will delay shipment until the check clears the bank. Some sellers agree, especially if you have a good feedback record. If the seller doesn't agree, pay according to the original plan.

Include Auction Information

One week, I listed twelve different Peaceable Planet plush collectibles on eBay. They all closed at my reserve price so I anticipated twelve payments in the same amount.

It went smoothly until I received one Postal Money Order with no note or address enclosed — only a small return address label on the outside of the envelope that had been mangled somewhere in transit. I had no idea who sent the payment or which plush item it was for.

I had to wait until I received the other payments to determine who sent the mysterious money order. I explained later to the buyer why her item took so long to arrive.

Remember Your Shipping Address!

Make it easy for the seller; include your shipping address with your remittance note. Everyone has their own system for preparing items for shipping and it helps to have everything on hand.

When I ship items, having the buyer's shipping address in the envelope with the payment makes it easy for me since I don't have to hunt through e-mail for it.

The seller shouldn't have to use your return address to ship the item. The envelope might not arrive the way you sent it. Your writing might be soiled or the envelope torn. Poorly gummed address labels sometimes get lost.

The best assurance you have that your item will ship promptly is to include with your payment everything the seller needs to know to get the package on its way.

Sending an E-mail Notification of Payment

After you send the payment, notify the seller so he or she can watch for it. If it went via registered or overnight mail, be sure to let the seller know.

Check Appendix C for sample e-mail messages to send to alert the seller that the payment is on its way.

☞Communicating With Your Buyer

Once you receive payment and prepare to ship the item, let the buyer know you'll be sending the treasure soon.

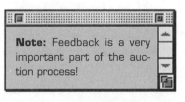

Note: Feedback is a very important part of the auction process!

If the payment arrived promptly, post positive feedback for the buyer right away. With a personal check, wait ten days for it to clear the bank before you post feedback. You'll read more about entering feedback for other users at the end of this chapter.

When you're ready to ship the item, call up your document program, open your shipping note template, and fill in the blanks.

Shipping Note

Here's what the transmittal letter you send with the item should include:

- Item name
- Auction number
- Ship date
- Your user ID
- Your phone number or e-mail address

Here is an example of a shipping note:

Note: Notice the mention of feedback.

Your Item has Arrived!
Enclosed you will find your:

_____

Auction number: _____
Today's date: _____

Please Let me Know When it Arrives!
Send email to Nancy (**Marble90@aol.com**) and let me know that you got the package. If you encounter any problems or you need to reach me sooner, please call me at: **1-800-555-1234**

If You're Happy with our Transaction:
Please post positive feedback for my user ID (**marble**). I have already done the same for you when your payment arrived. If not, let me know ASAP!

If You're NOT Happy with our Transaction:
Please notify me right away. I am an honest, experienced trader and will take whatever measures necessary to be sure we're all satisfied with the outcome.

Thanks!
(Signature)

Sample Shipping Note

The shipping note should reiterate the auction information. The buyer may want to save it for later reference, if necessary.

Ship Promptly

Once you receive payment or you've waited enough time for the personal check to clear, ship the item within 24 hours. Notify the buyer immediately of any unavoidable shipping delay.

Note: Only list items for auction that you have in your immediate possession. Avoid pre-sells!

Which Carrier?

Use the carrier that gives you the best service. Many sellers have good luck with U.S. Postal Service Priority Mail. You can track and insure items as needed. Frequent shippers can set up an account and receive free shipping supplies by calling 1-800-222-1811. You can also visit them on the Web at www.usps.gov.

You can arrange similar accounts with UPS or Federal Express. Both also track and insure parcels. Your buyer might even have an account number against which you can charge the shipping. UPS, Federal Express, and the U.S. Postal Service will pick up parcels from your home or office if you arrange it in advance.

Note: If the buyer's address is a PO box, you'll have to use the U.S. Postal Service. The USPS does not accept delivery from private carriers.

Avoid COD

I advise against COD (cash on delivery). As the seller, COD demands a lot more work from you than conventional shipping and puts most of the risk right back in your lap. It's also more costly and it takes much longer for you to receive your payment.

There have been cases recently where sellers have sent shipments by COD, and the carrier accepted payment by personal check. The check bounced, leaving the seller out of luck. Perhaps some drivers think COD means "check on delivery."

Note: The seller should avoid having both the item and the payment out of hand.

Send an E-mail Notification of Shipping

After you ship the item, let the buyer know. If you put a tracking number on the package, include this in your e-mail so the buyer has all necessary information in case the package doesn't show up within a reasonable time.

☛Good Packing

This is almost as important as describing the item well. If it arrives damaged, everything else was a waste of time. Use care in packing the item for shipping so it reaches the buyer in the same condition it was in when you sent it.

Use a box that's large enough to allow adequate packing material to cushion the item on all sides. Remember that you're responsible for getting the item to the buyer's shipping location in the expected condition. When you pack it for shipping, secure it sufficiently to withstand jostling.

It's far better to over-pack and possibly pay a little more for postage than to ship an item without adequate protection.

Preparing the Item

Getting an item ready for shipping is an important part of the process. If the item has accessories, keep a written or photographic record of everything you send the buyer. Here's an example of what you might include in the list:

- Original packaging
- Product documentation or certificates
- All necessary hardware, if the item must be re-assembled
- Assembly instructions
- Anything that came packaged with a collectible item, such as doll clothes and shoes (if your auction included them)
- A book's dust jacket
- Any protective covering or casing you sold with the item

Keeping record of what you send can also help safeguard you against fraud.

Marking Your Pieces

Be mindful of the bait and switch routine I mentioned in Chapter 3. One way to protect yourself is to mark your item in some way that will not void the mint status of the piece.

With plush toys, sew in a thin colored thread that you can see only if you part a seam. On figurines, pottery, or earthenware, make a small dot in an inconspicuous place that you can only detect under a black light. Scan the front and back of sports cards. Many people discreetly mark and photograph their pieces.

The bait and switch scam isn't that common with antiques and fine art, but it's still a good idea to keep your auction photos on file. This documents what you send to your buyers.

Packing Material

If it's breakable, wrap it in bubble-wrap and secure it with packing tape. If the item has several parts, such as a lid and a base, wrap each one separately. They might take longer to unwrap, but the buyer will be far more upset if the item breaks.

Nest the item in shock-resistant material. Line the bottom of the shipping carton with packing puffies, place the item

Note: Save packing puffies from shipments you receive. Most collectors who buy and trade through the mail have enough packing material around to last three lifetimes.

on them, and surround it with more puffies. Wadded newspaper can help fill in larger spaces.

If the item is bendable, be sure to secure it so it won't crease during shipment. If it's a figurine without a box, wrap it in bubble wrap, secure the wrap with tape, and nest it in plenty of puffies.

Adequate Cushioning

Use a shipping container big enough for the item, the product packaging, and plenty of puffies. Be sure the carton has adequate room for the item to "float" in the center of all the packing.

Some folks will double-box extremely fragile items. Pack the item securely in one box, then float that box in a slightly larger box by surrounding it with more packing puffies.

Make sure the item can't jostle inside the container once it's sealed. The carrier won't stamp it "fragile" if something bounces around inside when the package is shaken.

Do I Mind If You Smoke?

It's your business if you smoke, but I'd rather not be able to tell when your package arrives. Cigarette, pipe, and cigar smoke have a way of permeating porous items, such as fabric and packing material.

If you smoke, try to keep your packing materials in a well-ventilated area so they don't set off the smoke detector at your buyer's home. I'm not trying to be politically correct about smoking; I just speak from unpleasant experience. Those roller blades I mentioned in Chapter 1 and the box they came in smelled as if they used to belong to Joe Camel. Our family room reeked for days.

Don't Forget the Enclosures!

Tuck the shipping note where the buyer will see it when he or she opens the package. This is also a chance to promote good karma — and maybe more business — by enclosing a few other items with the shipment.

Business Card or Brochure

Do you run a collectible business? If so, including a business card or brochure with your shipment is a great way to generate more sales. Your customer will see it when he or she likes you the most — the day the item arrives!

Nice Touches

One seller I buy from writes her shipping letters on Kim Anderson note cards. I save all of them. Another collectible dealer includes two Andes Candies chocolate mints with each shipment.

Just for kicks, I included a few unopened packs of Pez candy with some old Pez dispensers I shipped out. That type of gesture can be meaningful for some folks, especially those still leery of buying things from the Internet.

Why not use this opportunity to put a little sunshine in someone's day?

Yes, Packing Can Be Fun!

When it's time to grab all the envelopes with checks and letters and head for my packing area, I'll line up the collectible items I'm sending to their new homes along with everything I need to get them there safely:

- The buyers' remittance letters
- Shipping cartons
- Bubble wrap
- Plenty of packing puffies
- Wadded newspaper
- Shipping labels
- Prepared shipping notes
- Packing tape

I use the buyers' remittance letters to make out the shipping labels.

Bubble wrap secures nicely with packing tape. Once the item is safely nestled in puffies or secured with wadded newspaper, I'll place the shipping note closest to the side I think the buyer will open; then seal the carton. A few pieces of clear packing tape over the shipping label ensure that the ink won't smear and be unreadable.

My buyers are typically happiest with me when their item arrives in the condition they expected. This definitely helps when the online auction transaction progresses to the final phase.

Feedback

There's no better way to judge someone's method of operating at an online auction site than by the testimony of someone who did business with the person. Many people read a seller's feedback comments before deciding to bid on his or her auctions.

Angie Jones occasionally buys collectibles on eBay, but only after checking the seller's feedback profile. "I usually feel confident buying on eBay because I only purchase items from sellers with positive ratings," she says. "I would hesitate to buy from someone without any feedback."

The first online auction site to use a peer rating system known as *feedback* was eBay, and it works. For an important process, it's very simple. When you transact with another user, you enter a one-line comment about how it went. Some sites let you judge on a scale from one to five; others, like eBay, simply have you declare the comment as positive, neutral, or negative. The comment becomes part of that user's permanent record at the site.

Remember that the decision to enter comments is up to the person doing it. If someone refuses to enter feedback for you, don't retaliate with negative comments. Some users choose to leave feedback only when they feel the person they dealt with went beyond the call of duty.

If another user posts positive comments for you, you're under no obligation to reciprocate. If the transaction completed with no problems, though, you should leave a good report for that person as well. You never know when you may be dealing with him or her again.

Open Feedback

When eBay first started its feedback system, you could leave any type of comment for any other user. The only restriction was that only one comment you left the same person would count toward his or her overall rating.

This means that someone you never dealt with could post a negative comment about you and it would stay on your record as long as that user ID was in the system. Feedback bombing, which you'll read about further on, was a problem at times.

Most sites, including eBay, no longer allow open feedback for negative comments. Some sites don't allow open feedback at all.

Transaction-Related Feedback

Many auction sites only let you leave feedback for someone with whom you did business. Unless you and the other person were the buyer or seller for the same successful auction, your comment won't register. Or, your comment will appear on the person's feedback page but won't count toward his or her overall rating.

With this method, you know when you review someone's feedback file that each comment represents an actual auction the person participated in, as either buyer or seller.

There are certain drawbacks to only allowing transaction-related feedback. If your high bidder backs out and the next highest bidder buys the item, you can't exchange feedback with that person no matter how well the transaction went. With open feedback, you can.

A Cyber-Tattoo

Once you enter feedback, it's usually there to stay. Most sites won't erase or edit it for you. There's a moral reason for this but also a legal one.

If the auction site starts messing with the feedback comments, they become responsible and possibly liable for them. If the comments remain unedited and appear just as the user typed them in, only the author is responsible for the content.

This is why auction sites advise you to "be sure you're saying what you want to say with this feedback." Knowing the remarks are permanent, users should carefully consider what they post about another person, especially since their own user ID stays attached to the comment forever.

Character Assessment?

No online auction site can guarantee that a positive rating means you won't have any problems with a particular user. A person could have a positive rating as a buyer, yet operate poorly as a seller.

Use feedback as a tool to help you make an informed decision about whether you want to bid on a person's auction, or accept his or her bid on an item you list for sale.

The Rules

All online auction sites have rules for using the feedback system. Here are some examples:

* You can't post positive feedback for yourself from a secondary user ID, if you use more than one.
* You can't leave negative feedback if a user fails to perform some action outside the scope of the auction.
* Some sites don't let you transfer your user feedback from another site.

If you earn too much negative feedback, you can lose your site privileges.

Note: Some of the newer sites allow users to import their feedback from other sites, but this is cause for contention as this book goes to press. Feedback importing may soon be regulated.

How to Post it

Once you find the feedback entry page, the rest is easy. You'll enter a one-line comment explaining how the transaction went and click "enter," or something similar. Your comment and your user ID are added to the person's feedback file, which any registered site user can read.

Finding the Feedback Screen

In Part 2, you'll see instructions for leaving feedback on some of the major online auction sites.

During my auction site research, I noticed that the most difficult page to find at some sites is the one where you enter feedback. Almost every auction

Note: Some sites let you hide your feedback. Most sites advise against this, though, because it raises suspicion about what you're keeping quiet.

site calls the peer rating system something else, which makes it even more of an adventure.

The first place to look for the feedback entry form is on the site's home page. I hope that auction site designers soon realize that feedback should be easy to post.

If that hasn't happened yet, start your hunt by clicking on the rating number after the person's user ID. If that doesn't take you to the right place, go back to the auction listing and see if there's a link there. You might also find it under Customer Service, Help, User Services, or Auction History.

It's often a challenge, but keep hunting — it's there somewhere. Once you find it, follow the instructions the site provides to enter the feedback comment. That part is always very simple.

Warm Fuzzies in as Few Words as Possible

Without limits, some users might elaborate with joy when an item arrives sooner than expected, when a payment arrives in overnight mail, or when e-mail is so friendly that the parties meet for sushi.

For this reason, most online auction sites give you an eighty-character limit with which to express your satisfaction. On a standard monitor — seventeen inches — eighty characters is typically one line of text in a maximized Web browser.

This is plenty of space in which to post an effective feedback comment.

What Do I Say?

Be as specific as possible within your character limit. With a little practice and by reading comments left for others, you'll get the hang of it quickly.

Phrases like these get right to the point:

> Fast pay, good communication, easy to deal with.
> Friendly e-mail, great packaging, an asset to online auctions.
> Item exactly as described, seller knows the market, fast shipping.

If you have any spaces left, throw in "A+++" or whatever tops off your comment.

Negative Feedback

It happens. Every online auction community has its share of grouches. It's aggravating, even painful when it happens, but don't let one negative comment placed on your record deter you from using the site. Keep doing business with stellar practices, and the comment will age into a pile of hyperlinks nobody will care about because they won't be able to find it. If I see a user with 1078 positive comments, do I care if some misanthrope left him or her a negative comment three months ago? No.

You have the right to be treated with dignity and respect, and this includes interaction on the Internet. When it comes to the complex world of online auctions, people are bound to make mistakes at first. I did, and maybe you will. When it happens, you'll want people to forgive and forget.

Remember this when you're an experienced user and someone messes up one of your auctions. It's easier to explain the proper procedure to the person than make a grand issue of it. You'll only make yourself look bad.

Most sites advise you, right on the feedback page, to try to settle the dispute off-line before you post negative feedback about the person.

I heartily agree. Off-line disputes can be resolved. Negative feedback is there to stay.

When It's Necessary

Be sure any negative feedback you submit reflects your experience with the person. Since you can't withdraw comments, enter negative feedback as a last resort. Try to settle the matter first on the phone or in e-mail.

Here are some instances where posting negative feedback about a user, as either the seller or buyer, is necessary to warn other users:

- Buyer refuses to pay
- Seller refuses to sell
- Seller fails to send item after receiving payment
- Seller sends an item that doesn't match the description and refuses to refund
- Seller refuses to accept return of an item within the three-day review period
- Any dishonest or illegal behavior

Users with too many negative comments may have their site privileges revoked.

Wording the Comment

The comment should get right to the point and not include name-calling or accusations. For example, if several weeks pass and a promised payment never arrives, a negative comment like this will suffice:

Waited one month and no payment arrived, only promises. Re-listed item.

Avoid any "beware" or "caution" statements. Anyone who reads the comment later can make his or her own judgment based on the facts you provided.

Feedback Scrooges

I asked members of my online collecting community if everyone with whom they transact posts feedback for them. I found that an average of 80% of successful auctions result in the users leaving each other feedback, positive or negative.

Feedback is a useful resource, but certain people bristle at it. Some folks have a "personal policy" against leaving anyone positive feedback. This can be for any number of reasons:

- The person hasn't figured out how to post feedback and doesn't want to ask directions.
- He or she is waiting for you to leave feedback first (wimp feedback).
- What, say something *nice?* Never!

Whatever you do, don't take it personally. If you liked the way the person did business, post a positive comment and move on.

Doesn't Have a Clue

When I sent out a Hallmark Kiddie Car Classic to my high bidder, the shipping note included my stock phrase:

> "I left feedback for you when your payment arrived and would appreciate if you would do the same for me if you're happy with our transaction."

A few days later, I got a rather terse e-mail from the fellow. He chastised me for requesting positive feedback from him. He intoned that leaving feedback was his decision and I had no right to pressure him into it. "After all," his e-mail berated, "you waited two full days to ship me the car!"

Yes, I waited two full days to ship the item. His check arrived on Saturday and the following Monday was Labor Day, a holiday that suspends postal service in the United States. I shipped his package that Tuesday.

While some online auction users are stingy with positive feedback, I'm tempted to assume that someone this cantankerous simply doesn't know how to enter it. I hope that by now, someone drew him a picture.

You Go First

Similar to the wimp trading I mentioned in *Collector's Guide to Buying, Selling, and Trading on the Internet,* we also have wimp feedback. Certain users won't enter feedback for you until you post a comment for them. Some people would rather pull out their toenails than be the first to offer a positive comment. They fear disappointment.

The best way to deal with someone like this is just go ahead and leave positive feedback if the deal went OK. If he or she doesn't reciprocate, at least you'll know you're not the one with the problem.

Feedback Misuse

Unfortunately, leaving feedback for a friend to increase his or her rating is not the purpose of the feature. Sure, I know, everyone does it. But that doesn't make it right.

On the other hand, if someone has 25 friends all willing to post pearls of praise, the popular recipient is probably a nice, honest person. There are far worse feedback misuses than having a trusted friend or fellow collector help boost your rating.

Feedback Bombing

This only happens at sites that allow open feedback for negative comments. One user has a grudge against another and arranges for several users to gang up and post negative feedback for that user ID.

Either that or one person opens several new accounts just to bomb the victim with a barrage of negative comments. This is definitely not good for the recipient, since auction sites may pull your account if you rack up too much negative feedback.

Several sites have a safeguard against this, one being that all negative feedback must be transaction related. You can only enter negative comments if you and the other party participated in the same successful auction.

In addition, some sites will not let you enter any feedback until the fifth day after you opened your account. This is clever, since that's usually how long it takes an auction to close and a new user to genuinely need to enter feedback.

Feedback Extortion

If someone wants you to operate outside the scope of the auction transaction and threatens you with negative feedback if you don't, this is feedback extortion.

It's very uncommon. If it happens to you, report it at once to the auction site administrator.

Feedback Surfers

This is common.

Some auction sites allow users to enter positive feedback that isn't transaction-specific. In other words, you can add to someone's feedback rating whether you dealt with the person or not.

To increase their own feedback score, some users troll the auction listings for users with high ratings — usually over 1,000 — and enter a positive feedback comment in hopes of getting one in return. They suspect that with such busy transaction turnover, the high-rated user will assume the comment is valid and reciprocate, without the time-consuming effort of checking past auctions. Low-rated users are targets too. The feedback surfer assumes that, possibly unfamiliar with the process, the user may oblige a comment in return.

A user with fewer than 10 feedback comments, most of which are not transaction-specific, could be a feedback surfer growing a positive record. Ask for online references before bidding on his or her auctions.

If you find a comment in your own file from someone you don't know, send the person e-mail and question the action. It could be someone you dealt with weeks ago, behind in transaction maintenance. It could also be someone trying to increase his or her own rating. If you never dealt with the person, don't reciprocate.

Remember Me, From Way Back?

This is another form of feedback surfing, only more interactive. A person trying to boost his or her rating leaves you feedback and then sends you e-mail. He or she will claim to have done business with you in the past (by drumming up something out of your auction history) but is certain you don't remember. You'll get an e-mail message like this:

> Hi! You and I traded Beanies back in 1997. You probably don't remember me but we traded bears and everything went fine. I'm trying to establish feedback

on eBay, so could you leave me a positive comment? I'm user "qwerty" on eBay. Thanks!

If you don't remember the person, don't leave feedback. Remember that you could be putting your own reputation on the line if this ends up being someone with an unsavory character.

Note: The user ID "qwerty" is fictitious and in no way reflects on any individual. If you read Chapter 2, you know how I came up with it.

☛Communicating with the Site

I've participated in hundreds of online auctions at numerous sites. I've found that if you employ good practices, auctions typically go off without a hitch. Here's how to make that happen:

- Represent your item accurately in the auction description.
- Stay in communication with the buyer or seller while the transaction is in progress.
- Leave positive feedback when it's merited.

Not everyone operates as well as you do, though. Sometimes things don't go the way you planned and you have to contact the online auction site administrators.

Complaints About Users

Most online auction sites have a "how to use the site" or "help" link or an e-mail address to which you can send requests for information. Those messages usually go directly to the folks running the show, the site administrators. They alone have specific capabilities at the site, such as:

- Canceling an auction in progress
- Sending e-mail warnings to users
- Revoking user privileges
- Adjusting a user's account

Unless there's a specific link for "complaints about users," use the main e-mail address when you need to contact the site for any reason.

You may not get a reply, or the answer you get will read like a form letter. Rest assured, however, that someone investigated your complaint and acted on it, if necessary. The folks who run auction sites want users with ill intent flushed out before they damage the site's reputation. You'll need to contact the site administrators under certain circumstances.

Buyer Doesn't Pay — You Need a Refund

Contact the site and request a refund of your commission fee. The site administrators can adjust your account accordingly and send warning e-mail to the buyer who backed out of the auction.

The site may require you to post negative feedback for the bidder before they'll refund your fees. This helps discourage fraudulent refund requests.

Blocking Bids

If you have problems with a particular bidder, contact the site administrators. They can send an e-mail request to the person instructing him or her to refrain from bidding on your auctions. If the user then violates that request, he or she can lose site privileges.

> **Note:** If you cancel a user's bid, be sure there's a good reason. Other users can track this action and you don't want frequent misuse to hamper your reputation.

Some sites let you cancel any user's bid, as long as you enter a few lines of text explaining the situation. Check the site's help pages to see if they offer this feature.

☞Keeping Good Records

Document your online auction transactions. Whether you maintain a photocopy of your shipping and payment notes or chronicle them in an accounting ledger, accurate records come in handy if you need to refer to the transaction later.

One way to keep track of your auctions, whether you're the buyer or the seller, is to print the main auction page to keep on file. That page usually has the winner's name and the amount of the high bid in case you need to refer to it later.

Managing Your Photos

Keep copies of all your auction photos. You never know when you'll need to refer to one. Plus, it's fun to review the items you've sold at auction months later.

Unless you're listing the same item again, delete the photo from your hosting location. This saves space and lessens the chance that someone will re-use your photo, since it will be unavailable to the public once you take it off the Web. Save the photos on your hard drive or on a floppy disk.

You may want to number the image files after the date you listed the auction, like this:

Image file	Date auction listed
12201999-1.jpg	December 20, 1999
02242000-1.jpg	February 24, 2000 – first one
02242000-2.jpg	February 24, 2000 – second one
04032000-1.jpg	April 3, 2000 – first one
04032000-2.jpg	April 3, 2000 – second one
04032000-2a.jpg	April 3, 2000 – second one, side view

Listing the image files by auction number would work, but it's slightly more difficult since you don't know the auction number until after you have the auction up and running, and the photo's already in your auction description.

With this system, there's a better chance of finding the picture if you need to refer to it long after the listing ages out of the auction site's file system.

Save All E-mail!

I save all e-mail that transpires from online auction activity. I keep it in special directories named after the auction site the messages result from.

Saved e-mail is helpful for many reasons:

- Finding an address or telephone number the person sent you
- Checking the date the person promised to send payment or ship the item
- Referring to the original agreement if a dispute arises
- Remembering a transaction with a particular user if someone asks for a reference
- Providing any necessary memory-refresher about the transaction

The other person may appreciate your saving the e-mail too, especially if it's the only record of the original agreement. Sometimes e-mail disappears accidentally.

I save auction-related e-mail messages on my hard drive for 12 months. Then I download them to a floppy diskette to keep on file. You never know when you might need to refer to an old e-mail message months after a transaction completes.

The preceding chapters explained the benefits of online auction sites for collectors. By now, you probably have some idea of what kind of auction site would be the most useful to you in managing your collection online. The next chapters comprise Part 2, where you'll examine some of the major auction sites and what they offer Internet collectors.

I hope you enjoy exploring them as much as I did!

Note: This is the author's personal opinion, but e-mail should be private. Posting e-mail messages on Internet bulletin boards or forwarding them to others without the sender's permission is bad form on the Internet, and may cost you the respect of others. It might be tempting to share e-mail, especially if the disagreement involves other people. Keep in mind, though, that you could mar your own reputation by publicizing a private e-mail message.

Part 2
Where the Auction Is

Chapter 7 — The Auction Sites

☞Online Auction Sites

There are hundreds of Internet auction sites, and there'll be even more tomorrow. A few authors have made valiant attempts to compile books that list all auction sites on the Internet, but the books go out of date before they're published. There's so much going on in the online auction community that it's next to impossible to catalog it and keep it up to date.

As an alternative to an online auction directory, I chose six auction sites that each operate differently and wrote a separate chapter for each one. The way the Internet works, one of them may disappear overnight or another megasite might emerge making this book seem incomplete without a chapter on it.

If you read, or at least skim, the six chapters that follow, you'll be able to participate at any online auction site no matter how long it's been running. The Internet auction industry is still evolving. While a site may no longer be in operation, you'll probably encounter the same or similar features and options at a new site. It's important to know how they work, and what to expect in the way of new online auction features that will develop over time.

Here in Part 2, we'll examine some of the major online auction sites in detail. You'll also find short blurbs on over fifty other online auction sites of interest to collectors, and some Web sites that provide services — some of them free — to help manage your auctions.

Note: Want more information about user support for online auctions? Check out the Online Auction Users Association at www.auctionusers.org and FairMarket, Inc. at www.fairmarket.com.

The Changing Internet

The Internet is alive with change. Sites that are there today might take you someplace else tomorrow, and new ones appear constantly. You're never bored on the Internet, and you'll always find plenty of auction sites at which you can manage your collecting.

The sites you choose to use depend on your personal needs as a collector. There are millions of registered users at all the major online auction sites. Many avid users of one site have user IDs at a few others. This is common, and fun if you can keep them all straight. As things change on the Internet, it helps to be flexible enough to change right along with them.

☞Major Auction Sites

Web sites dedicated to auctions, and only auctions, are what I call the "major auction sites." Some of these sites offer extra features for users, but they all relate to the auction community. The core business of the site is enabling users to list and bid on items.

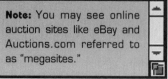

Note: You may see online auction sites like eBay and Auctions.com referred to as "megasites."

Critical Mass

It's best defined as a size, number, or amount large enough to produce a particular result, as in the *critical mass* of activity to render an event successful. The critical mass concept as it relates to online auction sites varies, depending on who's defining it.

The megasites, particularly eBay, supposedly epitomize the critical mass for the online auction industry. Some Internet pundits speculate that new auction sites must produce the critical mass that eBay has in order to be successful.

Whether the success of eBay is an industry fluke is subject to speculation, which I won't discuss here. I mention critical mass to offer collectors another angle from which to judge an online auction site. Remember that critical mass is subjective. If you're satisfied with the results you get using a particular site to manage your collecting, then the critical mass at that site is sufficient for you.

In Chapter 2, I outlined the benefits of major auction sites and lesser-known ones for collectors. Keep those in mind when an online auction site, or any Internet business, boasts about having critical mass.

Support on the Web

Sites like Honesty Communications (www.honesty.com) help by letting you track your current auction activity with tools at their site. Some of these Web-based auction services put additional strain on the auction site's server, but they help attract users.

Here's an example of what Honesty Communications offers:

• The ability to track your auction activity at several sites all at once
• Auction page-hit counters
• Message boards for online auction site users

These tools are invaluable to those who frequently buy and sell online.

Getting Help

The feature that sets major auction sites apart from portal auctions or newer sites is technical support online. If you need to "ask the site" a question, the megasites usually make it easy for you to get the assistance you need. While the smaller sites do have technical support available, you're more likely to get a fast — and personalized — response from a major online auction site.

☛Web Portals

Portals are designed to be your first stop on the Web. They're the Internet stepping stone to all other sites, and many of them offer their own services, including online auctions.

The term "portal" originates from the word used for a grand entranceway that entails many doors and rooms. Web portals are supposed to be your "doorway" to the Internet. Most of them debuted as search engines, and now provide a mix of other services — news, weather, entertainment information, stock market updates, chat rooms, message boards, free e-mail, shopping, and online auctions. Some of them give you free Web space for a home page.

They differ by how well they present and organize the services, and how diverse their offerings are.

Major Web Portals

Here are a few of the leading Web portals. You're probably already familiar with a few of them:

Uniform Resource Locator	Site name
www.yahoo.com	Yahoo!
www.excite.com	Excite
www.planetdirect.com	Planet Direct - Your Personal Web Service
www.lycos.com	Lycos - Your Personal Internet Guide
www.altavista.com	AltaVista Connections
www.enetcenter.com	eNet Center Portal
www.realinks.net	Realinks Internet Portal and Web Advertising Network

Web portals constantly change their content and services. When you access a portal, you may see a completely different page each time. That's just a way to keep things interesting and make sure you come back after you've surfed off to the other sites.

All portals have one thing in common. They want to be the first page brought up in your browser every time you launch it, and then be the epicenter of your Internet life.

Who Pays for Them?

Advertising pays for the site. You'll see banner ads on the pages that constantly change. Web portal services are typically free to users. When you use their services, such as e-mail or online auctions, each page contains an ad banner for one of the sponsors. If you use the sites regularly, visit a few of the sponsors. This helps keep the Web portal in business.

Some of the services require registration and user fees.

I mention portals here because some provide online auctions, many of which have respectable amounts of regular users. Auctions are one service where you might register and typically pay a fee — the usual listing fee and commissions — just as you would at any other auction site. Some of them offer free introductory listings and others entice users with free auction listings any time.

Many Web portals are sponsored by a major search engine or browser provider.

Auctions on Portals

Most of the portals use standard auction-site software to run their auctions.

Once you've used one of the major auction sites, you'll easily figure out how portal auctions work. You register a user ID and password, search for auctions, bid by proxy, and rate other users. Most portal auction sites have plenty of traffic. You can even find portals just for online auction activity, such as these:

Uniform Resource Locator	Site name
www.otwa.com	Online Traders Web Alliance
www.auctions-portal.com	Auctions Portal
www.auctionsonthenet.com	Auctions on the Net
www.webdata.com	Webdata.com®
www.online-auctions.net/Collectibles	Collectibles Auctions
www.collectiblesnet.com/ auctionportal.html	The Collectiblesnet.com
www.usaweb.com	Auction Community Web Portal
www.internetauctionlist.com	The Internet Auction List
www.shoppingspot.com/auctions.htm	ShoppingSpotAuctions

Auction portals typically include lists of hyperlinks to Web sites offering free auction software, item counters, HTML tutorials, and programs that generate auction descriptions that you can copy and paste as you enter an auction. Some of them even contain message boards and chat rooms where you can discuss online auction issues with other users. Whether it's a general use Web portal or one designed for business, you'll usually find links to online auctions from these sites.

Note: The Online Traders Web Alliance at www.otwa.com is a "centralized clearinghouse" for auction users who want to obtain help, get advice, or learn about some useful auction resources. You'll find plenty of online discussion forums there.

☞The Auction Site Chapters

The next six chapters cover some of the major auction sites on the Internet currently available for collectors and others.

Chapter	Site Name	Uniform Resource Locator
Chapter 8	eBay	www.ebay.com
Chapter 9	Amazon.com	auctions.amazon.com
Chapter 10	Auctions.com	www.auctions.com
Chapter 11	Live Auction Online	www.liveauctiononline.com
Chapter 12	CityAuction	www.cityauction.com
Chapter 13	Up4Sale	www.up4sale.com

Each chapter contains a table of site features and covers the standard and unique features of the site. Since the sites change their "look" and page layouts constantly, I only included a few page views from each site.

I also interviewed frequent users at each site and included their comments, experiences, and recommendations.

Note: Some of the auction site pages I included in the six chapters may look different when you access them, but the information you find will be similar.

You'll find specialized auction sites and some of those available on Web portals covered in Chapter 14. I also include links to sites that offer tools, features, and software to assist in managing your online auction activity.

☞How I Chose Sites to Include

Finding online auction sites to research was no problem at all. I did a search for "online auctions" with one popular search engine and came up with hundreds of selections. The first few were lists of auction sites compiled by independent Web site owners, or auction portals. I had plenty to choose from.

I also asked around in my own collecting community. While most of my Internet collecting friends admittedly use eBay, several use Up4sale, Auctions.com, and Amazon.com as well.

When I found a site that looked promising, I registered and bid on a collectible item. I made sure I was the high bidder at least once at each site I tested, and carried the transaction all the way through to leaving (and receiving) positive feedback when the deal completed.

If you're wondering what I did with all the items I purchased, I kept some, and sold others. After all, I wanted to buy *and* sell at each site, so I needed collectible items to list. I couldn't think of a better way to experience the sites than to buy and sell collectible plush (it's everywhere) or antique glass (my favorite).

Why a Chapter?

There are too many online auction sites out there to write a chapter on each one. I had to draw the line somewhere or this book would take several years to write and would become obsolete while still in manuscript form. However, I wanted you to know that as a collector, you have options when it comes to choosing an online auction site. But which ones merit a unique chapter?

Here are the criteria I used to decide:

- Plenty of categories for collectibles (as opposed to computers, electronics, automotive, etc.)
- More than 50 auctions with active bids
- Ease of use
- User confidence

• On-site assistance
• Unique features and options

The results were interesting. Some sites have names that sound like they cater to collectors, yet all auctions listed in any particular category appeared by the same user ID. This could mean a collectible dealer runs the site, which is fine for the dealer, but may not be what a collector wants from an auction site, especially to sell items.

Other sites had plenty of auctions listed by numerous users, but no active bids. I chose to spotlight online auction sites if they:

• Drew many people seeking both antiques and collectibles online
• Are dedicated to the business of auctioning goods

Why Not a Chapter?

I only included a few auction sites that run off of Web portals. They operate so much like the major sites do that you'll know how they work by the time you read these chapters.

I also passed up auction sites that loaded slowly, took forever to figure out, or rejected my site registration for any reason. Who needs that hassle?

☞Table of Features Explained

You'll find a table of features for each online auction site I cover in the next six chapters. Here's an explanation of each feature in the table:

Site URL: www.URL.com Time zone: Eastern, Central, Mountain, or Pacific	
Main page features	**Description**
Site links on main page	Set of easy-to-use navigation links on the home page that take you to the pages you'll use most.
Featured auctions	List of featured auctions on the site's home page.
Browse by category	Listing categories you can click on to start browsing auctions.
News	Any recent additions or changes to the site, or auction updates for your information.
Date of last update	When did they last change the site?
Copyright information	Copyright © 2000 Whoever
User recall	Does the site know you when you return or do you have to log in each time?
Link to personal activity page	"My Auctions" or "My Activity" page that lists everything you currently have going on at the site.

Search Features	Description
Search by keyword	Find listings that match words you enter.
Search by seller	Locate all auctions listed by a particular seller.
Search by bidder	View all auctions a particular user entered bids on.
Search by category	Find all current listings entered in a particular category.
All in one search	One search page that lets you find items by searching a variety of criteria.
Search title only	Match your search string to the auction title only.
Search auction descriptions	Match your search string to the auction title and the description text.
Search completed auctions	Conduct your search on auctions for which bids are no longer accepted.
Advanced search	Any search features beyond keyword, seller, bidder, and category such as price range, etc.

Auctions and Bidding	Description
Proxy bidding	Automatic bidding to match the maximum bid you entered when someone tries to outbid you.
Dutch auctions	List multiples of the same item in one auction.
Reserve price	Minimum price you'll sell the item for when you start the bidding at a lower price.
Mandatory reserve	You must enter a reserve price.
Adjustable start and end times	Schedule your auction to start at a time other than when you enter the listing.
View bidding history	See who bid, when, and how much.
Open-ended bidding	In last hour of auction, a certain amount of time (usually 5 minutes) added for every bid entered.
HTML in description	HTML code allowed in the auction description.
Featured auctions	Auctions that show up on the site's home page or other high-profile site pages.

Services	Description
Site Tutorial	Online site instructions to teach you how to use the site.
Personal Paging	Messages sent to your personal paging unit to notify you of an auction status change.
Escrow	Third-party service run by the auction site to handle the transaction. See Chapter 5.

Particulars	Description
Insertion Fee:	Non-refundable one-time fee for listing the auction.
Commission:	Fee based on the closing sale price.
Duration:	How long the auctions can run.

If I inaccurately listed a feature as "no" when it actually exists at that site, it's because I couldn't find it. In that case, you might not find it either.

I hope you find the following chapters useful as you use online auction sites to manage your collections.

And now — to the sites!

Chapter 8 — eBay

☞www.eBay.com

Launched in September 1995, the eBay auction site helps individual buyers and sellers, not large companies, sell items to one another over the Internet.

Seasoned Internet collectors know all about eBay. They lead the online auction business, with more than two million registered users and several hundred million completed auctions. In the time it took you to read this paragraph, about ninety new auctions started on eBay — it's *that* popular.

Each auction generates a consecutive serial number. When I last entered two auctions on eBay, the second auction's number was 895 numbers higher than the first one. I started them a little under *five minutes* apart.

Information included on the site's "About eBay" page indicates that over 50% of the items listed on eBay are sold, which is apparently a better conversion rate than any other electronic marketplace.

The eBay Internet auction site receives more than 300 million hits each month. This site's users conduct over ten million searches each *day*. It's fair to say there's a tremendous amount of traffic on eBay.

Sales at eBay are in U.S. dollars ($) or Pounds Sterling (£), as specified by the seller. All eBay fees are in U.S. dollars.

Designers for eBay change their site pages every few months but the home page consistently offers the same general information. Here's an example of what greets you when you call up www.ebay.com:

The eBay Home Page

You can reach any of the main pages on the site from this page. Copyright and other site information appear when you scroll down to the bottom. The site links at the top of the page appear on every eBay page. Site navigation is a breeze.

☞Table of Features

Site URL: www.ebay.com Time zone: Pacific		
Main page features	**Yes**	**No**
Site links on main page	X	
Featured auctions	X	
Browse by category	X	
News	X	
Date of last update	X	
Copyright information	X	
User recall		X
Link to personal activity page	X	
Search features	**Yes**	**No**
Search by keyword	X	
Search by seller	X	
Search by bidder	X	
Search by category	X	
All in one search	X	
Search title only	X	
Search auction descriptions	X	
Search completed auctions	X	
Advanced search	X	
Auctions and Bidding	**Yes**	**No**
Proxy bidding	X	
Dutch auctions	X	
Reserve price	X	
Mandatory reserve		X
Adjustable start and end time		X
View bidding history	X	
Open-ended bidding		X
HTML in description	X	
Services	**Yes**	**No**
Site Tutorial	X	
Personal Paging	X	
Escrow		X

Particulars	
Insertion Fee:	$.25 (min. bid under $10)
	$.50 (min. bid over $10)
Commission:	5% to $25
	2.5% to $1000
	1.5% over $1000
Duration:	3, 5, 7, or 10 days

☞What's Unique about eBay?

Things frequently change at eBay. They're constantly making the site easier to use. The eBay administrators take user comments seriously, incorporating many of them into the bidding and listing process.

Before a change is fully implemented, you'll see links on the auction pages inviting you to test the proposed new format. You can e-mail the site managers with your comments. It's definitely a two-way street at eBay, which is good for anyone who uses the site. And millions do!

Auction Features

Currently the standard among online auction sites, eBay pioneered many of the features now available at other online auction sites. This site adds more features every few months. When they do, you'll see announcements about them all over the site.

Update User Information

Once your auction is running, you can't go back and correct a mistake with your browser's "back" button. However, typos are embarrassing and can affect your credibility as a seller.

To help you out, eBay allows you to revise your item title, description, image URL, payment options, or shipping terms before anyone bids on your auction. On the auction-listing page, you'll see this:

Seller: If this item has received no bids, you may revise it.

Clicking on the word "revise" will take you to the Update User Information screen, where you can correct the information after entering your user ID and password. Once you revise your item, this line of text appears on the auction page:

Seller revised this item before the first bid.

The "seller revised" hyperlink takes you to the Explanation of Seller Revisions page.

Add to the Description

Once your auction has active bids, you can add text or an image to the description with an HTML-enabled form. The original text appears unchanged; your new text appends to it as a time-stamped addition to your listing.

This is a good feature to use if you need to modify your listing once someone bids on it.

You'll find the "Add to my item description" link under the eBay Services tab.

Change Category

Also on the Services page, you can change the category in which you listed your item. Sellers often use this feature if their auction isn't getting enough bids.

If the new category has a different fee structure than the original one, your account will be charged or credited for the difference.

The Gallery

As if there isn't already enough variety at eBay, they let you search for items by looking at the pictures.

For an additional charge, you can add your auction image to what eBay calls "The Gallery." Here, eBay presents a series of small pictures, called *thumbnails*, listed by auction category. The photos appear in rows on numerous pages, ordered by the closing date of the auction. Potential bidders can browse the photos instead of looking at text versions of the listing or viewing the auctions one by one.

To bid on the item, click on the photo, and you're taken right to the auction page where you can read the description.

Including my item's photo in eBay's Gallery definitely attracted bids. At least this is what my bidders told me in e-mail. Many of them found my listing by browsing through The Gallery.

Great Gift Icons

For an additional fee of $1.00, you can choose a special gift icon to appear next to your auction title on the listing pages. This is supposed to indicate that your item would make a great gift. Your auction also appears in the "Great Gifts" link on the search bar, in the appropriate price range.

You can choose from several little title icons, including a heart, birthday cake, Christmas tree, Menorah, pilgrim hat, or baby bottle. There are many different ones.

I'm not sure if this attracts bids or not, but it definitely adds a nice touch to search results.

User Services

The user services at eBay make the online auction experience safe and fun for both buyers and sellers.

About Me Pages

Any registered eBay user can create an "About Me" page on eBay, containing information he or she wants other users to know:

- Favorite Web links
- Currently running auctions
- Information about business or livelihood
- Hobbies and collections
- eBay user feedback

You can create and edit your About Me page using any of several different formats. You'll enter your user ID and password to edit the HTML file for your personal page.

The eBay Community

This site likes to inform users about what's going on in the world of online auctions. For that purpose, they provide a unique online auction information network.

The eBay Community page links you to places of interest at the site for updates and information:

- **News** – This has information bits about what's happening at the site.
- **eBay Life** – You can browse the site newsletter and read hints and tips for buying and selling at auction.
- **Charity** – Here you'll find links to charitable events taking place at eBay.
- **Suggestion Box** – This link takes you to a page where you can share ideas with the eBay site administrators.
- **Chat and Message Boards** – There's a chat room called the eBay Café; a cyber-café for AOL users, and message boards so users can post discussion topics.
- **Library** – Loads of articles about the products bought and sold at auction appear in the eBay library. You can even read articles about preparing antiques and collectibles for auction.
- **eBay Store** – What home is complete without eBay cups, shirts, duffel bags, and clocks? You can get that and more at the eBay store.
- **About eBay** – Follow this link to learn everything you ever wanted to know about eBay.

The eBay Community page also links to other instructional and informative pages at the site. You can post questions about including images with your auctions, how to use HTML, or when to contact the high bidder. It's all there.

Listing Icons

A series of little images appear adjacent to the listings to let you know at a

Chapter 8 — eBay

glance what features the auction includes. You'll see these images as you browse through search results. Here's an example of what they stand for:

- **Gallery** – The image for this listing also appears in the eBay Gallery.
- **Photo** – The listing includes a picture of the item.
- **Hot** – This auction generated 30 or more bids so far.
- **New** – The listing went up within the past 24 hours.

The listing icons vary depending on which search method you use, but the meaning is the same; eBay adds to and changes the listing icons periodically.

Using the Site

There's a unique arrangement for navigation links that appear on every page of the site. A link bar contains the major search links. When you click on one, a group of sub-links appears under the main link, much like a family tree of hyper-links would appear.

Help

There are many pages where you can get help using the site. For basic navigation, you'll find main site links that appear at the top of every page. Specialized links appear when you click on one of them:

- **Browse** – Categories, Featured, Hot, Grab bag, Great gifts, Big ticket
- **Sell** – Add your item for auction
- **Services** – Overview, Registration, Buying & Selling, My eBay, About me, Feedback Forum, Safe Harbor
- **Search** – Find items, Find members, Personal Shopper
- **Help** – Overview, Basics, Buyer guide, Seller guide, My info, Community standards
- **Community** – Overview, News, Chat, eBay life, Library, Charity, eBay store, Suggestion box, About eBay

Navigation throughout the site is easy, since you can get anywhere on the site from any page.

Searching for Auctions

The search pages are comprehensive. You can search for auctions almost any way. Each major search category appears on a separate screen and offers additional criteria. You can search in only one category but with any criteria selected:

- **Listing title search** (enter keywords)
  Search title and description
  Category (select from drop-down menu)
  Price range

Document...Part 2 — Where the Auction Is   Page 187

Regions (select from drop-down menu or search by country)
Order by (date, ascending, or descending)
View results (all items, items with Gallery preview, Gallery items only)
View text-only results
- **Item number lookup**
   Enter the auction number
- **Seller search (enter user ID)**
   Include bidder emails (Yes or No)
   Completed items too? (No, All, Last Day, Last 2 Days, Last Week, Last 2
      Weeks)
   Order by (Newest first, Oldest first, Auction end, Current Price)
   Number of items per page (select from drop-down menu)
- **Bidder search (Enter user ID)**
   Completed items too? (Yes or No)
   Even if not high bidder? (Yes, even if not the high bidder; no, only if high bidder)
   Number of items per page (select from drop-down menu)
- **Completed auctions**
   Search title only
   Order by (date, ascending, or descending)
- **International search**
   Category (select from drop-down menu)
   Country (select from drop-down menu)
   Order by (date, ascending, or descending)
   View results (all items, items with
      Gallery preview, Gallery items only)
   View text-only results

An option on the search page lets you specify whether the search results should contain the site images, or text-only.

> **Note:** Viewing Web pages in text-only mode makes them load faster.

Category Search

From the eBay home page, you can search for items in specific listing categories. Just click on the hyperlink auction titles for the items you seek.

You'll see pages of sub-categories to choose from until you select the branch with the listings. Icons by each listing let you know which features that auction includes — gallery, photo, hot, or new.

Gallery Search

At the eBay home page, you can click on "Shop by Photos in the Gallery" to browse the image thumbnails. You'll select a category just as you would with a regular search, only you'll see the images.

The featured auctions appear first, followed by the regular listings. It takes a little longer to load than a regular search, but what a great way to window-shop!

Going Going Gone

To search listings closing in the next 5 hours, select the "Going Going Gone" link from the header of your category search results. To affect last-minute bids and try to end up the winner, many experienced online bidders search exclusively from this category.

Your auction will automatically drop into the Going Going Gone category when only five hours remain on the auction clock.

Search User IDs

From the main search page, eBay lets you check out the bidding or selling activity of any eBay user. You'll see clearly labeled fields for this feature on the main search page.

To access sensitive information (your account status, your personal profile, or a list of feedback that you left for other users), you'll need to enter your user ID and password.

Bidding

When you bid on an item, you'll enter your maximum bid on the auction page. To confirm and enter the bid, type your user ID and password in the spaces provided on the review page. You may just log in rather than entering your user ID and password with each current bid.

On the confirmation page, you'll see if you're the new high bidder, or if another user's proxy bidding got there first. If you scroll down the page, you'll see a short version of the auction listing with the current high bidder's user ID in place.

Bidding screens at eBay have changed a few times and they're bound to change again, but the basic bidding process will probably remain standard for online auction sites.

Proxy Bidding

This concept was pioneered by eBay. If you're the first bidder, the amount shown as your current bid will probably be lower than your maximum bid. It will match the minimum price set by the seller. The only exception is if your maximum bid meets the reserve price; then your current bid matches reserve price, even if your maximum bid exceeds it.

If someone else bids on the item, your bid raises until your contender's amount exceeds your maximum. You'll then get an outbid e-mail notice from eBay, and you'll need to enter a higher maximum bid to stay in the game. In case of a tie for the highest bid, the earlier bid wins.

Proxy bidding does not work with Dutch auctions.

Bidding History Available

From the auction-listing page, click on the "Bid History" link beside the "number of bids" column. You can opt to see the information with or without the bidders' e-mail addresses. If you select this feature, you'll enter your user ID and password before the history page displays.

A list of users who have bid on the auction will appear. The bid amounts remain private until the auction closes. After closing they are listed by each bidder's user ID.

Retracting a Bid

From the eBay Site Map under "Services," scroll down to Buyer Tools and click on "Retract my bid."

Here you'll find the Bid Retraction Form, which you can use to retract a bid you made on an auction. You'll enter your user ID and password, the auction number from which you're retracting a bid, and an explanation.

Since all eBay bids are binding, you should only retract bids for a good reason, such as:

- The seller added something to the item description after you bid, causing you to reconsider.
- You made a grave error with a decimal point, like bidding $550 instead of $5.50 as you'd originally planned.

When you retract a bid, you'll eliminate all bids you placed on that auction. You must bid again to stay in the running for the item.

Your retraction appears in the bidding history for this auction, and the seller or other bidders may ask you to explain your action. For this reason, you must enter a one-line explanation of why you're retracting your bid.

Selling an Item

Once you register, you can click on the "Sell" link at the top of any eBay page. You're immediately taken to the "Sell Your Item" page. You'll enter all the necessary information about the item that you're listing:

- Item title (required)
- Category (select from list, required)
- Description (allows HTML, required)
- Picture URL (optional)
- Add auction picture to The Gallery? (yes or no, costs extra)
- Boldfaced Title? (costs extra)
- Featured in category? (costs extra)
- Featured? (costs a lot extra)
- Great Gift icon? (select by holiday, costs extra)
- Item location (city, state, zip code, country, required)
- Preferred payment method
- Where will you ship?
- Who pays for shipping?
- Quantity (required)
- Minimum bid (required)

- Duration (3, 5, 7, or 10 days, select from list, required)
- Reserve price (optional)
- Private auction (optional)
- User ID/Password (required)

> **Note:** eBay has a great Selling Tutorial that virtually walks you though the auction entry screen.

The entry page is user-friendly. There's a link to a help page near almost every field.

You'll click "Review and Place Your Listing" and then see a listing confirmation screen. The information you entered and your formatted auction description appears. The auction isn't running yet; if you need to change anything, hit the "Back" button on your browser. If the auction is OK as it is, click on "Submit my listing" and the auction clock starts running.

Editing Active Auctions

You can edit your listing before anyone bids on it from a link right on the auction page. You'll need to enter your user ID and password to edit your auction.

After the first bid, you can add to the description. Each addition will be time stamped so bidders know when you made the change. To add to the description, use the link on the auction page. You'll enter your user ID, password, and auction number.

Ending an Auction Early

Under "Services" from the eBay Site Map, select "End my auction early." From here you'll see the Ending Auction Early entry form, where you can enter your user ID and password, and the number of the auction for which you no longer wish to accept bids.

If you end the auction because you reconsidered selling your item, you must cancel all bids on your auction before it ends. If you don't, you must sell it to the high bidder.

Cancelling a Bid

Any bid placed by a user on your auction may be canceled. From the "Site Map" under "Services," select "Cancel bids on my item." This takes you to the Bid Cancellation page. Here you must enter your user ID and password, the auction number, the user ID of the person whose bid you wish to cancel, and an explanation.

You should only use this feature if you have a good reason, such as:

- The bidder reconsiders bidding and asks you if he or she can back out.
- You can't verify the identity of the bidder, after trying all reasonable means of contact.
- You have sufficient reason to believe the bidder is using a bogus account.

Because your cancellation appears in the bidding history for the auction, you'll need to enter a one-line explanation of why you're canceling the bid.

Once you cancel bids, you cannot reinstate them.

Fees

Bidders pay no fees to eBay — only to the seller in payment for an item won at auction. Sellers pay fees associated with the listing:

- Insertion fee
- Commission
- Optional display features (bold title, featured auction, etc.)
- Optional Great Gift icon
- Optional image inclusion in The Gallery
- Optional reserve auction fee (applies only if item does not sell)

I have little doubt that eBay will come up with more optional features in the future. If you select them, the charge adds to your basic insertion fee.

Insertion Fees

You'll pay an insertion fee for every auction you list. Ordinarily, the fee varies according to your auction's opening value and multiplies based on the amount of items you offer.

Opening Value or Reserve Price	Insertion Fee
$0.01 – 9.99	$0.25
$10.00 – 24.99	$0.50
$25.00 – 49.99	$1.00
$50.00 and up	$2.00

The insertion fee is non-refundable if your item doesn't sell.

Reserve Auction Fees

In mid-1999, eBay started charging for reserve price auctions. Here's the fee schedule:

Reserve Price	Reserve Price Auction Fee
$0.01 – 24.99	$0.50
$25.00 and up	$1.00

Reserve auction fee is refunded if the high bid meets the reserve price.

Optional Features

There's a charge for optional features used to draw attention to your listing:

- **Boldface title:** $2 per auction
- **Category Feature Auctions:** $14.95 per auction
- **Auction Home Page Featured Auctions:** $99.95 per auction
- **Great Gift icon:** $1

The fees for these options are non-refundable if your item doesn't sell.

Final Value Fee

The site final value, or commission, is five percent of the sale amount up to 25 dollars, plus 2.5% of the amount above that.

Range of Final Price	Final Value Fee
$0.00 - 25.00	5%
$25.01 - 1,000.00	add 2.5% of any amount over $25.00
$1,000.01 and up	add 1.25% of any amount over $1,000.00

For Dutch auctions, the fee depends on the amount of the minimum-winning bid multiplied by the quantity of items sold.

If the item doesn't sell, eBay returns your sales fee. If your item sells, the commission appears on your account. You can have up to ten dollars on your account or you can enter a credit-card number that's retained on file. You'll receive timely account statements via e-mail.

If your high bidder backs out of the sale, eBay will refund the fees if you contact them no earlier than seven business days after the auction closed. They'll instruct you to complete an online form to initiate the refund.

Payment Information and Terms

When you register at eBay, you have two different ways to pay your auction fees:

- **Credit Card on File:** You can make regular monthly payments with your credit card. You'll enter your credit card information at eBay's Secure (SSL) site. As long as eBay can authorize your card for each month's payment amount, you can list auctions.
- **Pay-As-You-Go:** You pay by check, money order, or one-time credit card payment. You can accumulate up to $10.00 in fees before payment is due. Once your account goes over $10.00, you can't list any new items until you send in a payment or enter a credit card number.

You'll receive an e-mail invoice the first week of each month. The invoice includes the previous month's account activity and any past due amounts.

SafeHarbor

The customer service and security system at eBay is called "SafeHarbor." Several elements of SafeHarbor protect eBay users from fraudulent transactions or other site misuse.

- **Feedback Forum** – This allows users to leave comments about each other after they transact.
- **Customer Support** – The customer support staff is available around the clock. Send e-mail to helpdesk@ebay.com. The eBay Help Desk addresses questions in the order received.
- **Understanding eBay Auctions** – You'll find a great tutorial on eBay that explains every aspect of the site in clear, understandable terms.
- **Escrow** – When buyers want to use an independent escrow service, eBay refers them to iEscrow.
- **Verified eBay User** – eBay partners with Equifax Secure, Inc. to verify information users provide about themselves. If you use the service, you'll have a special little icon after your user ID so others can be sure you are who claim to be.
- **Insurance** – This is available for all eBay users in good standing. Any purchases made from auctions listed on or after March 1, 1999 have free insurance coverage of up to $200, less a $25 deductible.
- **Authentication & Grading** – eBay provides a link to the International Society of Appraisers (ISA) and similar organizations so you can arrange for third party item verification.

The company's premise is the belief that "people are basically good." They endorse the tips on safe auction trading provided by the Internet Fraud Watch organization.

The Auction Listing

On the facing page is an example of what you'll see when you call up an auction listing.

Notice the Great Gift icon I added, which appears after the auction number. Some users add small images to the Location line, since that field accepts HTML. I included the part about Santa's North Pole.

The auction description I formatted appears below the main listing, when the user scrolls down the page.

Feedback

This was the first online auction site to use the peer-rating system, now known as feedback. Most other auction sites currently use a similar peer-rating system.

Feedback can be positive, neutral, or negative. The user's feedback score represents positive comments left by unique users, minus negative comments left by unique users. You can look at a feedback page by clicking on the number in parentheses after any user ID.

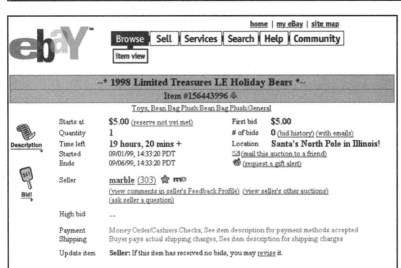

Auction Listing on eBay

High-rated e-Bay users are rewarded different colored stars, based on the level of feedback achieved.

- **Gold star** – 10–99 positives
- **Blue star** – 100–499 positives
- **Purple star** – 500–999 positives
- **Red star** – 1,000–9,999 positives
- **Shooting gold star** – 10,000 or more positives

In December 1999, "parrothead88" became the first "shooting star" user on eBay. I'm sure there will be more of them in the months and years to come.

Transaction Specific

Until recently, you could leave a positive comment for any user for any reason. However, that changed. Now all feedback, including neutral, must be transaction specific. Neutral feedback still doesn't affect the user's overall rating.

Each transaction-related feedback comment you post will increase the person's score by one, unless you already left that person an open comment before eBay instituted transaction-specific feedback. Any transaction-specific comment you

Note: Every comment you enter will appear on the person's feedback page whether it increments the final score or not.

enter after the first one will increase the user's rating. You can only enter one transaction-related comment per auction.

☞Meet Emily, A Frequent eBay User

Emily sells collectibles on eBay to subsidize her family's income. She buys wholesale from a collectible outlet and lists porcelain figurines on eBay with no reserve price. Her minimum bid is the suggested retail price.

"My auctions usually don't attract more than one bid each," she says, "but that's all I need to sell the item and not breach my agreement with the collectible company. Too many sellers are listing items below retail and that's not fair to those of us who follow the rules."

Wishing to accommodate and attract as many buyers as possible, Emily established a merchant account and accepts credit card purchases.

"People enjoy the auction experience," says Emily. "I can also make these items available to folks in remote areas who can't just drive down the street and buy any collectible item they want. Now that I take credit cards, business is booming!"

History with Online Auctions

Emily's neighbor offered to teach her how to use Windows 95. "I wanted to go back to work," she explains, "but I didn't know much about computers."

One afternoon, as Emily was learning the Excel Spreadsheet, a package arrived for her friend. Inside were five Cherished Teddies and a note from an eBay seller. Emily's friend told her about being high bidder and getting a great deal on several retired pieces. Intrigued, Emily asked to see how eBay works.

"To make a long story short," she continues, "once I saw how easy it is to sell on eBay, I got my own computer and went back to work — right at home!"

Lessons Learned

Emily started slowly. She bid on a few items and ended up the high bidder. Then she listed some old children's books she'd been meaning to get rid of. Once she felt confident with the process, she set up an account with a wholesaler and started listing auctions regularly.

She did learn one costly lesson. Emily discovered it wasn't a good idea to run concurrent auctions for the same item.

"I got a shipment from the distributor and listed every item in its own auction, all running at the same time," she says. "What a mistake! I only sold one of each style but I had to pay all those listing fees. Now I know better. I only have one active auction running for each design, or I use a Dutch auction. That way if several of them sell, I'm the one who sells them!"

Thoughts about eBay

As a red-star user with over four thousand positive feedback comments, Emily feels she's found her niche in the collectible business.

"I always wanted to have a collectible shop," she says, "but I didn't want to be married to it. With eBay, I can run a business that pays good money online and set my own hours.

Emily finds that she makes enough to supplement her family's income and never runs out of people to talk to. She corresponds with other eBay sellers and frequents the eBay chat rooms.

"This site is so well-known," says Emily. "Almost everyone I meet has an eBay account and sells online. I can't imagine a better way to run a small business than by listing items on eBay. There's so much traffic that I'd never even have to consider advertising. If anyone wants to know more about me, well, they can look at my eBay About Me page!"

Best Experience

"I'll never forget one lady I met through eBay," Emily says. "She discovered eBay by using one of her husband's Netscape bookmarks and found her way to one of my hinged box auctions. She sent me e-mail asking for more details and revealed that she was afraid to buy something from someone she didn't know."

Emily decided that she would let the woman get to know her through e-mail correspondence, and walked her through the bidding process. They exchanged daily e-mail and the woman ended up high bidder.

"She had gotten tired of collecting Beanie Babies," Emily said, "but she missed adding new things to her curio. So, I talked her into collecting my porcelains! Now she and I trade items and I helped her set up her own mini-business on eBay."

This made Emily proud. The woman, she later found out, had a debilitating condition that left her unable to leave home very often. Emily and eBay brought excitement into her life again.

Chapter 9 — Amazon.com Auctions

☞ auctions.amazon.com

"Hey, I like the way you guys have this place painted!"

That was my first impression when I surfed into the Amazon.com auction site. It's well laid-out, reminding me of a notebook kept by a tidy student. For a relatively new auction site, it's remarkably easy to use.

This is excellent for the first-time online auction user because you won't lose your place while navigating the site. You can get anywhere on the site right from the main page, and you can get back to the main page from anywhere on the site. As auction sites go, it's definitely one of the friendliest.

Amazon.com changes its "look" from time to time. Here's an example of what appears when you call up the home page. Notice that it greets me by name!

Amazon.com Auctions Home Page

Amazon.com has a great set of features and links that go all over the site and back home again. You'll see copyright information and the date of the last site update as you scroll to the bottom of the page.

Table of Features

Site URL: auction.amazon.com Time zone: Pacific		
Main page features	**Yes**	**No**
Site links on main page	X	
Featured auctions	X	
Browse by category	X	
News	X	
Date of last update	X	
Copyright information	X	
User recall	X	
Link to personal activity page	X	
Search features	**Yes**	**No**
Search by keyword	X	
Search by seller	X	
Search by bidder	X	
Search by category	X	
All in one search	X	
Search title only	X	
Search auction descriptions	X	
Search completed auctions	X	
Advanced search	X	
Auctions and Bidding	**Yes**	**No**
Proxy bidding	X	
Dutch auctions	X	
Reserve price	X	
Mandatory reserve		X
Adjustable start and end time		X
View bidding history	X	
Open-ended bidding	X	
HTML in description	X	
Services	**Yes**	**No**
Site Tutorial	X	
Personal Paging		X
Escrow	X	

Particulars	
Insertion Fee:	$0.10
Commission:	5% to $25
	2.5% over
Duration:	3, 5, or 7 days

☞What's Unique about Amazon.com?

Amazon.com differs from other Internet auction sites because the auctions link to another branch of the business – the very successful Amazon.com online bookstore. The bookstore branch is a pioneer in its class – the best known and widely used on the Internet.

Amazon.com launched their auction division in March 1999. All ten million existing customers became automatic registered users of Amazon.com auctions, giving the site a ready-made crowd of regulars. Since high traffic helps sell items, it was a hit from the start.

Internet auction users will find the site's ease-of-use helpful in managing collections online.

Auction Features

Many of the listing features at Amazon.com auctions correlate to the company's merchandise area. This helps to entice some of Amazon's ten million registered users to your auction.

To keep up with the busy online auction market, Amazon.com adds new features constantly. These state-of-the-art features keep the auctions running smoothly and easily for users.

Open-Ended Bidding

Whenever someone enters a bid in the last ten minutes of an auction, the clock automatically adds ten more minutes. All Amazon.com auctions run with open-ended bidding. This feature ensures that an auction can't close until ten minutes pass without a new bid. Amazon.com calls it "Going, Going, Gone."

CrossLinks

Amazon.com brings potential customers right to your listing. When a user searches for a product, several Amazon.com auction "CrossLinks" appear with each merchandise listing. Active auctions show up if they relate in any way to the subject matter of the book. Some generate at random, based on the listing category.

For example, if you conduct a book search for "Railroad Collectibles," one of several titles you'll see is *Railroad Collectibles: An Illustrated Value Guide* by Stanley L. Baker (Collector Books, 1989).

If you scroll down the page, here's what you might see:

Our auction and zShops sellers recommend:

- PENNSYLVANIA RAILROAD LANTERN (Current bid: $25.00)
- New York Central Railroad stock certificate (Current bid: $3.25)
- ALL ABOARD! The RR in American Life (Current bid: $10.95)

The auction listings are hyperlink text. If you click on one, you'll go right to the auction page where you can read the description – and bid.

What a wonderful way to coax buyers to your auction!

ISBN or ASIN Entry

Sometimes the CrossLinked auctions don't have anything to do with the book. The system "attempts" to match books to auctions. To ensure good matches, auction sellers can specify their own CrossLinks.

When you list an auction, you can enter the International Standard Book Number (ISBN) or an Amazon Standard Identification Number (ASIN) for any book you want as a CrossLink. A link for your auction will appear when an Amazon customer views the book listing. He or she can visit your auction and perhaps enter a bid. When your auction closes, the CrossLink will no longer appear.

You can change or add CrossLinks to your active auction listing at the "My Account" services page.

Take-It Price

You may elect to set a Take-It Price. This is the amount at which you're willing to end the auction.

If you offer a Take-It Price, you'll need to be available to get in touch with the winning bidder at any time. He or she may "Take-It" any time after the first minute of the auction.

You can alter the Take-It Price before anyone enters a bid. Once a bid is in place, the Take-It Price is locked in.

User Services

You'll find plenty of services at Amazon.com designed to make the online auction experience safe and fun for both buyers and sellers. The status quo at this site is "be friendly and helpful."

Since Amazon.com is a multi-feature site, you can click any tab on the main navigation bar and do some serious online shopping.

Cookie, Anyone?

Unlike most other major auction sites, Amazon.com "remembers" you after your first visit because it sends a "cookie" to your PC. This means you don't have to enter your user ID and password to log in — the site already knows who you are.

A cookie is a very small text file sent by an Internet site to your computer's hard drive. Its purpose is to track your visits to

Note: Since Amazon.com uses cookies, be sure you don't enter your user ID and password from a public PC, or a PC that anyone unknown to you might use after you do. If someone else accesses the Amazon.com site from the same PC, he or she could be logged in as you, and would be able to run up charges against your account and bid on items in your name.

the site. Most browsers accept cookies by default. You can set your preferences to deny them if you wish to remain anonymous at Web sites that use them.

zShops

Sellers can post items for sale at fixed prices without bidding. Once customers find something desirable, they can buy it immediately.

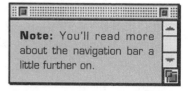

Note: You'll read more about the navigation bar a little further on.

To access zShops, click on the "zShop" tab. You'll find it on the Amazon.com Auctions navigation bar at the top of any page.

First Bidder Discounts

To attract an early bid, the seller can offer a 10% discount to the first bidder. If you're the first to bid on an item, you lock in a 10% discount from the seller if you win the auction.

As the first bidder, you earn a substantial advantage over rival bidders. If you bid early, you'll increase your chance of winning. If you win the auction, the site calculates your discounted winning price and notifies you via e-mail.

First bidders have a few other advantages, which change constantly. Visit the site to find out more.

Amazon.com Payments

If you're not set up to accept charge purchases, Amazon.com can help. When buyers use a feature called "Amazon.com Payments," Amazon.com can charge their credit cards for auction and zShop purchases and deposit the funds directly into your checking account.

This helps both buyers and sellers by eliminating checks and money orders. The transaction completes faster.

LiveBid

LiveBid.com, a Seattle-based company now part of the Amazon.com family, broadcasts their auction events over the Internet. Bidders participate as if physically present at the event. LiveBid's software also lets bidders review auction catalogs and post absentee bids before an event.

You'll see a link for LiveBid and more information about using the feature on the Amazon.com home page.

☞Using the Site

With a little practice, it's easy to navigate the Amazon.com auction site. At the very top of the site, you'll see four links:

- **Shopping Cart icon** – You'll see any items you've ordered from Amazon.com during your current browser session.

- **Your Account** – Review your order history, subscription information, or edit your 1-Click order settings. You can adjust a few other options as well.
- **Help** – Here's where you get started. It's also a page to consult when you have specific questions about the site.
- **Sell Items** – Click here to get that auction running!

Each auction page has a navigation bar at the top of the page. You'll find hyperlink tabs to the various entities of the Amazon.com site, such as books, music, e-cards, zShops, and other services.

Right under the navigation bar, you'll see another series of auction site links:

- **Search Auctions** – You can define your search several ways.
- **Browse Auctions** – Click on the category listings to browse active auctions.
- **Your Account** – This is your personal page with links to your auction activity.
- **Search zShops** – You can search for items in Amazon.com's zShops by several different criteria.
- **Browse zShops** – Browse zShop listings by item categories.

Amazon.com is rich with instructions on how to use each feature. If a new feature appears that I haven't included here, you'll find plenty of assistance in using it right at the site.

Help

When I called the telephone number listed at the Amazon.com site seeking auction help, I didn't wait long for assistance. I reached an attendant who said she could answer questions about auctions. She could not, however, tell me any in-depth information about the history of the site, nor would she direct me to someone who could.

Instead of an interview, I browsed the site for information. I found it easy to use.

Quick Tutorial

The "Auctions Quick Tutorial" appears on the Amazon.com Auctions home page. Here you'll find links to help pages:

- **Find it** – Helpful hints for searching auctions and zShops
- **Bid on it** – Advice for setting your maximum price and other bidding tips
- **Get it** – Instructions for contacting the buyer or seller after the auction closes
- **Trust it** – Read about the Amazon.com guarantee for purchases

The Top Five

The "Top 5 Questions" box shows up all site help pages:

1. How do I search?
2. How do I buy?
3. How do I bid?
4. How do I sell an item?
5. How do I create an auction?

Answers are just a click away.

Searching for Auctions

Using Amazon's basic search function, you can find select listings quickly. Type a text string or Auction ID number into the search box in the upper left-hand corner of every Amazon.com Auctions page; then click on "Go."

If you click "Auction Search" on the navigation bar, you can refine your search to include:

- Titles or titles and descriptions
- Specific categories
- Open or completed auctions

When you obtain the results you want, you can sort them in several ways:

- End date
- Start date
- Relevance
- Price
- Bid count

Category Search

From the Amazon.com Auctions home page, you can browse auction listings by category. Click on any category from the main list and you'll see a list of sub-categories and featured auctions.

You can select to have the listings sort by end date, start date, price, or bid count.

Advanced Search

If the basic search doesn't return the listings you're seeking, use the Advanced Search feature I mentioned earlier. You can search for auctions by several criteria:

- **Keyword or Auction ID**
- **Search by** (select one)
  Title
  Title and Description
- **Category**

- **Status** (select one)
  - Open
  - Completed
- **Country item can ship to**
- **Country in which item is located**
- **U.S. Zip Code**
- **Sort by** (select one)
  - End date
  - Start date
  - Relevance
  - Price
  - Bid Count
- **Ascending or descending** (select one)

You can search closed auctions from the Advanced Search link. With this information, you can calculate a secondary market price using the method described in Chapter 1.

Search User IDs

You'll use your e-mail address as your user ID at Amazon.com, or select your own "nickname." You can search user activity at the Advanced Search page.

To access sensitive user information like your user profile, your account status, or to change your password, use the links at the Account and Community Guide page, located with the Auction Help links. You'll need to enter your user ID and password to make any changes.

Bidding

Since the site already knows who you are, you don't need to enter your user ID and password to bid. If you didn't accept the cookie or the site doesn't recognize you for some other reason, click on the "Your Account" link from the navigation bar and log in. Then you can bid.

The bidding area is right at the top of the auction page. You won't scroll down looking for it as the auction clock ticks away precious seconds. If you are at the bottom of the page, you'll see another "bid box" there, too. Once you enter your bid, you'll see a confirmation screen where the link appears at the top of the page.

> **Note:** Amazon.com keeps the bidders' identities private until the high bid meets the reserve price, if one is set. This helps prevent bid siphoning.

I purchased quite a few items at this site during my cyber-travels through it. No wonder! I found it easier to bid at Amazon.com than any other online auction site I researched.

Proxy Bidding

Like most other Internet auction sites, this one has proxy bidding. They call their version "Bid-Click." Your maximum bid remains private. When you bid, you'll know right away if another user's proxy bidding outbids you.

If you're the first bidder, the amount shown as your current bid will probably be lower than your maximum bid. The amount will match the minimum price set by the seller. The only exception is if your maximum bid meets the reserve price. Your current bid then matches the reserve price, even if your maximum bid exceeds it.

Bidding History Available

You can review the bids placed on any auction. Just click on the "Bid History" link on the left side of the auction listing.

You'll see the bidder's user ID and amount bid, by order of bid placement. For reserve auctions, the bidder's user ID remains hidden until the high bid meets or exceeds the reserve price.

Bid Retraction

You can call back a bid under these circumstances only:

* Seller changes the auction description
* Error with bid amount (you bid $4,000 when you meant to bid $40.)
* Invalid seller e-mail address
* Seller's feedback rating changed negatively since your initial bid

Amazon.com is somewhat more lenient about retracting bids than other online auction sites.

Selling an Item

Once you register, you can click on the "Sell an Item Now" button on the navigation bar. You'll enter some details about the item:

* Item title
* Description (allows HTML)
* Picture (Optional)
* Category
* Minimum bid
* Reserve price
* Auction type
* Duration of auction
* Item location
* Shipping terms
* Accepted payment methods
* Display features (Optional)

The entry page is user-friendly. There's a link to a help page by almost every field.

If you want your listing to come up with Amazon.com book listings, you can enter numerous ISBN numbers for your CrossLinks. Whenever a user searches for any of those books, he or she will see a link to your auction as well.

Before you insert the listing, you can double-check the auction item page with the "Preview" button on the bottom of the auction entry form.

When you click the "Submit" button, the listing is live. You'll see the auction page right away.

Editing Active Auctions

You can make changes to the listing for up to 90 minutes after you enter it. After that, it's available in the database to come up in searches, and bidding can start.

You can also use the "View or modify an open auction" link under Seller Services if you need to make changes to one of your active listings.

Ending an Auction Early

If your auction hasn't received any bids, you can end it immediately. Click on "Your Account," and then go to "View/Edit Open Auctions." A list of your active auctions appears. If you click on "Modify this listing," you can change most of the information you entered.

End an auction early from the same link used to modify an auction. When you click on "Modify this listing," you'll see an "End this auction early" button. You'll be charged both listing and completion fees for auctions you close with winning bids.

If your auction has a bid that meets or exceeds any reserve you set, you can still close the auction early, but the winning bid stands. You must sell the item to the high bidder.

Fees

Bidders pay no fees; sellers pay listing and completion fees and any optional display features selected to enhance their listings.

Listing Fees

You'll pay a listing fee of ten cents for every auction you enter. This applies to both standard and Dutch auctions. Listing fees remain in effect even if your auction doesn't sell. Think of the listing fee as rent paid to the site for hosting your auction.

Optional Features

If you wish, you can highlight your auction in the following ways:

- **Bold Listings:** $2 per auction
- **Category Featured Auctions:** $14.95 per auction
- **Auction Home Page Featured Auctions:** $99.95 per auction

Optional fees are non-refundable if your item doesn't sell, and they don't apply to re-listed auctions.

Completion Fees

Amazon.com takes its commission based on the amount of an auction's winning bid. For a Dutch auction, the fee depends on the amount of the minimum winning bid multiplied by the quantity of items sold.

Range of Final Price	Closing Fee
$0.00 – 25.00	5%
$25.01 – 1,000.00	$1.25 plus 2.5% of any amount over $25.00
$1,000.01 and up	$25.63 plus 1.25% of any amount over $1,000.00

Payment Information and Terms

Sellers must use a credit card to pay for all auction fees.

Billing is once every month, with the first billing 24-29 days after you register, or whenever your fees and commissions reach $25.00. After that, you're billed on the same day each month, or whenever your balance goes over $25.00.

Security/Safety Features

Amazon.com has several security features in place:

- **Rating and Feedback** – You can rate users on a scale of one to five.
- **Identify Verification** – This happens with a credit card check. If you don't want to submit a credit card number, you can't participate at the site.
- **Online User Guides** – These are available for bidders and sellers.
- **Staff of Investigators** – They check out things from fishy-sounding auctions to copyright infringement.
- **Fraud Policy** – Zero tolerance policy against any user who defrauds or defaults payment. One violation and you lose your user ID.
- **Auction Guarantee** – If you believe a seller has defrauded you, Amazon.com will reimburse buyers up to $250 per claim, subject to certain guidelines.

The Auction Listing

Here's an example of what you'll see when you call up an Amazon.com auction listing:

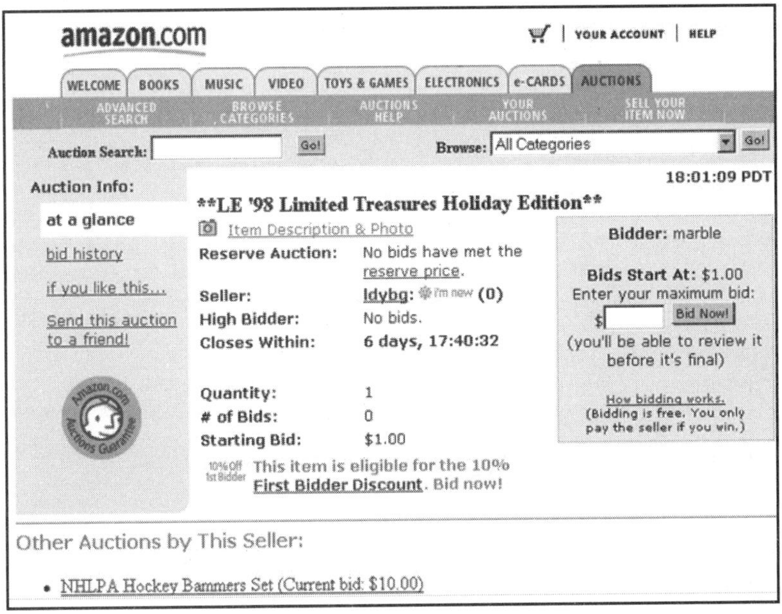

Auction Listing on Amazon.com

The auction description appears below this listing, when the user scrolls down the page. You'll also see another bid box near the bottom of the auction page, identical to the one shown above. Less scrolling!

Feedback

Amazon.com offers a unique feedback method. Instead of just good, bad, or neutral, you rate users on a scale of from one to five. Their rating shows up as a series of stars. Five stars indicate a stellar user of the highest integrity, and one star means you better watch this one.

For new users with no feedback, this darling little "I'm new" icon with a smiling sunshine face appears. See ldybg's example in the listing screen above.

Transaction Specific

You can enter feedback for any user, but the "one to five" stars don't apply unless the feedback relates to a successful transaction. If it's not transaction-related, the comment shows up when you view all the comments, but the feedback post won't increment the user's total rating score.

☛Meet Franziska, A Frequent Amazon Auctions User

"I collect mostly matches, postcards, keychains, and pens," says Franziska, a long-time collector, "but I didn't know much about their actual value. When I was younger, I collected whatever I thought would be worth something later, like World's Fair items." Using online auctions definitely helps Franziska determine the value of her collectibles.

As a hobby, she buys items from antique shops, Indian jewelry shops, junk shops, and bond shops, and resells them at Amazon.com.

"I don't know all the history of every item I sell," she says, "but I get information from people who bid on my auctions. They send me e-mail while the auction is running. I learned all about quilts, Limoges, crystal items, sunglasses, and watches this way."

History with Online Auctions

"For any collector," Franziska says, "part of the success is luck and instinct." She remembers two pairs of earrings she once bought in a resale store for eight dollars each. As she held them in her hand, however, she knew they were fine jewelry, handmade and very old.

"I bought them and then took them to my jeweler," she continues. "He confirmed what I thought. I remember that experience whenever I list auctions. Before I sell anything, I have the items verified so I can be honest with my sellers."

Franziska learned how auctions work by watching auction programs on television, and by asking other online auction users.

"I learned about quilts and their value through an online quilt dealer, and from my bidders too," she says. "I also have a book on quilting and a friend who's an expert. I constantly learn new things. I also get a lot of information about my collectibles directly from the Internet."

Thoughts about Amazon.com

"I find a high class of buyers at Amazon.com," Franziska says. "Most of my customers pay within three days of the auction closing. Then they write to tell me how thrilled they are with the item. That's the best part of it."

Franziska finds that well-formatted auction descriptions are necessary if you want to be successful.

"I write very good copy and only use excellent pictures. Sometimes I spend two to four hours just preparing one listing. I want my photos to be perfect so they show details of my items, such as the fire of a stone. What I write is welcoming and friendly, and I put as much information as I can into it."

Lessons Learned

A quilt buyer posted a negative feedback for Franziska.

"I didn't deserve it," she says. "The woman insisted we use escrow so she could look at a quilt pattern. I agreed, and she set up the escrow."

Later, the buyer contacted Franziska in e-mail, claiming she didn't like the quilt. She said she found cat hairs all over it and didn't like the pattern, although Franziska had included a photo of the quilt in her auction. She also thought it looked used. Franziska tried to explain that handmade quilts are never "brand new," but the buyer apparently expected something sealed in a manufacturer's package.

"The woman who made the quilt worked on it for a year," Franziska explains. "The buyer simply did not understand what 'new' means when dealing in handmade quilts. She's used to the store-bought quilts in plastic."

Franziska received the returned quilt a week later. "I removed it from the box in front of two witnesses," she says, "and there were some cat hairs on it, but they sure didn't match *my* cat! I always wondered how she could be so certain that it was cat hair. I had a feeling she really did like it, and used it a little, but when her husband found out she paid over $400 for it, he made her send it back."

Best Experience

Despite the isolated incident with the quilt, Franziska is very pleased with the results of her auctions on Amazon.com.

"I sold three Rutellated quartz gems for over $80 each," she explained. "I only paid eight dollars apiece for them. I was stunned. I hesitated about listing them because I always thought they were ugly stones with straw in them, but that was why I bought them — I thought they were so unusual. The buyers were thrilled with them. I learned not to rely on my own likes and dislikes to know what another person might want."

Franziska found out why online auctions are so successful. One person's castoff is another person's prized collectible.

Chapter 10 — Auctions.com

☞www.auctions.com

Auctions.com is one of the fastest growing online auction networks. They provide online auction services and support for consumers, affiliated newspapers, and merchants. Formerly known as Auction Universe, the site re-launched as Auctions.com in mid-November 1999.

> **Note:** Auctions.com in the UK operates at www.auctionuniverse.co.uk. In Australia, look for Auctions.com under www.sold.com.au.

Auctions.com is a division of Chicago-based Classified Ventures, Inc., a consortium of more than 130 daily newspapers that compete together in the online classified advertising marketplace. The company plans to host auctions for several retailers who advertise and promote products in their local newspapers. Offering consumer merchandise adds a unique component to the site.

Auctions.com also hosts charity auctions that typically capture a good deal of revenue and attention for the site. Auctions.com recently hosted an auction of over 71 life-size cow statues that were artfully painted and graced the streets of Chicago during the summer of 1999.

Auctions.com Home Page

Auctions.com is part of the Auction Universe Network. All sales at Auctions.com are in U.S dollars.

Auctions.com's fee schedule and method of operation are similar to many other popular auction sites. Membership is free and there are no listing fees to pay, only commissions. Once you register and establish a user ID and password, you have an initial account of $10. If your site fees exceed that amount, you must submit payment or a credit-card number.

Auction sites constantly change their home page layouts to entice users. An example of the Auctions.com home page is on page 216.

Explanations of the small listing icons appear at the bottom of the page, along with site links and copyright information.

☛ Table of Features

Site URL: www.auctions.com Time zone: Eastern		
Main page features	**Yes**	**No**
Site links on main page	X	
Featured auctions	X	
Browse by category	X	
News	X	
Date of last update	X	
Copyright information	X	
User recall		X
Link to personal activity page	X	
Search features	**Yes**	**No**
Search by keyword	X	
Search by seller	X	
Search by bidder	X	
Search by category	X	
All in one search	X	
Search title only	X	
Search auction descriptions	X	
Search completed auctions	X	
Advanced search	X	
Auctions and Bidding	**Yes**	**No**
Proxy bidding	X	
Dutch auctions	X	
Reserve price	X	
Mandatory reserve		X
Adjustable start and end time	X	
View bidding history	X	
Open-ended bidding	X	
HTML in description	X	

Services	Yes	No
Site Tutorial	X	
Personal Paging	X	
Escrow	X	

Particulars	
Insertion Fee:	Free
Commission:	2.5% on closing price
Duration:	1 – 14, 30 days

☛What's Unique about Auctions.com?

In addition to an Internet auction site, Auctions.com has a traveling road show that hosts auctions at trade shows. If you attend an event that features Auctions.com, you can register and participate in one of their auctions right at the show. They also offer seminars on how to use the site.

Auction Features

Auctions.com has a number of useful listing features not found at some of the other major online auction sites. Some are quite helpful; others are fun.

The auctions run with open-ended bidding. Auctions close at the scheduled closing time or five to ten minutes after the last bid, whichever is later. As long as people are bidding within five minutes of each other, the auction doesn't end. The Auction Payment and Terms form, where you select several of the following auction features, is on the next page.

Automatic Auction Renewal

You can select the "Auto Relist" option when you list your item. If your auction doesn't close successfully, Auctions.com will automatically re-list it for you with the same information you originally entered, including the duration, up to four times. You'll select how many times to re-list the auction when you enter it. There's no additional charge.

When the auction re-lists, it retains all bid history from the action's first run.

Flexible Auction Duration

Auctions.com provides a flexible length of time for auctions to run — from one to 14 days. You'll select the auction duration from a pull-down menu when you enter the listing.

This feature is helpful for sellers who don't want to conform to the usual 3, 5, or 7-day durations offered at some of the other sites.

Additional Category Listings

For twenty-five cents, you can list your item in one additional category. You'll select this option at the "Auction Terms" area of the auction-entry page. With this feature, your auctions can show up on several different category searches.

Adjustable Start and End Times

You can schedule an auction to start and end at any time of the day. When you're entering the auction, the start time defaults to whatever time it is "now." You can adjust the time so the auction starts later.

You must pick a start time later than the present time. If it's currently 6:00 PM and you want the auction to start at 11:00 AM, it will start at 11:00 AM the next day. See the area on the auction-entry form below where you adjust the start and end time of your auction.

Auction and Payment Terms Selection at Auctions.com

Know-The-Code

Instead of hunting through all the categories when you list your auction, you can simply enter the 4-digit category code and go right to the auction-entry page.

This saves time for sellers who constantly list items in a select few categories.

Managing Your Auctions

The "My Auction.com" link allows sellers to edit an active listing, add to an item's description, or link a picture to an auction already running. You can also close an auction early.

You can only make these adjustments before the auction receives a bid.

ForSale

This is Auctions.com's version of straight sales listings, available exclusively to their Bid$afe™ Gold members. The first bid on a particular ForSale™ listing secures the merchandise at the specified price. If you bid, you agree to buy it at the seller's listed price.

> **Note:** You'll read more about the Bid$afe program at Auctions.com further in this chapter.

You can use a ForSale auction for Dutch listings. Each bid counts down the number of items available until all of them sell. The auction ends when the specified duration expires or when all items sell, whichever happens first.

ForSale auctions have a little orange "F" by the listing.

User Services

You'll find plenty of services at Auctions.com designed to make the online auction experience safe and fun for both buyers and sellers. If you're a collectible dealer, check out the "Merchant Central" site link where you can take advantage of special benefits.

Bid Protection

Auctions.com uses something called "10X Bid Protection" software to help prevent bidding errors. The program detects a possibly misplaced decimal point when you enter a bid.

If you bid $300 and the minimum bid is $30.00, the software detects a bid amount ten times more than the minimum bid and asks you to confirm the amount before the bid registers.

Block Non-Rated Users

Auctions.com lets you choose not to sell to members who don't want to be rated. You can block bids from users who have their rating hidden. You'll select this feature when you enter your listing.

Personal Paging

Auctions.com offers a member paging service, which works in tandem with your personal e-mail enabled pager when someone bids on your auction (or outbids you).

Auctions.com needs your secondary e-mail address or your pager's phone number, your PIN number, and your pager company's URL. You can learn more about personal paging if you decide to sign up for it. Check the site for information.

Note: Your pager company must offer Internet paging services in order for you to use this feature.

You can also request e-mail notification at an alternative e-mail address when someone bids on your listing, or when you're outbid.

Feedback Notification via E-mail

Auctions.com notifies you by e-mail whenever someone posts feedback for you. The message includes:

- Rater's e-mail address
- Date the message was entered
- Auction the rating is from
- Item auctioned
- Text of the feedback comment

If you have any questions about the feedback or rating, you can send e-mail to the person who posted the comment.

Retractable Feedback

From the Site Help link, you can delete any feedback comment you made about another user. You'll enter your user ID and password to access a page where you can select which comment you want removed.

> **Note:** Even if a site allows you to delete feedback, you should still use care when entering comments about another user. As long as the comment appears in the person's file, others can read it.

Merchant Central

This is a special offering for sellers with merchant accounts. Auctions.com provides the following online auction benefits:

- **Merchant Package** – Enjoy twelve months of unlimited free Auctions.com basic listings and a few other perks.
- **Merchant Page** – This is a special auction page that Auctions.com designs, hosts, and maintains for your company.
- **Merchant Site** – Take advantage of your own private-label auction Web site that Auctions.com designs, hosts, and maintains for your company.
- **Merchant Manager** – With this feature, you can maintain complete control over your inventory.

Auctions.com generates these services with special auction-management software. You can find out how to enroll by clicking on the Merchant Central link at the top of any page.

☞Using the Site

When I contacted Auctions.com, I immediately heard back from an account representative from PR 21, the public relations firm that promotes Auctions.com. I received answers to all of my questions within 24 hours. I made one site suggestion and received a "thank you" message the same day.

You'll find a link to "My Auctions.com" on every page. This brings up a search page for your personal auction activity. You can track your current and past auction activity, and check the status of your Auctions.com account. If you need to change information in your account or user profile, plenty of links help you access the right pages.

Help

For help using the site, there's a row of links across the top banner of every page. This navigation bar takes you to places of interest at the site:

- **Home** – If you click on the Auction.com image at the top left, it returns you to the Auctions.com home page.
- **How To Sell and Bid** – Takes you to the site tutorial pages.
- **Register Free** – In case you haven't already.
- **List an Item** – Have your auction description ready, and get that auction running. This link takes you right to the auction-entry pages. You'll stop briefly to enter your user ID and password.
- **Site Help** – Contains links to every important page at the site.
- **Contact Us** – You'll find out how to contact the site administrators, register, rate another user, buy and sell, site security information, the FAQ, and news about special features. This link gets you in direct contact with the site administrators.

Under the main navigation bar, you'll see a search box and a link to Bid$afe, the site's user protection program. Then you'll find another row of site links:

- **Advanced Search** – There's more about this further in this section.
- **View All Categories** – This returns a page showing every listing category. Click on one to see the auctions.
- **My Auctions.com** – Manage or track your personal auction activity.
- **Merchant Central** – Let Auctions.com help you increase your sales and marketing exposure.
- **Showcase Auctions** – View all listings in the premium categories.

Navigation is easy, since you can get anywhere on the site from any page.

Searching for Auctions

Auctions.com provides a search box on every page where you can enter a search string. Results will display listings that match your criteria by searching both the auction titles and the descriptions.

Category Search

Categories and sub-categories appear on the Auctions.com home page. If you click on the "View all categories" link, under each category you'll find another link to "Auctions Ending Today" in that section.

If you click on the main category, you'll see a list of every sub-category in that group, followed by links to Showcase auctions in the main branch.

If you click on any sub-category, you'll see more categories if any exist, or Showcase listings followed by standard auctions that appear with that group.

Clicking on "Auctions Ending Today" produces a list of auctions scheduled to close within the next 24 hours. Some buyers search exclusively in these listings so they don't have to wait long for the results.

 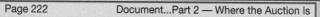

Advanced Search

Auctions.com has a very comprehensive Advanced Search feature. You can hunt for auctions by almost every possible criterion:

- **Description** (Enter keywords)
- **Item Number**
- **Category** (Select main category from drop-down menu)
- **Zip/Postal Code**
- **State/Province**
- **Country**
- **Listings Per Page** (Select amount from drop-down menu)
- **Search by:** (select from list)
  - Title
  - Description
  - Both
- **Seller's e-mail**
- **Bidder's e-mail**
- **Bid$afe Auctions Only**
- **New Auctions Today**
- **ForSale Auctions Only**
- **Ending within:**
  - Any time
  - 14-1 days
  - Today
  - 1 hour
- **Auction Status:**
  - All open
  - Last 30 days
  - Last 60 days
  - Last 90 days
  - Last six months
  - All closed auctions
  - All auctions
- **Columns To Display:** (select from list how you want the listings to appear)
- **Sort results** by:
  - Ending date
  - Start bid
  - Bid @
  - Category
  - Seller
  - Item #
  - State
  - Rank
- **Ascending or descending** (select one)

Fill in all fields, or just one or two relevant to the type of search you want. When you click the "Search" button, your customized results appear if any Auctions.com listings match your criteria.

Search User IDs

At Auctions.com, your e-mail address is your user ID. You can search user activity with the Advanced Search feature.

To access sensitive information like your user profile or account status, or to change your password, use the "MyAccount" link at the "My Auctions.com" page. You'll need to enter your user ID and password.

Bidding

You'll bid on an item much like at any other online auction site. Enter your maximum bid, your user ID, and password on the auction-listing page; then click "Place Bid."

Auctions.com makes bidding easy by letting you enter this information at the top of the auction page, instead of scrolling down to locate the fields. This saves time if you're doing a lot of bidding.

Once you place your bid, there's no separate confirmation screen — you're back at the auction page. The bid-entry area now contains the confirmation and status of your bid. If someone outbids you, you'll know right away. If you're the new high bidder, your initials and state or province of residence appear in the Leading Bidder field by the listing.

Note: Auctions.com keeps the bidder's e-mail address private. This helps prevent bid siphoning.

Bidding at Auctions.com involves a lot less scrolling and searching for fields than at other sites. The site design makes bidding easy.

Proxy Bidding

Auctions.com calls it RoboBid™ but it does the same thing any proxy-bidding feature does. It automatically handles the bidding in your absence, upping the ante incrementally until it reaches your maximum bid amount.

If you're the first bidder, the amount shown as your current bid will probably be lower than your maximum bid. The amount will match the minimum price set by the seller. The only exception is if your maximum bid meets the reserve price — your current bid matches that, even if your maximum bid exceeds it.

Bidding History Available

To check the bidding history for any auction, click on the "Bid History" link beside the current bid amount. You'll see all bids entered for the auction so far. The bidders' identities show up as their initials and state or province of residence; user IDs don't appear.

Calling Back Bids

You can cancel a bid, but it's not that easy. Auctions.com will only cancel bids at the request of the seller. You have to contact him or her and explain why you need to call back your bid and request cooperation. This helps prevent frequent bid retractions.

10X Bid Protection helps prevent drastic errors so it usually isn't necessary to retract accidentally high bids.

Selling an Item

Click on the "List Item" link on any site page. First, you'll enter your user ID and password.

Next, you'll see a page asking for the item category. Select one from the menu. The following page lets you break down the category even farther, if choices exist.

From there, you'll enter specifics about the auction:

- Title
- Description (HTML-enabled description entry area)
- Featured listing choices (Optional)
- Link to your Web site (Optional)
- Item photo URL (with a special preview button)
- Shipping and payment information
- Auction Terms:
  Minimum bid
  Optional reserve
  Quantity for Dutch auctions
  Duration, Auto Relist
  Adjustable start date
  Adjustable start time
  Adjustable end time
  Block bidding from users who choose not to be rated

The next screen allows you to review your auction. If you like what you see and all information is correct, press the "Start Auction" button. If you need to make changes first, use the Back button on your browser to edit the previous screens.

Editing Active Auctions

After you log in with your user ID and password, you can make any changes to your description through the "My Auctions.com" link as long as no one has bid on your item yet. You can change any information about the listing.

If there is bidding activity on the item, then it's too late to make changes, but you can append comments to the description. Each addition is time-stamped. Anyone viewing the listing will know when you added the information.

Ending an Auction Early

You can end an auction early as long as there are no active bids. After you log in, follow the "My Auctions.com" link and select the auction you wish to remove.

If there's an active bid on your item, you can end the auction but it's a little more difficult. First, bid on the item yourself. Place an enormous bid to take the item off the market. Then contact the bidders and to let them know you intend to end the auction early.

Note: Your bidders will appreciate knowing why you decided to pull the listing.

Then forward the end-early request to Auctions.com, along with the auction number. Auctions.com will then end the auction, with a slight delay if you end it during late evening hours or on weekends.

Cancelling a Bid

Auctions.com allows sellers to cancel bids placed against their auctions. The seller must contact the service department to request a bid retraction. If buyer wishes to call back a bid, he or she must contact the seller. Only the seller can request a bid retraction.

Entering a bid on an item for sale constitutes an agreement between buyer and seller. Auctions.com urges users to enter bids only on items they intend to purchase.

Fees

Bidders pay no fees; sellers pay completion fees and any optional display features they use to enhance their auctions. Fees are charged to the seller's account when he or she enters the auction listing, based on any optional features selected.

Listing Fees

Auctions.com recently eliminated listing fees. You pay commission only on the final sale and the fee for any optional listing features you select. This keeps Auctions.com very competitive in the online auction market.

Optional Features

If you wish, you can highlight your auction. You'll pay some additional fees:

- **Boldface title:** 25¢
- **Italic title:** 25¢
- **Showcase auction:** $100
- **Showcase category auction:** $9.95
- **Optional Web site URL:** $1.00
- **Extra categories:** 25¢ per category

The fees for these optional features charge against your account even if your item doesn't sell. If you selected Auto Relist, the options carry over (if your auction re-lists) at no additional charge.

Commission

Auctions.com charges a straight 2.5% of the final selling price. If your item doesn't sell, you will only pay for any optional listing features you selected.

Payment Information and Terms

To list auctions, you have to maintain an account balance to cover fees associated with the listings. You can replenish your account in $10, $25, $50, $100, or $500 increments with a minimum replenishment of $10. You can enter a credit card to retain on file at Auctions.com's Secure (SSL) page.

You can also add to your account by sending a check to the Auctions.com business office in Yalesville, CT. The full address is available at the site. You'll find a printable form on the "Paying by Check" page that you can complete and send along with your check.

Security/Safety Features

Auctions.com offers a unique customer service and protection program called Bid$afe. In Bid$afe auctions, Auctions.com serves as a financial intermediary, guaranteeing the transaction for both buyers and sellers.

For a membership fee of $19.95 a year, Bid$afe bills your credit card for any auctions you win and sends the payment to the seller. It's essentially an escrow service, presumably run by Auctions.com.

Your annual membership entitles you to $3,000 in insurance coverage, free listings, and a few other benefits. Your credit card is billed 3.5% of the merchandise value per transaction, for shipping and handling costs.

The Auction Listing

On the next page is an example of what you'll see when you call up an auction listing at Auctions.com.

When you scroll down the page, you'll see the auction description and another site navigation bar.

Feedback

Auctions.com calls its user feedback the "Rating Services." You can rate any user you've dealt with in a successful auction.

You'll enter feedback for another user from the Rating Services link, although I had a hard time finding it from one of the site pages. It appears under the Site Help link.

You can refuse rating comments, but then the auction community can't determine your credibility as a buyer or seller. If you choose not to be rated, "NR" appears after your user ID. Auctions.com lets sellers block bids from users who hide their feedback.

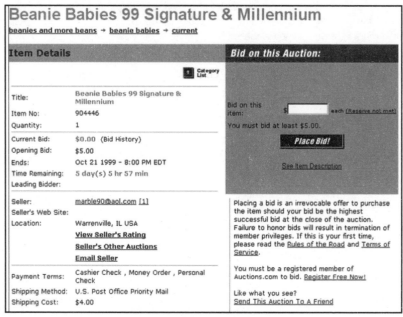

Auction Listing on Auctions.com

Transaction Specific

You can only enter rating comments for a user with whom you completed a transaction. Each time you transact with someone, the feedback you post for the person increments his or her overall rating score.

Feedback Retraction

Auctions.com lets you retract any comment you left for another user if you change your mind later. From the Site Help link, select "retract" under Rating Services. This produces a list of all rating comments you entered. You can click on the checkbox by any you wish to delete; then click the button to submit the form. The comment disappears from the user's record.

☛Meet Dan, A Frequent Auctions.com User

Dan is a 55-year-old Auctions.com user who has at least 1,000 active auctions running at any given time. Dan suffers from multiple sclerosis and prefers to operate a business at home. He's been a sports card collector for 15 years and recently started selling online.

"I don't do it to make a profit," Dan says. "I do what I do for therapy, to keep my hands and my mind busy. I am a very slow typist but people on the other end don't know how long it takes me to type an e-mail message, so it's transparent to them. I'm just like any other seller online. My customers want the cards they pay for, and that I can handle very well."

History with Online Auctions

Dan did a lot of selling on eBay before switching to Auction Universe, which is now called Auctions.com. He found that Auctions.com better suited his interest in collectibles. Dan also appreciates how easy it is to enter and track his listings at Auctions.com.

He knows about all the other auction sites on the Internet but claims that none has quite the personal touch of Auctions.com. His e-mail requests for information and assistance receive prompt and personalized answers. Dan feels the Auctions.com help staff treats him with respect. He also likes the other auction users with whom he's done business.

"I've developed a good customer base, and they all know where to find me," Dan says. "My customers know I'm not going to disappear with their money."

Thoughts about Auctions.com

"Online auctions are wonderful for folks in my situation," Dan says. "I participate when I feel up to it, and nobody knows when I'm suffering. I prefer that. I feel like I fit right into the online collector community."

Despite his disability, Dan finds that he can still actively participate in a hobby he loves — dealing sports cards.

"Plus," Dan adds, "I love the way Auctions.com runs their site!"

Lessons Learned

While few and far between, Dan has encountered some negative feedback.

"On any online auction site you'll run into people who are disagreeable," Dan warns, "and people who bid with no intention of paying if they win. This should be somewhat expected. I go to extremes to give people the benefit of the doubt before posting negative feedback, but sometimes there's no other way to warn others about a non-paying bidder."

Online, Dan is just as shrewd as any other auction seller is because he *can* be.

Best Experience

Dan claims his favorite aspect of online auctions, particularly Auctions.com, is the venue it provides for meeting people he'd never ordinarily have a chance to know.

"I have developed a few pen-pal type relationships while using Auctions.com," Dan relates. "Some are very interesting, and they have lasted a long time. My online auction friends don't care how slow I type, and they understand when I tell them I have to type in all upper case."

Dan plans to stay active at Auctions.com since he enjoys it for so many different reasons.

Chapter 11 — Live Auction Online

☛www.liveauctiononline.com

"Most Live Auction Online users are in the U.S." says Dave D'Archangelo, "but we're based in Kelowna, British Columbia. Dave, a former eBay user, is part owner of this Canadian-based online auction site, operating since mid-1997. Live Auction Online, or L.A.O. to those familiar with it, has 14,200 registered users as of this writing, with 25-50 new users every day.

Check Our Hottest Items!!!!

Item #	Item Name	$$$$$	Bids
315031ja	Birthday Bear No Reserve 3 Days	$15.25	7
305808fo	Britannia !!! Retired Bear !!!	$25.25	7
323776be	Britannia Bear -retired *3 Days*	$35.50	5
301445fo	1998 Teddy The Ty Holiday Bear	$19.50	5
333014oi	$1.00 Silver Certificate Bill****	$4.25	5
232620FW	Ty Beanie 98 Teddy Mint	$21.75	5
211918ja	Flitter The Butterfly	$15.00	4
282140ro	Pokemon "charizard" Holofoil	$22.75	4
332732go	Spangle-new Ty Beanie- No Reserve	$10.00	4
297862FW	Ty Beanie Glory Retired Mint	$25.25	4
81878ju	Clubby 2	$14.00	4
352329oi	$1.00 1935 Silver Certificate Bill*	$5.75	4
266739Ho	New * Osito * Mexican Bear	$15.00	3
141426sh	Flitter & Lips	$30.50	3
324720pc	20 M. Jordan Cards Worth $2 Each	$7.00	3
357853oi	$1.00 1957 Silver Certificate Bill*	$2.75	3
355845jm	Unused Hitler Block Of 4 Postage St	$2.50	3
332753re	-----flitter-----lips---- M.w.m.t	$40.50	3
282804FW	Inch Beanie Buddy Hardtofind	$20.50	2
326196lo	~~ty's New Lips The Fish~~ Mwmt.	$19.00	1
327068in	Hippity - Mint/tag Prot!$2 Ship?	$9.00	1
333439eh	Ty Wiser The Owl, Mwmt No Reserve	$6.50	1
75474do	Spangle	$15.00	1
282893bu	25 Bank Notes Diff Countries	$5.00	1
186821ja	Spangle No Reserve	$9.99	1
132836ra	Fuzz The Bear	$9.00	1
306421Ch	Weedle Mint Pokemon (rare) N/r	$0.25	1
333364in	Quackers! Mint/tag Prot! $2 Ship?	$5.50	1
347837Ch	Farfetched Mint Pokemon (rare) N/r	$1.00	1
337774Ch	Bulbasaur Mint Pokemon (rare) N/r	$0.35	1

For All The Hot Auctions --- *Click Here*

NO LISTING FEES -- ENJOY THE AUCTION ACTION!!

Register Here!!

Auction Help

If this is your first visit go to our Help Pages and check our *FAQ's*!

Featured Categories

Autographs

Beanies Retired & New

Bears

Coins, U.S.

Comic Books

Figurines & Miniatures

Gems, Faceted Cabochon

Fine Jewelry

Gold Jewelry

Hallmark Collectibles

Hot Wheels

Memorabilia

Militaria

Stamps - Non U.S.

All Categories

L.A.O. NEWS

L.A.O. gets top marks from members, *more info*....

Link Your Site

Link your site to your auctions, *more info* ....

Anchor Tenants

Run your own auctions, at L.A.O. *more info* ....

Need Help

E-mail Support!!

Your good fortune will be clearly evident soon!

Live Auction Online Home Page

"We're growing," Dave adds, "and just experienced our first company buy-in. We're hoping to go public soon." According to Dave, L.A.O. has between two hundred and four hundred new listings every day.

All transactions at L.A.O. are in U.S. dollars.

Live Auction Online has convenient feature tabs at the top of every site page, making navigation easy. If you scroll to the bottom of the home page, you'll see the site links and copyright information. Question and answer pages for buyers and sellers help new users get started.

Table of Features

Site URL: www.liveauctiononline.com Time zone: Pacific		
Main page features	**Yes**	**No**
Site links on main page	X	
Featured auctions	X	
Browse by category	X	
News	X	
Date of last update		X
Copyright information	X	
User recall	X	
Link to personal activity page		X
Search features	**Yes**	**No**
Search by keyword	X	
Search by seller	X	
Search by bidder	X	
Search by category	X	
All in one search	X	
Search title only		X
Search auction descriptions	X	
Search completed auctions	X	
Advanced search		X
Auctions and Bidding	**Yes**	**No**
Proxy bidding	X	
Dutch auctions	X	
Reserve price	X	
Mandatory reserve		X
Adjustable start and end time		X
View bidding history	X	
Open-ended bidding		X
HTML in description	X	

Services:	Yes	No
Site Tutorial		X
Personal Paging		X
Escrow		X

Particulars:	
Insertion Fee:	Free
Commission:	5% to $25 2.5% on $25 – 1,000 1.25% over $1,000
Duration:	3, 5, 7 – 14 days

☞What's Unique about Live Auction Online?

LAO caters to people who wish to use online auctions to manage their collecting. The site encourages both dealers and independent collectors to add a link to LAO on their personal sites in return for a link exchange with HotBot, a popular search engine.

Auction Features

This growing online auction site plans to add bold-faced and featured listings very soon, and offers free listings to anchor tenants, those sellers having at least 50 auctions running at any given time. They also plan to install auto-listings, a program that allows you to list multiple auctions with one click.

L.A.O. also offers several user-friendly features for private sellers.

Link Your Site to Your Auctions

You can copy a "View my Auctions at L.A.O." icon from the L.A.O. site to add to your personal site. When you request the free service with your user ID and password, L.A.O. sends you the code to add to your page that makes the icon a hyperlink to your auctions.

You can use the same code and L.A.O. icon in bulletin board or collector exchange posts (where it's allowed) to lure collectors to your auctions.

Auction Rating

From the tab at the top of any site page, you can enter comments about individual auction transactions, or about another user. L.A.O. is one of few sites I researched that included the user feedback link on every page of the site.

User Services

L.A.O. has several unique services designed to make the online auction experience safe and fun for both buyers and sellers. The special link exchanges alone help to lure bidders to your auctions.

Defined Rating System

Most online auction sites indicate a user's feedback with one number. This is the total of all positive comments minus any negative ones. You'll typically see a number in parentheses or brackets by a user ID, like this:

sparky (908)

While "sparky" has 908 positive feedbacks, you don't know until you check the feedback page that he actually has 920 comments. Twelve negative comments, however, reduce his overall rating to 908.

L.A.O. reveals all your feedback, or "rating," at one glance. Instead of one number you'll see three, which represent positive/negative/neutral comments:

sparky 920/12/0

This system gives you a quick summary of the person's overall performance at L.A.O.

Auto-Feedback

When you enter feedback comments for users you've dealt with, you don't have to type in the comment each time you enter feedback. The text field automatically populates with any text you entered there during your current browser session. If you want to leave a different comment, backspace through the comment or highlight it and type over it.

Next time you visit the site, the field will be blank until you enter the first comment. Then that text appears for the next feedback post.

Multiple Bids

If you want to bid the same amount on several different auctions, L.A.O. "remembers" your bid amount, user ID, and password. Those fields will populate with the information you entered previously for any auction during your current browser session.

If you want to change your bid, backspace through the numbers and enter a different amount.

Feedback Editing

From the Auction Edit tab, you can change the comments you left for other users. You'll need to select "Edit your comments" from the menu, log in, and click the "Enter Auction Edit" bar.

You'll see more about editing feedback comments later in this chapter.

Hot Items

As you saw on the home page on page 232, listings classified as "Hot Items" appear on the home page. Hot Items are standard, non-reserve auctions with the highest bids, listed in order of bids entered. L.A.O. displays Hot Items on the home page so more users can get in on the action!

Domain Forwarding

L.A.O. owns over 50 high profile domains that forward to their online auction site when users enter them in the address line on their browsers. For example, the following URLs take you directly to the auction listings at L.A.O.:

www.beaniedealers.com
www.clothingauctions.com
www.beanie-auction.com
www.antiques-auction.com
www.stamps-auction.com
www.autographsauction.com

The popular HotBot search engine picks up the L.A.O. domain, which brings even more collectors to your auction listings.

☞Using the Site

My first impression is that with a little practice — once I looked around and asked a few questions — the site is very easy to use. I went back and bid on a few items while completing my research. I liked it that much!

Plus, the help staff is very friendly and personable. My e-mail received answers the following business day. Dave spent plenty of time on the phone with me explaining L.A.O. and its many features.

Help

For help using the site, each page has a group of link tabs at the top. These are the main links to interesting places at the site:

- Auction Categories – Displays all listing categories and the number of live auctions appearing in each one.
- Hot Auctions – Shows standard non-reserve auctions in order of number of bids received.
- New Auctions – Lists all auctions entered within the past 24 hours.
- Cool Deals – Businesses can link auctions to their Web sites.
- Start an Auction – Have your auction description ready, and get that auction running. This link takes you right to the auction-entry page.
- Search – Search listings to find just the right stuff.
- Auction Edit – From this link you can edit your auction description, end your auction early, re-list a closed auction, or edit feedback you left another user.
- Auction Rating – Use this link to rate another user.

Moving around the site is easy because navigation tabs appear on every page.

Searching for Auctions

From the navigation tabs, click on "Search." You'll see the "Welcome to Auction Search," where you can hunt for the auctions you wish to view.

L.A.O.'s search feature examines both auction titles and descriptions. You don't have to explore them separately or specify which one to include.

You can search for auctions by several criteria:

- **Keyword search for any item**
- **Buyer's Auction Search**
  Current auctions you are high bidder on
  Current auctions you have been outbid on
  Check your secret maximum bid
  Past auctions you have won
- **Seller's Auction Search**
  Check your current auctions running
  Your past auctions with bids
  Your past auctions with no bids
- **Auction search** (enter item number)

You can make only one selection in each search criteria. For instance, you can search current auctions a seller has running, but not both current and closed in the same search.

Category Search

Click on the "Auction Categories" from the L.A.O. navigation tabs. You'll see a table of listing categories and the number of auctions currently running in each one.

If you click on any category link that contains active listings, you'll see the auctions listed much like you would at any other online auction site. If you click on the auction number, you're taken right to the auction page to view the details and description. You can then bid if you choose.

Search User IDs

You can search the current or past activity of any registered user. To search by user ID, click on the "Search" tab.

Enter a site name into the space provided on the "Welcome to Auction Search" page in either part of the form:

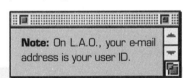

Note: On L.A.O., your e-mail address is your user ID.

- Buyer's Auction Search
- Seller's Auction Search

You'll see the appropriate listings on a new screen.

Bidding

Once you find the right auction, bidding is easy. On the main auction-listing page, scroll down to the field labeled "Your maximum bid." Enter the most you're willing to pay for the item. Then enter your e-mail address and password, and click on the "Place your bid" bar.

Review your bid information on the next screen. If everything is correct, click on the "Place Your Bid" bar and your bid takes effect. If you need to change the amount of your bid, hit the Back button on your browser to go back to the auction page where you can scroll down and enter the correct amount.

Once you enter your bid, you'll see a confirmation screen. Review the auction to see if you're high bidder or if proxy bidding outbid you by clicking the "View Your Bid" bar.

Invisible Seconds

As the auction closes, the clock does not display the countdown in seconds, only minutes. This deters anyone from using sniper programs. The L.A.O. administrators feel this is a fair way to present auctions.

When the "Time Left" shows 0 minutes, the auction has closed. It will drop out of the active auction list at the next midnight.

Proxy Bidding

L.A.O. calls it "auto bid" and it works like any other proxy bidding. It automatically handles the bidding in your absence, upping the ante incrementally until it reaches the maximum amount.

If you're the first bidder, the amount shown as your current bid will probably be lower than your maximum bid. The amount will match the minimum price set by the seller. The only exception is if your maximum bid meets the reserve price — then your current bid matches that, even if your maximum bid exceeds it.

Bidding History Available

From any auction listing page, click on the link that says "If you are not high bidder, click here." You'll see a list of users who have bid on the auction. The bid amounts remain private until the auction closes; then they appear.

Bid Retraction

You can't cancel a bid at L.A.O. You can only raise an existing one by bidding a higher amount on the same auction. L.A.O. considers each bid an agreement to purchase the item at your maximum bid amount.

Selling an Item

Once you register, you can click on the "Start an Auction" tab at the top of any page. This action takes you to the "Pick Your Category" page. From here, you'll choose your item's category from Door #1, Door #2, or Door #3.

Next, you'll enter your user ID and password, and some details about the auction:

- **Starting price**
- **Type of auction:** (select one)
  Standard
  Reserve
- **Reserve price** (if applicable)
- **Length of auction:** (select from drop-down menu)
- **Item to be shipped from:** (enter your city and state)
- **Shipping costs included:** (select one)
  Yes
  No
- **Item name** (this is where the auction title goes)
- **Description** (HTML-enabled description entry area)
- **URL to photo**
- **Category** (select from menu)

Once you've entered the correct information in all the fields, click on the "Start my Auction" button. You'll see your formatted auction. Once you check the listing, you'll click on another "Start my Auction" button and the auction clock begins.

Editing Active Auctions

From the Auction Edit tab, select "Update" from the list and click on the "Enter Auction Edit" bar after entering your user ID and password.

You'll see a list of all your currently running auctions. You can edit the item description, change your auction category, or add a photo by clicking on the auction number.

End an Auction Early

You can end an auction early the same way you edit an active auction. Use the Auction Edit tab and select "End Your Auction." Click on the "Enter Auction Edit" bar after entering your user ID and password.

You'll see a list of all your currently running auctions. Select from the list which auction you wish to cancel.

If any bids have been entered on the auction, you must e-mail the bidders and inform them of your reason for ending the auction.

Fees

Bidders pay no fees; sellers pay commission fees only on the items that sell. Users replenish their accounts with a U.S or International money order, or a personal check.

Listing Fees

L.A.O. has no listing fees and, according to Dave, has no plans to institute them in the near future.

Commission

L.A.O.'s site commission schedule is similar to other online auction sites:

Range of Final Price	Closing Fee
$0.00 – 25.00	5%
$25.01 – 1,000.00	2.5% of any amount over $25.00
$1,000.01 and up	1.25% of any amount over $1,000.00

Payment Information and Terms

Sellers can accrue a $3 account, which must be paid for with a U.S or International money order, or a personal check. Site fees can be pre-paid.

You'll receive an account status in e-mail every month.

Security/Safety Features

L.A.O. has a number of security features in place. They investigate all complaints as soon as possible and attempt to revoke site privileges of suspected users before anyone gets "ripped off."

Bidding for:	** Flitter & Lips **		
Start Price:	$25.00	Current Bid:	$36.50
High Bidder:	sunshineflowers@writeme.com	Bidders Rating:	0/1/0
Sellers Email:	shey69@aol.com	Sellers Rating:	12/0/0
Time Left:	2 Hours, 35 Minutes	# of Bids:	5
Auction Closes:	09/10/1999 20:36	Bid Increment:	$.50
Item #:	141426sh	Auction Type:	Standard

If You Are Not High Bidder Check Here ...

Bidders Options

SELLERS OTHER AUCTIONS	SELLERS CREDIT RATING	ASK A QUESTION

Bidders Options: click on the links above to see other auctions this seller has running now. See what others have to say about the seller by checking their Credit Rating and view the positive/negative/neutral comments that have been made. E-mail the Seller if you have questions about this item before bidding, keep all correspondence between you and the seller. The seller assumes all responsibility for listing this item.

Item Category:	Beanies-Retired-New
Item Subcategory:	Sea-Beanie

Product Description:
These beanies are MWMTs & come from a non-smoking home. Buyer to pay $5 shipping. Money orders only. Please respond within 5 days of auctions end. Check my other auctions to save on shipping. Thanks for looking.

Additional Comments:
None

Auction Listing at Live Auction Online

In addition to that, you'll find some of the standard regulatory features:

- **Rating and Feedback** – You can rate other users with positive, negative, or neutral comments.
- **Online User Guides** – These are available for bidders and sellers, in the form of frequently asked questions (FAQs).
- **Staff of Investigators** – They check out fishy-sounding auctions or copyright infringement, and cancel any auctions that appear fraudulent.
- **Fraud Policy** – L.A.O. has a zero tolerance policy against any user who defrauds or defaults on payment. One violation and you lose your user ID.

The Auction Listing

An example of what you'll see when you call up an auction listing at Live Auction Online is on page 240.

The "If you are not high bidder check here" link shows you the auction's current bidding history. You'll enter your maximum bid, user ID, and password to view the current bids.

Feedback

Access the page to leave feedback by clicking on the "Auction Rating" tab at the top of any page. Enter your user ID and password, and follow the steps.

You can also get there by clicking on the feedback numbers after anyone's user ID.

L.A.O. reveals all your feedback, or "rating" as they call it, at one glance. Instead of one number you'll see three, which represent positive/negative/neutral comments. When you click on a user's feedback numbers, you'll see a "Check Comments and Rating" page.

Edit Comments

If you left a negative comment and later settled the dispute, you can edit the remark from the "Auction Rating" tab.

After you log in with your e-mail address and password, click on the "Go to Edit Comments" bar under "Edit Your Comments." From here, you'll see the "Auction Edit" screen where you can edit comments you posted for other users.

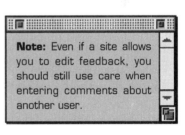

Note: Even if a site allows you to edit feedback, you should still use care when entering comments about another user.

You'll need to enter your e-mail address and password again; then click on the "Enter Auction Edit" bar. The next page displays a list of all feedback comments you've entered. Each one has a track number assigned to it. If you click on the track number, the comment appears. You can backspace through the text, or highlight it with your mouse and hit "return." Then you can enter new text.

If necessary, you can change the comment to positive, negative, or neutral from any other category. Then when you click on the "Edit Your Comment and Rating" bar, the information enters the system, and the comment is now changed.

Transaction Specific

Feedback doesn't have to be transaction-specific to increment the user's overall rating. Before you post the feedback comment, though, you'll be asked to select whether the transaction resulted in a sale or not.

Each comment you enter will increment the person's score, but you can only enter feedback that isn't transaction-related for a user once every 10 days.

☞Meet Christina and Heather, Two Frequent LAO Users

Dave put me in touch with Heather and Christina, who are both regular users of Live Auction Online. He classified them as "anchor tenants," sellers with at least 50 auctions running at any one time.

Both were kind enough to let me take up some of their valuable auction time with an interview.

History with Online Auctions

Heather has been using Live Auction Online for two years. "We have used many auction sites in the past," she says. "We currently also use OneWebPlace and Beanie Nation."

Christina's been active at L.A.O. since mid-1998. L.A.O. introduced itself with a "mass e-mailing," so Christina decided to check out the site. She also uses Yahoo auctions, Auctions.com, CollectingNation, NoBidding.com, eBay, and Up4Sale.

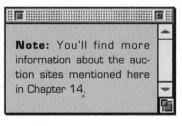

Note: You'll find more information about the auction sites mentioned here in Chapter 14.

Thoughts about Live Auction Online

Christina appreciates that L.A.O. plans to upgrade its technology. She also likes not paying a listing fee.

"Free listing makes it easier for us dealers who want to list a lot of items," she explains. "It also helps that Live Auction Online is far less complicated than some of the other sites."

In addition, she finds that the saturation present at some of the other auction sites isn't as much of a problem at L.A.O.

"You don't see hundreds of auctions for the same item all at once," says Christina. "We sellers have far less competition. Some auction sites are totally overloaded with hundreds of the same item, which drives the price way down. This is bad for anyone wanting to make a profit on an item. I don't have to compete with other people on L.A.O. Almost all my items are unique on that site."

Christina likes the response she gets from buyers at L.A.O. She finds that fewer people back out of sales there than compared to some of the other online auction sites. She's also a fan of L.A.O.'s customer service.

"It's very easy to locate their customer service e-mail address and you actually get a response back quickly. Other sites tend to make it very difficult to find their e-mail address and I rarely get a response from them."

Lessons Learned

Heather has some advice for users at L.A.O. that applies to online auction users in general.

"So far the only problem I've run into," says Heather, "is with people who bid and don't pay. Occasionally the price of an item will jump up to twice what it's worth without any real explanation. When this happens, I usually don't see the payment.

"Watch out for off-auction people who e-mail you with offers that are too good to be true," she warns. "You might see an auction saying something like 'I must sell my entire Beanie collection of 300 Beanies for $300.' These usually come from scam artists looking to make a fast buck on unsuspecting people. If you watch out for that," she continues, "you'll that find buyers and sellers at L.A.O. are very honest."

Heather also warns against agreeing to unusual payment methods. "Avoid wiring people money if you do not already know them personally," she advises.

Christina has a levelheaded approach to her online auction business. "There will always be a bidder that doesn't follow through with payment," she says. "Getting angry will just lead to what I call a feedback war. I allow a certain number of days for payment to arrive. If it doesn't show up, I re-list the item."

Best Experience

"Online auctions represent almost 75% of my sales," says Christina. "People can shop the online auctions instead of Web sites because they will find everything they could possibly want at one auction site. It's far easier than searching through hundreds of Web sites. They can also do market comparisons and get some very good deals on items.

"I love selling at online auctions," she adds. "I meet very nice people from all over the world. It's so much fun!"

Chapter 12 — CityAuction.com

☞www.CityAuction.com

Using CityAuction is similar to browsing live auctions in your own community. You can search for auctions listed by sellers in a specific radius relative to where you live.

Run by CityAuction, Inc. in San Francisco, California, CityAuction is a user-friendly site. You'll find buying and selling at CityAuction rather simple. Their auction software is similar in concept and appearance to some of the other sites, so if you've bought or sold collectibles at an online auction site before, CityAuction will be even easier for you to use.

However, there's also plenty of opportunity for the new online auction user to get his or her cyber-feet wet at this site. CityAuction explains online listing and bidding in detail.

Here's an example of what you'll see when you call up www.CityAuction.com:

CityAuction.com Home Page

You'll find an explanation of the auction listing icons and page update information as you scroll down the page.

Table of Features

Site URL: www.CityAuction.com Time zone: Eastern		
Main page features	**Yes**	**No**
Site links on main page	X	
Featured auctions	X	
Browse by category	X	
News		X
Date of last update	X	
Copyright information		X
User recall	X	
Link to personal activity page	X	
Search features	**Yes**	**No**
Search by keyword	X	
Search by seller	X	
Search by bidder		X
Search by category	X	
All in one search	X	
Search title only		X
Search auction descriptions	X	
Search completed auctions		X
Advanced search	X	
Auctions and Bidding	**Yes**	**No**
Proxy bidding	X	
Dutch auctions	X	
Reserve price	X	
Mandatory reserve		X
Adjustable start and end time		X
View bidding history	X	
Open-ended bidding		X
HTML in description	X	
Services	**Yes**	**No**
Site Tutorial	X	
Personal Paging		X
Escrow		X

Particulars	
Insertion Fee:	None
Commission:	5% to $25 2.5% to $1,000 1.5% over $1,000
Duration:	1 hour to 21 days

☛What's Unique about CityAuction?

CityAuction definitely has its share of noteworthy features. For instance, sellers can designate their selling accounts as "merchant" or "private seller," so you know some key information about the seller before you bid. The Bidder Credit Card Requirement option allows sellers to charge purchases to a buyer's credit card. If you select this option, any users interested in bidding on your item must have a valid credit card number on file with CityAuction.

Auction Features

On each listing, you'll see a clock running in real time. This means you don't have to keep refreshing the page to see how many minutes and seconds remain on an active auction — you can keep your eye on the clock and watch the auction close as the time runs out.

CityAuction has several useful listing features, and plenty of help pages explaining them.

Quick Win Auction

In this type of auction, the seller declares an opening bid and a threshold price, which is hidden. Bidding proceeds as normal until a bidder matches the threshold price. Then the auction closes immediately and that bidder wins.

Falling Price Auctions

The price lowers rather than rises as the bidding progresses in a falling price listing. Merchants enter auctions offering a group of products at an opening price, which then drops after a specific time interval passes. On the listing page, you can see when and how far the price will drop. A bid guarantees you the item, and you agree to purchase it at the specified price. The listings close when the quantity remaining drops to zero.

Mass Uploading

The mass uploader allows you to enter a large batch of listings at once. The process uses a spreadsheet you upload to CityAuction's server.

Image Uploading and Hosting

CityAuction can host your image on their server. If the picture is on your hard drive, you can upload it directly to CityAuction. You can manage any images you upload and reuse them in other auctions as long as you're an active user.

User Services

You'll find plenty of services at CityAuction designed to make the online auction experience safe and fun for both buyers and sellers.

The convenient My CityAuction link is located in the navigation links that appear at the top of every site page. This directs you to log in with your user ID and password; then brings up a page showing all your current auction activity — and it greets you by name!

Watch List

This function allows you to track and return to auctions of interest to you. While browsing through the listings, you can add items to your Watch List if you want to keep an eye on them and perhaps bid in the last few minutes before the auction closes.

To remove an item from the watch list, just check the box to the left of the Watch List entry and click on the "Delete" button.

My AuctionPlace

This is your own personal home page on CityAuction that you can link to from other places on the Web. You have complete control over the contents of the page. All your open listings will automatically appear at the bottom.

Users who have a My AuctionPlace page will have a little "house" icon appear beside their user ID at the site. Clicking on the icon takes people to that user's My AuctionPlace page.

Near Me

The "Near Me" link appears along the right margin of each site page. This feature allows you to search for auctions listed by sellers near a particular geographic location, such as within a specific radius of your home.

Glossary

Buying and selling at auction has a language all its own and CityAuction's glossary does a great job of explaining the terms. By following the Glossary link from the Help page, you'll find definitions for online auction concepts such as these:

• Cookies
• Mass Upload
• Hot Items
• Threshold price

If you decide to check out the glossary, plan to spend some time because there is such a wealth of online auction information to read!

☛Using the Site

I found the site easy to navigate, with adequate help pages. From the home page, you can click on any link and the next page displays a row of site links across the top. These navigation links appear on all CityAuction's internal pages and take you to interesting places at the site.

- **Home** – Return to the CityAuction home page to check out featured listings, or to search for auctions by category.
- **Categories** – Check out all active listings by clicking on any auction category. You'll also find links to Hot Listings (those with a lot of bidding activity) and Featured Listings from each category page.
- **Search** – Search active and closed auctions by number, keyword, user ID, or various other criteria.
- **My CityAuction** – This is your "account control panel," designed to help you keep track of your CityAuction activity. After entering your user ID and password, you can check your active listings, view any bids you have placed on auctions, manage your user information, create and manage your Watch List, and set several other options.
- **Sell** – Use this link to start an auction.
- **Watch List** – If you have a Watch List created, this page lets you use it to track auctions you find particularly interesting.
- **Account** – This page offers the same information you'll find by clicking on the My CityAuction link.
- **Help** – Read more information about buying, selling, or managing your CityAuction account.

Each of these pages offers a special "Help" link located near the main navigation links. This "Help" link takes you to a page with expanded information about the function that you've selected. For instance, if you click on the "Sell" navigation link, you'll find the special "Help" link on that page. When you click there, you'll find detailed information about how to enter a listing at CityAuction.

You can get anywhere at the site from any page, and many of the pages offer their own hints and tips.

Help

You'll find several informational pages located in the "Help" links, located in the right margin of every page.

- **Getting Started** – This page offers information about the three basic functions of CityAuction. On each of these pages, you'll find a link to the main site glossary, which works as an all-in-one reference guide to help you understand auction terms:
    Buying an item
    Selling an item
    Managing your account
- **FAQ** – Includes frequently asked questions with detailed answers. This section lists by topic:
    Registration
    Bidding
    Selling

- **Terms and Conditions** – Here you'll find the CityAuction user agreement and the standard details of their services.
- **Seller Fees** – This page provides the fee schedule for the various charges assessed to your account when you list auctions.
- **Questions & Comments** – If you click on this link, a mail window pops up. If your browser is set to send and receive e-mail, you can send a message to CityAuction's Support Team.

Searching for Auctions

The regular search page has a field for a keyword search. You also have four other search options:

Listings near me
Just opened (Listings that opened today)
Closing soon (Listings that close today)
Closing this hour (Listings that close within the hour)

The "Listings near me" option allows you to search for auctions entered by sellers whose user profile shows their location within a radius of a specific place, like your home. You specify the location and distance of the radius, in miles.

Advanced Search

Beside the keyword search box, you'll see an Advanced Search link. With this search tool, you can hunt for auctions in several ways. Each major search category offers additional criteria with it.

Here's how you can hunt for listings at CityAuction:

- **Product Information**
    Category (Select from drop-down menu)
- **Listing Information**
    Description (Enter search string)
    For Sale By (Merchant, Private, Either)
    Type (Select from drop-down menu)
    Price (Set high and low amounts)
    End Date (Set start and finish date)
    Listing Number
    Reserve Price (Yes, No, Either)
- **Seller Information**
    Seller Username
    Seller Rating (All sellers, or only those with positive ratings)
    Seller Location (Select from drop-down menu)

• **Geographic Information**
Zip/Postal Code
Search Radius (Select from drop-down menu)

You can make multiple selections in all search criteria before you hit the "Search" button at the bottom of the page. The results will reflect every criterion you chose in any search category.

Category Search

From CityAuction's home page, select a listing category to see that group of products. Then click on the hyperlink for the items you seek. The search results list in chronological order, with the auctions closing soonest listed first.

When you use the search box at the top of a page of listings generated by a category search, the keywords you enter will only apply to the current category you're searching. To carry out a keyword search of all listings on CityAuction, you must click on the "Search" link from the main navigation links. You can then conduct your keyword search from the main search page.

Search User IDs

At CityAuction, your e-mail address can be your user ID, or you can select a unique user name. You'll establish your user name when you register.

To follow a seller's auction activity, use the "Seller Information" search category on the advanced search page. Enter the person's user ID to retrieve a list of his or her active auctions.

I couldn't find a link to search for a buyer's current auction activity. I tried to enter my user ID "marble" as a keyword search and I saw five auctions involving — can you guess? That's right — marbles.

Auction Agent

If you want to track auctions that interest you, select "Auction Agent" from the "My Account" link. This feature notifies you by e-mail when a newly listed auction or classified listing meets your criteria.

You can select, in any combination, the item category, keywords, seller status, price range, presence of a reserve price, and listing type.

Bidding

When you see an auction for something you want, read the description thoroughly. Be sure to contact the seller with any questions you have before you bid. When you're ready, click on the "Bid Now" link just under the main listing, right above the description area.

On the next screen, enter your maximum bid and click on "Confirm." You'll see a confirmation screen where you can review your bid. If the amount you entered isn't correct, use your browser's Back button to make changes.

If the amount shown as your bid is correct, click on "Submit." A new page comes up with the high bid amount for the item and tells you if you're the new high bidder. If you're not and you need to enter a greater amount, you can use your browser's Back button to enter a new bid.

From the Submit page, you can click on "View Bid History" to see a summary of bids placed on the item so far. If you're the high bidder and another user outbids you later, the site lets you know via e-mail.

Automatic Bidding

This is CityAuction's term for proxy bidding. It works the same way as proxy bidding on other online auction sites.

If you're the first bidder, the amount shown as your current bid will probably be lower than your maximum bid. The amount will match the minimum price set by the seller. The only exception is if your maximum bid meets the reserve price, then your current bid will reflect that — even if your maximum bid exceeds it.

If someone else bids on the item, your amount raises to bid against the person until his or her amount exceeds your maximum. You'll then get an outbid e-mail notice from CityAuction, and you'll need to enter a higher maximum bid to stay in the running. In case of a tie for the highest bid, the earlier bid wins.

Proxy bidding works in any auction except a Dutch auction.

Calling Back Bids

At CityAuction, you can only retract bids in exceptional circumstances, such as if the seller significantly and materially changed the item description after you entered your bid. However, whether the bid is actually called back is up to the site personnel.

According to the CityAuction Support Team, "If the bidder would like to cancel a bid, he or she must contact our department stating why the bid should be canceled. We do not make any promises that a bid will actually be canceled. In most cases, as stated in our terms, the bid will not be canceled."

As with any online auction site, request bid cancellation only as a last resort. Doing so may subject you to negative feedback from the seller, which can damage your reputation in the online auction community.

Selling an Item

Once you register, click on "Sell" in the main navigation links and you'll go right to a page where you can add your listing. From there, you'll see an item category listing. Click on the category that applies to the item you're selling.

In order to sell items on CityAuction, you must have a valid credit card on file

> **Note:** CityAuction allows you to upload many auctions at once. Use the link at the bottom of the main "Sell" page and follow the online directions if you want to list a batch of auctions.

with them. If you don't, the site prompts you to enter one on their SSL site before you can access the page where you list an item.

CityAuction will ask you to enter your user ID and password. Next, you'll see the auction listing entry page where you'll enter the following information about the your item:

- **Listing Information**
  Type of auction – Choose from English, Quick Win, Dutch, or Classified.
  Title – Make it a good one.
  Start Time and End Time – Select each time from drop-down menu. The fields will default to a 7-day auction.
  Available Quantity – Enter number of identical items you're selling.
- **For Auctions Only**
  Opening Bid
  Reserve/Threshold Price
  Minimum Quantity
- **For Classifieds Only**
  Desired Price
  Negotiability – Is the price firm or negotiable? (Select Yes or No.)
- **Product Information**
  Auction Description – Limit 8,000 characters, HTML permitted.
  Picture URL
  Specification of product – Condition (Select from menu), Mint (Yes or No), Item Type (Select from menu, varies with category.)
- **Payment/Shipping Information**
  Preferred payment method – Select all that apply.
  Enter your City, State, and Country
  Shipping methods – Select all that apply.

When you finish entering the information, click on "Review Listing." From the next page, you can view your formatted auction. You'll also see more seller options:

- **Merchandising options**
  Home Page Featured
  Category Featured
  Bold Faced Title
- **Bidder Requirements**
  Click box if buyer must have a credit card on file to bid.

Once you've reviewed your listing and selected any other options, click on "Place Listing," and you'll see a confirmation screen telling you that your auction is either active, or scheduled to start at the time you specified.

Editing Active Auctions

If you have an active or scheduled auction running, you'll see a link called "Edit Listings" as an option on your MyAccount page. Enter any necessary criteria to search your auctions, or default to "All" and click on the "Submit" button at the bottom of the page.

When the list of your auctions comes up, click on the auction number you wish to edit. When the auction page appears, scroll to the bottom and click on "Edit Listing." You'll see the auction entry page with the fields filled in as you populated them, and you can make any changes and re-submit the listing.

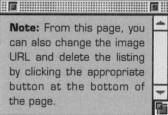

Note: From this page, you can also change the image URL and delete the listing by clicking the appropriate button at the bottom of the page.

Fees

Bidders pay no fees to CityAuction, only to the seller in payment for an item won at auction. If you participate at the site, you're responsible for paying any applicable taxes and for any costs you incur to buy items or list auctions at CityAuction. Sellers pay fees associated with the listing:

- Seller transaction fees (commission)
- Optional display features (bold title, featured auction, etc.)

Insertion Fees

There are no insertion fees for auctions or classified listings at CityAuction. Sellers pay only for optional display features selected to enhance their listings.

Optional Features

If you wish, there are a few ways you can highlight your auction for an extra charge:

- **Home Page Featured Listing** – $25.00 Per Listing
- **Category Featured Listing** – $10.00 Per Listing
- **Bold Face Title** – $2.00 Per Listing

To use any of these features, select them when you enter your auction. These special merchandising fees are not refundable if your item doesn't sell.

Seller Transaction Fees

The seller transaction fee, or commission, is calculated according to this schedule:

Range of Final Price	Final Value Fee
$0.01 – 25.00	5%
$25.01 – 1,000.00	2.5%
$1,000.01 and up	1.25%

For Dutch auctions, the fee depends on the amount of the minimum winning bid multiplied by the quantity of items sold.

If the item doesn't sell, CityAuction returns your sales fee. If your item sells, the commission appears on your account. You can have up to $10 on your account or you can enter a credit card number that's retained on file. You'll receive timely account statements via e-mail.

If the buyer formally backs out of the deal or remains uncommunicative after two weeks, you can obtain a seller credit. You'll find instructions for requesting a seller transaction credit on the "Help for Sellers" page.

Security/Safety Features

Many of CityAuction's safety features appear in their Terms and Conditions statement.

- **User privacy** – You many not disclose personal information about any user to a third party for any reason, and you cannot use CityAuction to "farm" e-mail addresses for spamming. Furthermore, CityAuction prohibits bid siphoning.
- **Illegal or questionable items** – You may not list any auction selling illegal items or anything CityAuction deems "questionable."
- **Online user guides** – CityAuction's Terms and Conditions appear at the site.
- **Staff of investigators** – If problems arise, send e-mail to admin@CityAuction.com.

CityAuction can cancel your account for any breach of the Terms and Conditions agreement or if they are unable to verify or authenticate any information you provide when you establish your user ID.

The Auction Listing

On the next page is an example of what you'll see when you call up a listing at CityAuction.

Notice the auction clock. On your screen, the minutes and seconds tick off in real time. When there is one hour left on the auction, the numbers change from black to red.

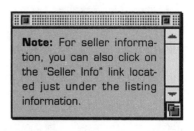

Note: For seller information, you can also click on the "Seller Info" link located just under the listing information.

As you scroll down the page, you'll see the seller's information and links to the seller's other auctions and feedback comments. The payment and shipping specifications appear further down on the page.

Feedback

After two users complete a transaction, each has the option to submit a comment about the other. Your feedback rating increases every time someone

CityAuction   *citysearch.com*   **match.com**

Auction Home > Toys & Beanies > Beanies Plush > Listing 6662114

Home   Categories   Search   My CityAuction   Sell   WatchList   Account   Help

Clubby I Beanie Buddy ++MWMTS++

Listing Type:	English	Time Remaining:	1 day, 00:14:46
High Bid:	$20.00	Open Date:	1/10 1PM EST
No. of Bids: (history)	1	Close Date:	1/16 1PM EST
Opening Bid:	$20.00	Quantity:	1
Bid Increment:	$1.00	Listing #:	6662114

Bid Now   **Seller Info**   Email This Listing to a Friend

Add to Watch List   **Shipping/Payment**

Product Detail

Description	Clubby I beanie buddy is in mint condition with mint tags. Lives in a smoke-free, adult environment and never been played with. Stored in an air-tight container and will be shipped in a plastic bag with a free tag protector. Add $4.05 for priority mail ($3.20) and insurance ($.85). Prepaid money order must be received within 7 days after close of auction. Buddy will be shipped immediately upon receipt of payment.
Condition	New
Tag Type	
Beanies Plush Type	Ty Beanies
Title	Clubby I
Year	1999

Seller Information

Auction Listing at CityAuction

posts a comment for you, but only once per unique user. You can enter user comments through the "MyAccount" link by clicking on "User Info" and then "Comments."

Feedback is positive, neutral, or negative. The user's final rating is a cumulative score. Positives count as one, neutrals as zero, and negative comments subtract one from the overall feedback score.

Transaction Specific

You can post comments only about users with whom you have completed a transaction.

☞Meet Lydia, A CityAuction Regular

Simplicity and ease of use drew Lydia to CityAuction. She previously sold art glass and limited edition cookware at an Internet collector forum, but found it difficult to appease everyone when they bartered for her items.

"I'd list items and the price I wanted," she explains, "but as soon as I posted that the item was sold, someone e-mailed me offering more. Of course I wanted more money for it, but I had to accept the first offer."

Lydia heard about an auction site called eHammer, and another one called CityAuction. She surfed into both sites, read the introduction pages and tutorials, and registered at both of them.

Note: You can read more about eHammer in Chapter 14.

History with Online Auctions

Similar to numerous other online auction users, Lydia is an off-line auction veteran. She and her sisters spent many Sunday afternoons at estate auctions in rural Pennsylvania, and she even trained to become an auctioneer.

"I love people," she says. "I love getting all the attention up on stage! But no matter where I went in my county, I'd see the same kinds of stuff come up for auction repeatedly. I think people bought things and then returned them to the auction pile when nobody was looking. It seemed as though nothing new ever entered the area." Lydia found a much different experience on the Internet.

"Suddenly, I'm looking at pictures of things I never saw before. The sellers are so friendly. I sometimes worry that I bug them too much with all my e-mail questions, but nobody's complained yet. I've made so many new friends!" Lydia plans to stay active at CityAuction because she likes the format.

Thoughts about CityAuction

"I like CityAuction's glossary of auction terms," says Lydia. "There are some things I'm too embarrassed to ask people so I look for them online. CityAuction has a FAQ and a tutorial, so I was able to learn everything I wanted just by reading the site."

Like many users, Lydia judges an online auction site by how easy it is to use. "I knew the system would bid for you if you entered a high amount," she confesses, "but I called it 'automatic bidding.' I had no idea it had another name until I went to CityAuction's online Glossary to look up something called 'Automatic (proxy) bidding.' Was I ever surprised!"

Lessons Learned

Unfortunately, Lydia admits to getting a slow start leaving user feedback. She didn't know how the process worked until one of her buyers asked why she hadn't posted a comment for him yet.

"I was so ashamed that I hadn't left anyone feedback!" Lydia says, "I thought when they wanted good feedback, they meant I should give them a good reference if someone asked. Now when I receive the payment from my high bidder I always leave the person good feedback as soon as I get the money order, or as soon as the personal check clears the bank."

Best Experience

Who wouldn't love an auction sleeper? Lydia listed a set of Looney Tunes drinking glasses that she collected at a Hardee's Restaurant back in the late 1970s. She set the reserve at $20 and decided she'd accept any offer, even less than her reserve price.

"I hadn't used them since college," she said, "but didn't think they had any value. I just wanted to free up space in my kitchen cabinet."

Lydia was shocked when the set of six glasses closed at $65. "I think it was a matter of serendipity," she laughs, "and being at just the right auction site!"

Chapter 13 — Up4Sale

☛www.Up4Sale.com

Up4Sale is owned by eBay Inc. and is one of the first auction sites on the Internet to boast "free auctions forever." You'll see their ad banner all over collector and auction portals on the Internet. Up4Sale is the original user-friendly online auction site, having experienced several format changes since its debut in 1998.

The only transactions for which you'll pay are the featured auctions. All transactions between the buyer and seller are in U.S. dollars.

Here's an example of what you'll see when you call up the www.Up4Sale.com home page:

Up4Sale.com Home Page

You'll see page links and copyright information as you scroll down the page. There's also a link to eBay.

Table of Features

Site URL: www.up4sale.com Time zone: Eastern		
Main page features	**Yes**	**No**
Site links on main page	X	
Featured auctions	X	
Browse by category	X	
News	X	
Date of last update		X
Copyright information	X	
User recall		X
Link to personal activity page	X	
Search features	**Yes**	**No**
Search by keyword	X	
Search by seller	X	
Search by bidder	X	
Search by category	X	
All in one search		X
Search title only		X
Search auction descriptions	X	
Search completed auctions	X	
Advanced search	X	
Auctions and Bidding	**Yes**	**No**
Proxy bidding	X	
Dutch auctions		X
Reserve price	X	
Mandatory reserve		X
Adjustable start and end time		X
View bidding history	X	
Open-ended bidding		X
HTML in description		X
Services	**Yes**	**No**
Site Tutorial	X	
Personal Paging		X
Escrow		X

Particulars	
insertion Fee:	None
Commission:	None
Duration:	3, 7, or 14 days

☞What's Unique about Up4Sale?

You'll find an interesting method of formatting your auction description — they don't allow HTML tags. Instead, you'll enter essential information about your item and the auction formats automatically with Up4Sale's unique auction software. It's a nice presentation.

Auction Features

Up4Sale apparently wants you to learn the workings of the site so well that you can enter your auctions correctly the first time. There are plenty of instructions available. Up4Sale offers an interactive tutorial where you can bid on fake auctions and enter fake bids just to get the hang of it. I didn't see this helpful feature at any other online auction site I researched.

Self-Bidding

Sellers may place one bid against their own auction to take the item off the auction market in case they find a buyer off the Internet. This is the equivalent of ending an auction early.

Multiple Item Auctions

You can list more than one item, but it's not an actual Dutch auction. It's comparable to Auction.com's ForSale feature. The seller sets the price, and you bid that price on however many of the items you want.

The bid entry page asks if you'll accept a lesser quantity of the items you bid on, and you'll select "yes" or "no." Proxy bidding doesn't operate with a multiple-item auction. You're simply "bidding" the set price of the item on a first come, first serve basis.

This is a great way to list multiple items with just one auction.

Auction Add-ons

For a small fee, you can select little icons to dress up your auction listing. These appear next to your auction when it comes up in searches, or if you made your listing a Featured Auction.

The images help draw attention to your auction. Up4Sale has a nice variety of little icons available that add appeal to your listings.

Interactive Confirmation Screen

Change or add to your proposed auction listing right from the Auction Confirmation Screen. It presents the information you entered as an online form.

On Up4Sale, you don't have to hit your browser's "Back" button to make the corrections. This saves time when you're entering numerous auctions.

User Services

You'll find plenty of services at Up4Sale.com auctions designed to make the online auction experience safe and fun for both buyers and sellers. The theme at this site appears to be "learn by doing."

Personal Photo Gallery

At your request, Up4Sale hosts your auction images in your own private gallery. You can upload them to Up4Sale's server directly from your hard drive, and then use them with your auction listings.

If you're using an older browser version, e-mail the image file to Up4Sale, and they'll put it on the Web for you. However, there's no reason to be using an older version of Netscape or Internet Explorer. You can download the most current versions of both from links available at Up4Sale's "Viewing Tips" page.

Fraud Alert

Up4Sale has a page that lists tips for avoiding scams. Follow the link from any auction-listing page to "Fraud Alert," where you'll read several important items:

- Warnings about bid siphoning
- Advice to telephone the seller before you send money
- Caution about users with negative or hidden feedback comments
- Reminder to avoid sending money to an address different from the one Up4Sale sends you when the auction closes
- Sound advice about being wary of users with free e-mail service addresses, like bigfoot, yahoo, hotmail, etc.
- Request to report all fraud to Up4Sale at watch@up4sale.com

Similar to most online auction sites, Up4Sale does not prescreen sellers who post items for auction on Up4Sale. Members are therefore encouraged to exercise extreme care in all dealings.

The News Room

Find out about new features and options available at Up4Sale, and check out the honors and awards the Up4Sale online auction site has won. You can find The News Room from the Site Map link on the "How To?" page. You'll read more about that further in this chapter.

Link Partners

In return for other Web sites hosting articles about Up4Sale, you'll find a link to those sites on Up4Sale's Link Partner list.

From the Up4Sale home page, select "Links and Resources." You'll see the Up4Sale Directory, where you can select a directory of items listed at the site. When you choose one, you'll see a page of links to sites that mention Up4Sale and offer information or online articles about the items you selected.

From these pages, you can also copy special Up4Sale link buttons (they're animated) to use on your own Web page.

☞Using the Site

Up4Sale has a great navigation bar that appears on every page of the site. The actual "bar" itself is color coded so you know which part of the site you're visiting. The links also appear in text form at the bottom of each page. Up4Sale makes it easy for you to find your way around the site.

Here's where the navigation links at Up4Sale take you:

- **Listings** – Visit the Featured Auctions, or browse the listing categories.
- **Auction Item** – Go right to the auction-entry page. Know the URL of your image and get ready to describe and list facts about your item. Up4Sale doesn't allow HTML in the description area since they have their own formatting style.
- **Register** – What are you waiting for? Sign up!
- **How To?** – This page has plenty of links that answer any Frequently Asked Questions. There's even a FAQ.
- **Member Center** – Check the status of your bids, or follow the bidding on your auctions. You can also search for listings by item number, change your user information, or manage your online feedback. If you forgot your site password, Up4Sale will e-mail it to you.

> **Note:** You'll read more about Up4Sale's voting process further on in this chapter.

- **Member Ratings** – Here's where you find out who you can "vote" on and how to post comments about another user.

Home Page Links at Up4Sale, with "How To" Selected

These navigation bar links also appear on the Up4Sale home page, enhanced by a special Java program. If you pass your cursor over any of them, you'll see a little explanation of each one. The home page screen on page 262 shows the default text to the right of "Auction Arnie," Up4Sale's mascot auctioneer. The Arnie detail on page 266 shows the hint that replaced the default text when I passed my mouse cursor over the "How To?" link without clicking the button.

When I clicked on the "How To?" link, a page appeared with many helpful site links. All of the help pages at Up4Sale give you fast access to the information you're seeking.

Help

For help using Up4Sale, click on the "How To?" link that's on the main navigation bar. You'll see a page with links to other information pages, such as:

- **Free Membership** – Learn the particulars about registering at the site and the information you'll need when you list items for sale.
- **Formats** – You'll read an explanation of the auction format Up4Sale uses. You won't code it in HTML as you do at other online auction sites.
- **Bidding and Buying** – This page explains standard bidding, proxy bidding, and the steps to follow if you're the winning bidder.
- **Selling Your Item** – Find out what Up4Sale expects of you when you list items for auction. You'll also see selling tips, instructions for including an image, and advice for making your listings stand out among the others.
- **Rates and Reasons** – Here, Up4Sale explains their free listing policy and offers a link to where you can learn about Premium Listings and the fees for using them.
- **Shipping** – Read about shipping methods and the recommended inspection interval to offer your high bidder when he or she receives the item you sent.
- **Merchant Accounts** – Up4Sale plans a great interface to allow Merchants to use the Up4Sale online auction system easily.
- **Security and General** – If you need more information about Up4Sale's Secure (SSL) server or their bidding policy, this page has several blocks of valuable information.
- **Prohibited Items** – View a non-exhaustive list of items that may be illegal, potentially infringing, or prohibited by Up4Sale. The site administrators will delete any auctions involving prohibited items.
- **Terms and Conditions** – Every online action site has them. Be sure you're familiar with the terms and conditions at Up4Sale before you bid or list auctions.
- **Viewing Tips** – Up4Sale advises you to refresh the auction page to check for bidding activity. You can also download the latest versions of Netscape and Internet Explorer from this page.
- **Site Map** – Lost? Here's a list of links to every information page at the site.

For updates and current information about the site, check out Up4Sale's News Room. You'll find a link to it from the Site Map.

Searching for Auctions

At Up4Sale, you can search for auctions a few different ways. You can use the "Listings" link on the navigation bar to view the main featured auctions. Below that appears a list of auction categories through which you can browse.

You can also do a text search. Some of the site pages let you enter a search string in a one-line text form and click on "Search." This examines auction titles and descriptions for any that contain your keywords. The results display on a new page.

Category Search

To search auctions by category, click on "Listings" from the navigation bar and you'll see them when you scroll past the Featured Auctions.

You'll also find "Hot Categories" on the Up4Sale home page. There's a link for auctions closing within the next 24 hours followed by categories with plenty of listings and bidding action.

Use the "Links and Resources" link from the home page for another kind of auction category search, with links to some great sites to browse while you're waiting for auctions to close.

Advanced Search

Up4Sale's Advanced Search is simple, yet adequate. Find the "Advanced Search" link on the Up4Sale home page, right under the search box.

You'll find several Advanced Search options, including:

- **Power Search** – You can search for items while eliminating others from the results. For instance, if I enter this search pattern:

  Search for: Hammer
  But not this: MC

  The results display auctions for hammers – but no listings for musical artist MC Hammer.

- **Search for Items by Seller** – Enter the seller's user ID or e-mail address and click on the "Search" button. You'll see all auctions currently listed by that seller.
- **Search for Items by Number** – You'll find ten fields in which you can enter Up4Sale auction numbers. Any that are valid will display as one search result. This is a great way to keep an eye on certain auctions. The only drawback is that you have to know the auction number. However, once you obtain the results in a listing, you can bookmark that page so you can return to it later.

Any of these will find the currently running auctions you want, if someone listed them at Up4Sale.

Search User IDs

There are two ways to search for auctions by user ID. You can use the Advanced Search, or click on the Member Center link from the navigation bar.

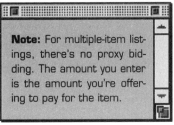

Note: You can only search your own auction activity from the Member Center, but you're doing the search by user ID.

Bidding

Once you find the right auction, bidding at Up4Sale is very easy. You can't miss the "Click Here to Bid!" button because it's located right under the title on the auction page.

This takes you to an on-screen form where you'll enter your user ID and password and the amount of your bid. If it's a multiple-item listing, you'll enter the number of items on which you wish to bid.

For a standard auction, you'll enter your maximum bid amount and proxy bidding does the rest until someone bids more than your high bid.

Note: For multiple-item listings, there's no proxy bidding. The amount you enter is the amount you're offering to pay for the item.

Click on "Submit Bid" to see the "Please Confirm your Bid" page. You'll see the amount you're about to bid. Your bid registers when you click "Submit This Bid."

Proxy Bidding

Up4Sale calls this feature "BidBot." If you're the first bidder, the amount shown as your current bid will probably be lower than your maximum bid. The amount will match the minimum price set by the seller. The only exception is if your maximum bid meets the reserve price — then your current bid will reflect that, even if your maximum bid exceeds it.

If someone else bids on the item, your bid will raise to bid against the person until it reaches your maximum and outbids you. You'll then get an outbid e-mail notice from Up4Sale, and you'll need to enter a higher maximum bid to stay in the game. In case of a tie for the highest bid, the earlier bid wins.

When you bid on an item, proxy bidding may outbid you right away. Up4Sale lets you know on the bid confirmation page and encourages you to try again.

Bidding History

For closed auctions, the bidding history displays right on the listing when you scroll down the page.

For open auctions, you'll see a "Click for more bid info" link by the "Number of bids" field on the auction page. The link displays all bids placed on that auction in chronological order, along with the bidder's user ID and the date and time he or she placed the bid.

Retracting a Bid

You can only retract a bid if the seller changed the auction description. If you're the current high bidder when this happens, Up4Sale sends e-mail letting you know about the change. You'll see instructions for canceling your bid if you reconsider after viewing the auction description changes.

Selling an Item

Once you register at Up4Sale, you can list items for auction by clicking on the "Auction Item" link on the navigation bar.

First, you'll read site selling policies and helpful posting tips. Then you'll scroll down to enter your user ID and password. Next, you must enter certain information the site uses to create your listing:

- **Title Your Auction** – Enter the auction title you prepared for your listing. Up4Sale reserves the right to remove what they call "SKREEMing" titles – those entered in all capital letters. Entering text in all upper case is always bad form on the Internet.
- **Describe Your Item** – You can't use HTML at Up4Sale, and they recommend a limit of 50 words in this field.
- **Choose a Category for Your Item** (Select one from the drop-down menu.)
- **Enter Optional Picture:** (Select one)
  No image. (No way!)
  Enter the URL of your image.
  Use a picture from your personal Up4Sale image gallery.
- **Minimum Bid** (Required)
- **Quantity** (Required)
- **Sell as a Block** – Yes or no
- **Reserve Price** (Optional)
- **Accepted Payment Methods** (Required, select from list)
- **Preferred Shipping Methods** (Required, select from list)
- **Enter the features of your item.** You have ten 80-character maximum fields in which to enter all the special information about your item that you'd normally format into your auction description. Up4Sale gives you plenty of room to describe your item irresistibly.
- **How Long Would You Like to Post Your Item(s)** – Select 3, 7, or 14 days from the drop-down menu.
- **How Would You Like to be Notified of Bids Placed Against your Item(s)** – Decide whether you want e-mail notification, or if you'd rather monitor the auction yourself.

Read the user agreement at the bottom of the page, and then click the "I Agree – Take me to the Confirmation Screen!" bar.

The Confirmation screen is an online form that presents all the information you entered. You can make changes or additions right in the appropriate fields.

Once everything is correct, click on "Post this Item" and the Up4Sale auction clock starts ticking.

Editing Active Auctions

Edit your auctions from the "Sellers" option under the "Member Center" link.

Select "Change/Add," which allows you to list your item in a different category, or add information to the auction description. The amendment will be time-stamped on the auction listing.

Your high bidder will learn of the change via an e-mail message automatically sent from Up4Sale.

Ending an Auction Early

Edit your auctions from the "Sellers" option under the "Member Center" link.

Select "End Auction." Up4Sale then lets you select an auction to close before the clock officially runs out.

Fees

Bidders pay no fees at Up4Sale. Sellers pay for optional display features selected to enhance their listings.

If you participate at the site, you're responsible for paying any applicable taxes and for any costs you incur to buy items or list auctions at Up4Sale.

Premium Listing Features

Up4Sale lets you highlight your auction in the following ways:

- **Bold Listings:** $.50 per auction
- **Category Feature Auctions:** $4.95 per auction
- **Auction Home Page Featured Auctions:** $9.95 per auction

You can select a little listing icon to appear by your auction title when it comes up in searches for an additional $1. If you want a larger image, you'll pay $2. You'll see the selection of listing images on the auction confirmation screen.

Payment Information and Terms

To use Up4Sale's premium listing features, you must open an account. The first time you attempt to use one of the optional features, you'll see a page where you can register to use them. Each user has an initial $10 credit limit unless you have a credit card number on file with the site.

You can also open an account before you use one of the features. From the Seller page, select "Premium Listings" and then click on "billing policy." You'll see Up4Sale's billing information. A link takes you directly to Up4Sale's Secure (SSL) site where you can enter your credit card information.

You can also send a check after generating a coupon at the site to remit with your payment.

Security/Safety Features

At the bottom of any auction-listing page, you'll see a link for Up4Sale's Fraud Alert page. You can read information about protecting yourself from Internet fraud. Up4Sale offers several features designed to make your online auction experience safe and secure.

Read the "Security and General" information at the "How To?" page for more information about Up4Sales security policies.

The Auction Listing

Here's an example of what you'll see when you call up an auction listing at Up4Sale:

Spun Glass Christmas Tree   Item #4233809

Click Here To Bid!   ✒ mail this auction to a friend!

See other auctions in this category!

Bid Needed to Win: $10.00
Starting Bid: $9.75
Quantity: 1
Number of Bids: 1 (click for more bid info)

Auction Ends: Thursday, 9/16/99 at 11:36:46 PM EDT
Auction Started: Monday, 9/13/99 at 11:36:46 PM EDT
Payment: Prepaid Check, Prepaid Money Order
Shipping: USPS

Seller Information: ☆ NEW USER! BLAKETD ⊙
Ask Seller a Question: Victory@theheadoffice.com
Other Sales: Click to See Other Sales By This Seller
Seller From: PHOENIX, AZ

Description

Description:
A unique Christmas creation of spun-glass, this beautiful tree is bedecked with all the trimmings and topped by a bright yellow star. 2 3/8 inch pink mirrored base, 3 inch high.

Features:
• A unique christmas creation of spun glass.
• Your satisfaction guaranteed or your money back, no questions asked.
• Buyer pays $6.00 shipping cost.

Auction Listing at Up4Sale

This listing also shows the description formatting Up4Sale uses based on what you enter when you list the auction. The image appears when you scroll farther down the page.

The bidder's identity is available at the "click for more bid info" link by the "Number of Bids" field. The winning bidder on this auction was user "NLHIX," who absolutely loves this handmade Christmas tree.

> **Note:** If you haven't figured out who NLHIX is, check the cover of this book.

Notice that you don't see the count-down. You'll have to synchronize your Microsoft Windows clock with the auction timing at Up4Sale.

Feedback

Up4Sale calls comments left by one user about another "votes." Members who have done business with each other can post a positive or negative vote for each transaction that takes place between them.

Votes

From the "Member Ratings" link, you can generate a list of the Up4Sale members on whom you're eligible to vote.

The votes you receive determine your overall rating score. Up4Sale deducts any negative votes from the positive votes to calculate your rating.

> **Note:** At Up4Sale, you'll lose your member privileges if your rating falls to minus three (−3). If this happens, your active auctions will close and any bids you have placed on open listings purge from the system.

General Comments

Anyone registered at Up4Sale can comment on any other user. These comments appear next to the votes on that user's rating page. However, the comments do not register when Up4Sale calculates the user's overall rating — only the votes figure in. This prevents users from helping each other establish a good rating without conducting actual transactions at the site.

You can respond to all comments and votes posted about you by other users. This lets members state their side of the story.

Star Rating

Up4Sale uses a "star rating" to reward members with high ratings. A user may have between zero and five stars.

The star rating tallies up all votes, both positive and negative, and then converts the numbers into a percentage. That percentage then determines the star rating.

Transaction Specific

Any registered member can choose to leave a general comment about any other member. However, only members who have transacted with each other can place a vote.

☞Meet Billy, A Frequent Up4Sale User

"If you told me five years ago that I'd buy this much stuff on the Internet," Billy says, "I'd have jumped for joy. I love collecting! I'm totally addicted to buying and selling stuff online."

Billy found out about Up4Sale through an ad in a collector magazine. He collects die cast cars and trucks, stamps, Boyd's Bears resin, and NASCAR items. Only when it's dragged out of him will Billy admit to being a former beanbag plush collector.

History with Online Auctions

"When the bottom fell out of the beanbag market," Billy says, "I wanted to get something for this pile of plush toys before they'd be worthless. I saw the ad for Up4Sale and checked it out. I can only describe the site by saying it looked inviting. I reminded me of an auction site for first-timers, and that's exactly what I needed."

Billy sold his entire collection of beanbag plush, in several lots.

"Apparently the bottom hadn't fallen completely out," he admits. "I made a fortune and my comment file grew. When the plush was gone, I went around looking for things I could sell at auction. When the basement and both crawl spaces were empty, I started poking around at yard sales."

He didn't limit his participation to selling, however.

"There are a few listing categories I look at daily, sometimes hourly. My collections are growing like crazy. I keep some items permanently, and others I enjoy for awhile and then list them for someone else to buy. I could never do this if it weren't for sites like Up4Sale."

Thoughts about Up4Sale

Billy likes the way Up4Sale gets his attention when he calls up the site.

"At some of the other auctions sites," he says, "I have my personal account page bookmarked. But at Up4Sale, I always go right to the home page so I can see the Tip of the Day and the featured listings. I like the way it's all presented. There's something really appealing about that little auctioneer."

Lessons Learned

From his experiences at Up4Sale, Billy discovered that it's imperative for a seller of any type of collectible to know the market.

"When Puffkin collectors say they want the tag in mint condition, with no bends," he explains, "that includes the bend in fold-over tags. The tag protectors I used caused the tags to lie very flat because they were too tight. This caused a break in the paper along the fold. I listed a Bandit the raccoon and said it had a mint tag with no breaks or bends. My high bidder had a fit when she saw the fold. I almost didn't believe her until she explained what part of the tag she meant. I had to refund her money."

Billy says he frequents many collector sites on the Internet and posts at a few bulletin boards.

"I find out what's important to collectors," he says, "and I know what to look for when I buy things for myself."

Best Experience

Billy fondly remembers selling his beanbag plush collection. He earned much more for it than he predicted and had a lot of fun in the process.

"My daughter helped me pack them up and ship them out," he says. " It was a real 'together' time for us. I think she also learned a lot about business. We made sure each package had a nice letter in it thanking the customer. She wrote all the letters and I let her sign them, but the customers knew an adult was supervising everything."

Billy has over 400 Up4Sale votes on his user ID record.

Chapter 14 — More Online Auction Sites

☞Auction Sites for Collectors

Electronic commerce is on the rise. It seems like everyone has some new and different way to market his or her products online. Internet auctions are by far the hottest new trend in Internet marketing. They're successful because they combine the ease of home shopping with the excitement of bargain hunting. They're also perfect for collectors, since 85% of the items sold at online auctions are collectibles.

The Internet hosts hundreds of auction sites for collectors. You may find that one online auction site looks and operates just like the next one with only slight differences in the page layouts. This doesn't mean one copied the other. They simply used the same or similar commercial online auction software.

I couldn't possibly cover all online auction sites in detail. As soon as I'd have them all alphabetized and categorized, more would appear. I limited this chapter to a few that looked like they would be of interest to collectors.

You may want to explore these sites to conduct your own online auction research.

Auction Features

The highlights and features I mention about each site are subject to change, since Web sites update constantly. Some of the sites might add or regroup their listing categories over time.

I included enough information about the sites to give you an idea about what each one offers for collectors. If one of these sites looks appealing, call up the URL in your browser and see what's happening in that auction community.

You never know what features they may have added just recently!

☞Online Auction Sites

In this section, you'll read the particulars of several online auction sites you may find interesting if you're an antique collector or dealer. Many of the sites will also interest folks who collect items that are part of a manufactured collectible line.

Here's an explanation of the information I include about each site:

Site Name: What's the site called?
Time Zone: The US time zone that generates the auction clock.
Main Interest: Enthusiasts who might like the site, antique collectors, numismatists, Boyd's Bears fanatics, etc.
Categories: Number of categories the site offers in which to list items for sale.
Unique Features: Does the site let you transfer your feedback rating from another auction site? Do they send you e-mail notification of listings that might interest you? Do they offer free listings with no commission charges? Do they come over and feed your pets while you browse the listings? I'll let you know.

Comments: My overall assessment of the site and its value as a medium to help you manage your collecting with online auctions.

If you find a site that looks promising, drop a bookmark there so you can visit them again later. Some of the sites require you to register before you can view listings.

auctions.excite.com

Site Name: Excite Auctions
Time Zone: Eastern
Main Interest: Antiques, Collectibles, Sports Memorabilia, Porcelain & Glass, Dolls & Toys, Art
Categories: 497
Unique Features:
- Access to portal facilities, such as free e-mail, message boards, chat, news and updates
- Geographic search – find items in your area
- Create a custom page for your auctions.

Comments: The Excite portal runs this site. You'll find thousands of active listings and a plethora of registered users. Plenty of bidding action. The site uses common auction software that's easy to use. There's also a good site tutorial and a page where you can track your auction activity.

myauction.warehouse.com

Site Name: Auction Warehouse
Time Zone: Eastern
Main Interest: Contemporary Collectibles and Antiques
Categories: 20
Unique Features:
- Live auction clock
- English auctions
- Site-run escrow service
- Base fees waived
- Straight-sales and merchant listings
- Classified and listings

Comments: Click on "General Merchandise" to visit auctions for Collectibles. If you select "Collectibles and Memorabilia," you'll see the listings you want. Uses standard auction software that's easy to operate. You'll need to register before you can view listings.

www.allstarauc.com

Site Name: All Star Auctions
Time Zone: Pacific
Main Interest: Comic Books, Comic Art, Strip Art, Sci-fi, Fantasy, Posters, Toys, Animation
Categories: N/A
Unique Features:
- Simulcast auctions with other online auction sites
- Fixed price sales
- Sell on consignment
- Telephone and faxed bids accepted
- Link to the site owner's eBay auctions
- Appraisals

Comments: Very interesting! It works differently from most online auctions. A little confusing to find my way around, but probably a breeze for regulars. Looks like a great place to manage your collection of Comic Art and Science Fiction items.

www.auction2000.net

Site Name: Auction Interactive 2000
Time Zone: Eastern
Main Interest: Antique and Collectibles
Categories: 5
Unique Features:
- Auction Chat
- Live auctions
- Auctions by licensed auctioneers
- Listings include thumbnail images
- News and site updates via e-mail
- New user referral incentive

Comments: Auction Interactive 2000 is a subsidiary of The Auction Company in Knoxville, Tennessee. This site has a unique and user-friendly auction format. There's a fair amount of listings with moderate bidding action. The emphasis is on bidding, not selling.

www.auctionaddict.com

Site Name: Auction Addict Online Auction
Time Zone: Eastern
Main Interest: Antiques, Collectibles, Hobbies, Books & Music, Coins, Currency & Stamps

Categories: 292
Unique Features:
- Fixed-price listings
- Virtual store front listings – view products and buy them online
- Search listings by geographic region
- Great quick-search function
- Optional listing features for a fee
- Special vendor listings
- Community center with message boards

Comments: Nice site layout with auction software similar to Amazon.com auctions. It's easy to navigate with site links on every page. There are plenty of listings with bidding activity. Most of the listings are under "Collectibles."

www.auctionanything.com

Site Name: AuctionAnything.com
Time Zone: Eastern
Main Interest: Sports Collectibles, Sports Memorabilia, Trading Cards
Categories: 21
Unique Features:
- Classified ads
- Open-ended auctions
- No listing fees or commissions
- Investor opportunities
- Business relations
- News and press releases

Comments: You'll find mostly sports-related items here. There are plenty of listings and lots of action. AuctionAnything uses a unique and sophisticated auction software program that's easy to use, and reliable. The item photo shows up on its own page when you click on a link, which cuts down on loading time. Great feature! Navigation is easy.

www.auctionfrenzy.com

Site Name: Auction Frenzy: Your Neighborhood Auction Partner
Time Zone: Mountain
Main Interest: Contemporary Collectibles, Trading Cards, and General Interest
Categories: 150
Unique Features:
- Auction stats on the home page
- Auction Watch to track your personal auction activity
- User ID is a six-digit identification number, not a name

- Merchant mart of fixed price items available
- Add yourself to their mailing list for news, site updates, and notification of special deals
- One-click viewing of all closed auctions
- Multi-bid feature

Comments: For a small site, I like the layout. There are links to the main pages right on the home page and plenty of instructions without a lot of confusion. There are links at the bottom of every page, but they disappeared when I passed my mouse cursor over them. Moderate bidding activity, easy to navigate.

www.auctionport.com

Site Name: Auction Port Online Auction House – Your Online Auctions
Time Zone: Eastern
Main Interest: Antiques, Collectibles, Coins, Currency & Stamps
Categories: 112
Unique Features:
- Appraisal service
- Message boards and live chat
- Bookstore
- Personal shopper
- Competitive listing fees, free basic auctions
- Free classifieds
- New user referral incentive
- Live auctions in online rooms

Comments: This is a full-function auction site with plenty to offer collectors, with emphasis on antiques. It's easy to navigate the site with the no-frills set of links on each page. Auction Port uses standard auction software, so it's very easy to bid. I found plenty of active listings and bidding action. They appear to have many registered users.

www.auctionware.com

Site Name: AuctionWare Online Auctions
Time Zone: Eastern
Main Interest: Collecting
Categories: 34
Unique Features:
- Fixed price listings
- Discussion forum
- No listing fees or commission
- Want ads

• Links to interesting Web sites
• Quick re-list if your item doesn't sell

Comments: This site uses a primitive but functional auction format. You'll find links that take you to news and articles about collecting antiques online.

www.auctionworks.com

Site Name: Auction Works – Online Interactive Auction
Time Zone: Eastern
Main Interest: Collectibles, Antiques, Memorabilia
Categories: 49
Unique Features:
• E-mail notification of auctions
• Build a wish list on a message board
• Personal shopper
• No listing fees – only commission
• Competitive insertion fees
• Live auctions in online rooms
• Fixed-price listings

Comments: This is a low-key auction site with an easy pace. They use standard auction software for listings. In each category, you can see the number of active and closed auctions.

www.beckett.com

Site Name: Beckett Collectible Auctions
Time Zone: Eastern
Main Interest: All types of Collectibles
Categories: 75
Unique Features:
• Online price guides
• Buy, Sell, and Trade with other collectors
• Grading
• Online store
• Collector's Page Builder to create your own collectibles Web page
• News and information

Comments: From the Beckett Collectibles Online home page, click on "Auctions" and you'll reach Beckett Collectible Auctions. Choose "Beckett Auctions" and you can check out items listed by professional auctioneers or select "Collector-to-Collector" and bid on other collectors' items.

www.bid.com

Site Name: Bid.com
Time Zone: Eastern
Main Interest: Computers, Sports Collectibles, Beanie Babies™
Categories: 14
Unique Features:
- "While supplies last" listings
- Message board
- News and information

Comments: Bid.com is a Canadian based online auction site. They use auction software similar to Up4Sale's. A navigation bar uses pull-down menus at the top of most pages. The site lists the auctions, and you bid on them. No private selling.

www.bidaway.com

Site Name: BidAway – Internet Collectibles Emporium
Time Zone: Eastern
Main Interest: Collectibles and Sports Memorabilia
Categories: 108
Unique Features:
- Auction by lots
- HTML code for their banner ads

Comments: You'll register via their secure server. You have to enter a credit card number to register. You can list only Dutch and Lot auctions. I couldn't reach the auction-entry page because of system errors. Moderate amount of auctions listed with light bidding activity.

www.biddingtons.com

Site Name: Biddington's Online Art & Antiques and Books
Time Zone: Pacific
Main Interest: Art, Antiques, Books
Categories: 39
Unique Features:
- Sellers pay 10% commission on all items over $100
- Mandatory site-run escrow
- On-site art gallery

Comments: Biddington's has easy-to-use auction software. The search results offer more information about the item listed than most others do. All transactions handled through Biddington's escrow service. They do not accept credit cards.

www.bidoncollectibles.com

Site Name: Bid on Collectibles
Time Zone: Eastern
Main Interest: Collectibles
Categories: 182
Unique Features:
- No listing fees or commissions
- Personal Auction Watch page
- Bid on multiple items
- Test auctions so you can practice bidding

Comments: Bid on Collectibles uses an auction software package I've seen at several other online auction sites. It runs smoothly and bidding is easy. Each time I check this site, I see more listings and bidding action. It's catching on! Navigation bar and page-bottom links make it easy to tour the site.

www.boxLot.com

Site Name: boxLot Auction Online
Time Zone: Pacific
Main Interest: Collectibles, Memorabilia, Antiques
Categories: 212
Unique Features:
- Spotlight auctions with photos on the site home page
- Daily drawings for prizes
- Auction Network categories
- Dynamic auction software

Comments: boxLot.com uses dynamic auction software similar to Amazon.com auctions. The listings are clear and concise, and bidding is easy. You'll find many listings with plenty of bids. This one's great for dealers!

www.buffalobid.com

Site Name: Buffalo Bid Antique and Collectible Online Auction
Time Zone: Mountain
Main Interest: Antiques, Collectibles, Western Memorabilia
Categories: 90
Unique Features:
- Auctions by lots
- Registry for wholesale or retail organizations
- Free regular listings

• Free image hosting
• Photos on a separate page from auction listing

Comments: Buffalo Bid uses common auction software that's easy to use and understand. Basic but functional site links on every page guide you through the pages. I found plenty of active listings in every category with lots of bidding action. You can browse through the category with the First, Previous, Next, and Last links on each auction page — no need to keep hitting your "Back" button. Great idea! I spent plenty of time at this site just browsing and being outbid!

www.cityauction.com

Site Name: CityAuction – Auction Classifieds
Time Zone: Pacific
Main Interest: Antiques, Collectibles, Hobbies, Books & Music, Coins, Currency & Stamps
Categories: 108
Unique Features:
  • Feedback at a glance shows number of auctions/positive/neutral/negative
  • Daily auction digest via e-mail
  • Monthly newsletter via e-mail
  • Comprehensive advanced search function
  • Cyber café
  • Message board
  • Dynamic auction software

Comments: CityAuction uses an auction program that looks a lot like eBay or Gold's. This is a full-function auction site with plenty of features and lots of regular users, listings, and bidding action. You'll see auctions all over the world that sellers chose to show in your area. While most auctions are worldwide or nationwide, some auctions of large or valuable items are restricted to a local area. I won an item as high bidder at this site, and the transaction was flawless.

www.collectingnation.com

Site Name: Collecting Nation – The Ultimate Online Auction Community
Time Zone: Eastern
Main Interest: Contemporary Collectibles, Action Figures, Collector Cards, Comic Books, Die Cast, Pokémon, BeanBag Plush
Categories: 134
Unique Features:
  • Each category is a separate auction site

- Featured auctions on home page
- Weekly contests with prizes
- Message boards
- News and information
- Dynamic auction format

Comments: This is a wonderful place! I spent hours going through each separate auction site affiliated with Collecting Nation. I found Beanie Nation, Comic Book Nation, Trading Card Nation, and the others. They're separate but all the same site. Any feedback you earn counts toward one rating no matter which "Nation" you use. You'll find auction software similar to eBay. Plenty of auctions listed; thousands of users. Check this one!

www.collectorsauction.com

Site Name: Collector's Auction – The High End of the Internet
Time Zone: Pacific
Main Interest: Coins, Currency, Stamps, Sports Collectibles
Categories: 309
Unique Features:

- Specializes in high-end collectible items, not those manufactured as part of a line
- Offers grading and authentication for coins, sports cards, and autographs
- Select a collector's universe from a long list for news, updates, hot auctions, and information
- Premium auctions
- Auction lingo directory
- Selling by lots
- Dealer auction services
- Price and market guides
- Photo gallery

Comments: Run by Collectors Universe (collectors.com), a high-end collector portal worthy of a bookmark. Set aside an hour or so to browse and read all the articles. You'll find information, stories, and a site tutorial. They even have an online lingo directory to help you learn the catchy online auction phrases. Plenty of bidding action. I'll definitely visit this one again.

www.collectex.com

Site Name: CollectEx
Time Zone: Eastern
Main Interest: Collectibles, Sports Memorabilia

Categories: 19
Unique Features:
- Image hosting
- Place multiple bids
- Fixed-price items available at online store
- Personal auction watch
- Special link to view auction winners
- New User's page with site information

Comments: CollectEx uses common auction software that's easy to use and understand. Primitive but functional site links on every page guide you through the pages. You'll find a separate category just for Emmett Kelly Jr. This is a very active auction site. Worth a look!

www.collectit.net

Site Name: Collect It
Time Zone: Central
Main Interest: Collectibles, Coins, Antiques, Stamps, Comics
Categories: 70
Unique Features:
- List of upcoming auctions
- Classified ads
- Optional open-ended auctions
- Personal Auction Watch feature

Comments: Collecting portal site run by Krause Publications. Heavy emphasis on visiting their main Web site. I saw plenty of listings and bidding action, but not as much as I expected. Still, this online auction site has promise. Collect It uses common auction software that's easy to use and understand. Cute little animated icons indicate user feedback ratings.

www.comspec-marketing.com

Site Name: Comspec Marketings: Florida Auctions Online
Time Zone: Central
Main Interest: Collectibles
Categories: 29
Unique Features:
- No listing fees or commissions
- Auctions close 5 minutes after last bid
- Handy site links
- Message boards for auction information
- New user referral incentives

Comments: Only a few active auctions, all by the same seller. This would be a nice online auction site if more folks would register and list items. There are convenient Next and Previous links on each auction page so I didn't have to hit my "Back" button as I browsed the categories.

www.edeal.com

Site Name: eDeal Auctions – InterActive Classifieds
Time Zone: Eastern
Main Interest: Antiques, Collectibles, Hobbies, Books & Music, Coins, Currency & Stamps
Categories: 198
Unique Features:
- Trade in global currency
- Live chat
- Competitive listing fees and commissions
- Online newsletter
- Interactive classifieds
- Site-run escrow
- Image hosting
- Dynamic auction software
- Frequent user reward program
- New user referral incentive
- Personal user control center

Comments: Auction software is similar to eBay and Gold's Auction. This full-function site is easy to use. Plenty of auctions alive with activity. Tell your friends about eDeal, have them register, and you can earn incentive points. There are handy site links at the bottom of each page. This one will definitely go places. Maybe it's there already!

www.ehammer.com

Site Name: eHammer, Online Auction of Antiques and Collectibles
Time Zone: Eastern
Main Interest: Antiques and Collectibles
Categories: 483
Unique Features:
- Convenient Log on/Log off button
- Links to professionally owned and run virtual auction halls
- Monthly featured auction halls
- Friendly and concise site tutorial
- Listing fees comparable to other popular auction sites

- Upload images to their server
- Dynamic auction software
- Specific instructions for AOL users
- Suggested shipping resources
- Comprehensive search function

Comments: This is an ultra-sophisticated full-function auction site with plenty of listings and lots of bidding. Great navigation bar of page links. It's very easy to get around. You'll find more antiques than collectibles here. Easy to register and bid. A definite must-see!

www.firstauction.com

Site Name: First Auction
Time Zone: Adjustable
Main Interest: Home Shopping, Contemporary Collectibles
Categories: 114
Unique Features:
- Dealer auction services
- First Auction lists the items and you bid
- No selling
- Flash auctions (they only run for 30 minutes)
- Adjustable time zone auction clock
- Personal page (displays your auction activity)
- Auction Newsletter
- Spotlight on Cool Stuff (featured listings on the home page)
- Rotating selection of goods

Comments: This one's part of the Internet Shopping Network (www.isn.com), which is part of the Home Shopping Network. Most of the auctions are for household items and apparel, but you'll find collectibles, jewelry, gemstones, coins, and stamps. Not much in the way of antiques. This is an interesting site to visit if you're into shopping from your workstation.

www.global-auction.com

Site Name: Global Auction Online
Time Zone: Central
Main Interest: Collectibles and currency
Categories: 46
Unique Features:
- Featured auctions
- No fees
- Home page auction stats (learn the number of registered users and how

many active auctions currently run)
- Charity auctions
- Want ads
- View hot auctions
- Message boards and chat
- News and announcements

Comments: Not much bidding action, but it has promise and it's easy to use. Fast navigation from site links. Nothing complicated about it.

www.goldnage.com

Site Name: Online Auction at Golden Age Antiques and Collectibles
Time Zone: Eastern
Main Interest: Antiques and Vintage Collectibles
Categories: 9
Unique Features:
- Frequent buyer incentives
- Fixed-price items available at online store
- Animated picture gallery on home page
- Link to closed auctions with high bidders

Comments: Golden Age lists items and you bid on them. You'll find loads of listings for some great items at reasonable starting bids. The navigation bar makes it easy to get around the site.

www.goldsauction.com

Site Name: Gold's Auction
Time Zone: Eastern
Main Interest: Contemporary and Classic Collectibles & Antiques
Categories: 198
Unique Features:
- Featured auctions
- Import your feedback rating from another auction site
- Free hit counters
- Free automatic re-list
- Bid Block (prevent a user from bidding on your auction with one click)
- My Page (your personal Web page at Gold's)
- Retractable Feedback
- User recall
- Bulletin boards and Live Chat
- Dynamic auction format

Comments: If you like eBay, you'll like Gold's. It runs a little slower but you'll find plenty of items to bid on, and thousands of registered users waiting to pounce on your listings. Easy navigation from links at the top of every site page. Gold's uses the dynamic auction format.

www.haggle.com

Site Name: Haggle Online
Time Zone: Pacific
Main Interest: Computers, Collectibles, Sports Memorabilia
Categories: 97
Unique Features:
- Publish, rebut, or hide feedback comments made about you
- Featured listings
- Dynamic auction format
- Comprehensive advanced search

Comments: Haggle Online is a full-function online auction site with plenty of registered users, active auctions, and bidding action. You'll find the categories for collectibles tucked under all the computer listings, but there are plenty of them!

www.interauction.com

Site Name: interAUCTION
Time Zone: Eastern
Main Interest: Collectibles, Trading Cards
Categories: 18
Unique Features:
- Dealer auction pages
- Discussion forum for collectors
- Bids are anonymous except to seller
- Seller can accept offers
- No listing fees or commission
- Automatic re-listing

Comments: interAUCTION has an interesting way of listing search results. You see a fast-loading description of the item, and then you can click on a link to view the image and bid. Uses common auction software that's easy to figure out. You can visit links to special dealer auctions.

www.internetauction.net

Site Name: Internet Auction Inc.
Time Zone: Eastern
Main Interest: Collectibles, Antiques, Eclectic
Categories: 38
Unique Features:
- Bid on lots
- Advanced search function
- Competitive listing fees and commissions
- Featured auctions

Comments: Internet Auction Inc. uses standard auction software that's easy to use once you read the instructions, if you can find any. They use a cute set of little icons to indicate the auction features. Their "adult" category link is prominent on the home page, so pick another site for family viewing.

www.justbeanies.com

Site Name: Just Beanies
Time Zone: Eastern
Main Interest: Beanbag Plush Collectibles
Categories: 10
Unique Features:
- No listing fees during first 90 days of membership
- Competitive listing fees and commissions
- Dynamic auction format
- Multiple item listings
- Weekly contests and prizes
- News and articles

Comments: You'll need to register before you can view auctions. Just Beanies uses auction software similar to eBay or Gold's. Navigation links on every page make touring the site easy. Plenty of registered users and bidding activity.

www.justglass.com

Site Name: Just Glass Auctions
Time Zone: Eastern
Main Interest: Contemporary and Antique Glass Auctions
Categories: 32
Unique Features:
- Straight sales and auctions

- Dealer auction pages
- On-site reference library
- Bookstore
- News and Press Releases
- Articles about glass and glass history
- Links to Web sites of interest to glass collectors
- Auction and user stats on home page

Comments: Specialty Internet Auctions, Inc. runs the Just Glass Auctions site with a user-friendly auction program. You can either bid or buy direct, depending on how the seller listed the item. There's loads of glass here. You'll see Fenton, Depression glass, Bohemian, and Czech pieces, and much more. I wonder if anyone lists red fan vases.

www.keybuy.com

Site Name: Key Buy Auction House
Time Zone: Eastern
Main Interest: Antiques, Collectibles, Dolls, Figurines, Art, Trading Cards
Categories: 17
Unique Features:

- No listing or commission fees
- Image hosting
- Mega list of all current auctions
- Neat online card trick
- Good help links
- Dynamic auction format
- Live chat and message boards

Comments: Key Buy uses auction software much like eBay, even the same colors. They appear to have many registered users, plenty of listings, and a good amount of bidding action. You'll find a page with an interesting card trick. Can you figure it out? Amazing! This site is definitely worth a look.

www.mistervintage.com

Site Name: Absolute Vintage Auctions by Mister Vintage
Time Zone: Eastern
Main Interest: Vintage Collectibles ONLY
Categories: 92
Unique Features:

- No-fee auctions for bidders and sellers
- Categories by decade
- Discussion boards and chat

- Time Capsule articles
- Guestbook
- Registration gets you a free e-mail address
- Links to user home pages .

Comments: The auctions work a lot like eBay or Gold's. This is a perfect site for anyone into vintage collectibles. There's no wading through endless listings for beanbag plush. I'd love to see this one succeed. It's easy to use and would support a collecting community. Check it out!

www.netcollect.com

Site Name: NetCollect – Where the World Shops Collectibles
Time Zone: Central
Main Interest: Antique, Classic, and Contemporary Collectibles
Categories: 125
Unique Features:
- Classifieds
- Trading boards
- Live chat
- Member control panel

Comments: You'll find plenty of listing categories at NetCollect. They use standard auction software that's easy to use. This site could go places if more people knew about it.

www.ohioauction.com

Site Name: The Ohio Auction & Classifieds
Time Zone: Eastern
Main Interest: Antiques, Trading Cards, Comic Books, Collectibles, Dolls
Categories: 54
Unique Features:
- Auctions and classified ads
- No listing or commission fees
- Personals

Comments: Ohio Auction uses common auction software that's easy to figure out. This is definitely a no-frills online auction site, with limited action. They have plenty of categories, though, so it's all a matter of time before collectors find it.

www.onewebplace.com

Site Name: One Web Place – Premiere Auction Site

Time Zone: Pacific
Main Interest: Art, Antiques, Collectible Card Games, Classic Collectibles, Decorative Items, Trading Cards
Categories: 430
Unique Features:
- Spotlight auctions
- Sophisticated advanced search function
- Image hosting
- English auctions
- Free listings in most categories
- Discussions and Live Chat
- FAQ

Comments: This is a full-function online auction site, and it's hopping with activity. There are many registered users and lots of bidding going on. You'll find plenty of categories and tons of listings. Look for more contemporary collectibles under the Decorative & Household category.

www.palmbeachauctions.com

Site Name: Palm Beach Auctions
Time Zone: Eastern
Main Interest: Art, Antiques, Sculpture
Categories: 8
Unique Features:
- Site links to places of interest
- Bid tracker

Comments: Gift shops and boutiques list items, and you bid on them. You'll find mostly high-end art here, and plenty of it. This is a very attractive and well-run site. It's easy to bid once you register.

www.popula.com

Site Name: Popula Auction for Vintage Antiques and Collectibles
Time Zone: Eastern
Main Interest: Books of all types, Vintage items, Miscellaneous
Categories: 52
Unique Features:
- Private Eye feature for tracking auctions
- Message board
- News and Articles
- Online reference library

Comments: This is an excellent auction site if you want to buy or sell reading material of any kind, particularly books. You can track any auctions that interest you with Popula's Private Eye feature. Post discussion items at the Vox Popula bulletin board and check out their reference library. Lots of links to sites owned by vintage item specialists.

www.potteryauction.com

Site Name: Pottery Auction
Time Zone: Eastern
Main Interest: Art Pottery
Categories: 68
Unique Features:
- Free image hosting
- Live chat
- Success stories
- No listing fees or commissions
- Dynamic auction format
- Optional featured auctions and bold listings
- Advanced search

Comments: You'll find every type of pottery imaginable, including Weller, Hull, and Roseville. They use auction software that's just like eBay or Gold's. The navigation bar helps you get around the site. If you collect any type of pottery, this auction site is definitely for you.

www.sellandtrade.com

Site Name: The Sell And Trade Internet Marketplace
Time Zone: Eastern
Main Interest: Trading Cards, Automotive, Collectibles, Coins, Sports Memorabilia
Categories: 200
Unique Features:
- No listing fees or commissions
- Want ads
- List items for trade
- Site contests for prizes
- Opinion forum
- Customized search results
- Link to Top 25 Sellers
- Special category for Canadian users

Comments: Sell And Trade uses interesting auction software that's simple enough to use if you've bid online before. At this site, you can sell items, bid on auctions, and trade item-for-item with other collectors. This is unique!

Sell And Trade has easy navigation links on every page. All items end at 12pm EST, but they plan to add "rolling listings" soon. The site is funded by advertisements.

www.sellathon.com

Site Name: Sellathon Auction Services, Inc.
Time Zone: Eastern
Main Interest: Collectibles, Baseball Cards, Toys/Fast Food, Diecast Cars
Categories: 109
Unique Features:
- List of Top 10 Sellers
- Competitive listing fees and commissions
- Contests and drawings
- Multiple fields for image URLs in listing
- Free automatic re-list feature
- News and announcements

Comments: This is the friendliest site I previewed! It reminds me of an online auction site designed by a cohesive nuclear family. Sellathon uses common auction software that's easy to use and understand with titles in the friendly Comic Sans font. This would be a great site to use your first time in the online auction world.

www.soldusa.com

Site Name: SoldUSA
Time Zone: Eastern
Main Interest: Hunting & Fishing Collectibles, Coins & Stamps, Contemporary Collectibles
Categories: 224
Unique Features:
- Catalog and Personal Auctions
- Authentication and Grading
- Competitive listing fees and commissions
- Live chat
- Online shop and bookstore
- Site-run escrow service
- News and information
- Advanced search function

Comments: SoldUSA has easy-to-use auction software. The site presents nicely and has plenty of registered users and bidding action. SoldUSA takes possession of catalog items to sell, presumably on consignment. You can also bid on and list user-to-user auctions as well. Wonderful row of navigation links makes getting around the site very easy.

www.sportsauction.com

Site Name: SportsAuction
Time Zone: Eastern
Main Interest: Anything to do with Sports
Categories: 32
Unique Features:
- Open-ended auctions
- User testimonials
- Items sold in lots
- Auction Express
- Photo appears on separate page

Comments: This one is part of the AuctionAnything network. I love the site layout. For a second I thought I was at the Baseball Hall of Fame in Cooperstown, NY. You'll bid on sports collectibles sold by SportsAuction. There are plenty of listings and lots of action. They use a unique and sophisticated auction software program that's easy to use, and reliable. The item photo shows up on its own page when you click on a link, which cuts down on loading time. Great feature!

www.stampauctions.com

Site Name: StampAuctions.com
Time Zone: Eastern
Main Interest: Postage Stamps from all over the world
Categories: 60
Unique Features:
- Cyber café
- Free classified ads
- Links to related Usenet newsgroups
- Want list
- Stamp collecting glossary
- Comprehensive advanced search
- Open and live auctions
- Competitive listing fees and commissions
- Unique user rating system

Comments: StampAuctions is part of the boxLot network. They use a common auction software program that's simple to use once you read the site tutorial. Users have feedback like any other online auction site, but there's also a system with colored stars that I wasn't able to figure out. I saw plenty of listings and bidding action. Whoever wrote the FAQ has quite a sense of humor.

www.steinauction.com

Site Name: Stein Auction
Time Zone: Eastern
Main Interest: Anheuser Busch Steins, Nascar, Fine Collectibles
Categories: 3
Unique Features:
- Consigned items can pay your winning bids
- Charge cards accepted

Comments: SteinAuction is a buy-only site, but you can sell on consignment. They list the goods, and you bid. If you win, SteinAuction adds a 10% buyer's premium onto your high bid. It's a nice-looking site with standard auction software, but there's not a lot of information about the site available. They have a nice navigation bar but not many links.

www.uauction.com

Site Name: uAuction.com
Time Zone: Eastern
Main Interest: Antiques, Computers, Jewelry, Collectibles
Categories: 243
Unique Features:
- Banner exchange
- Classified ads on home page
- Live chat

Comments: uAuction.com uses a very basic auction program. You'll see the listing on one page and bid on another. There are plenty of listings, though, so you might land some good buys. Links at the top of every page make navigation easy.

www.vanceauctions.com

Site Name: Vance Auctions Philatelic Mail Auctions for Stamp Collectors
Time Zone: Pacific
Main Interest: Stamps and Postal History Memorabilia
Categories: N/A

Unique Features:
- Links to upcoming auctions and shows
- Telephone bids accepted
- "Or" bids for two or more similar lots
- Bids conducted in Canadian funds
- Enter a bid sheet for absentee bids
- Sell on consignment

Comments: This Canadian-based site runs differently from most online auction sites. You bid on specified lots, one at time or in multiples. Vance Auctions runs philatelic Mail Auctions eight times a year. No online bidding.

www.viabid.com

Site Name: ViaBid – Online Auctions, Online Commerce
Time Zone: Eastern
Main Interest: Antiques & Collectibles, Books & Literature, Jewelry & Gems, Trade Cards, Autographs
Categories: 277
Unique Features:
- Dealer auction services
- Price and market guides
- Charity auctions
- Bid Blocking (keep a troublesome user from disrupting your auction)
- Selling by lots
- Link page
- Set price selling (show or hide price and accept offers)
- Firm price selling (straight sell, no bidding)
- No listing or commission fees
- Easy to navigate with links on every page

Comments: You can also reach ViaBid at www.gle.net. There are plenty of listing categories, giving this site lots of promise. You'll find many active auctions with a fair amount of bidding. I'll use this one to sell items in lots. Good site for dealers.

www.yahoo.com

Site Name: Yahoo! Auctions
Time Zone: Pacific
Main Interest: Everything
Categories: Too many to count
Unique Features:
- Part of the famous Yahoo Web portal

- Charity auctions
- Success stories online
- Image hosting
- Free listings
- Detailed help pages
- News and information

Comments: Yahoo! Auctions are very popular. Any avid online collector needs to give this one a look. From the Yahoo! home page, click on the "Auctions" link and then bookmark the main auction site page. They use a standard auction program similar to Live Auction Online that's very easy to use. Yahoo has thousands of registered users, a multitude of current auctions, and enough bidding action. This is a great auction site for managing your collection online. The only thing I'd recommend is better navigation links.

☞No Bidding Sites

Why not dare to be different? You'll find increasingly more sites on the Internet that use standard auction software, but alter the process a little. Look at these sites for online auctions with a unique twist.

www.classifieds2000.com

Site Name: Excite Classifieds
Time Zone: N/A
Main Interest: Collectibles, Stamps, Antiques, Coins, Toys
Categories: 68
Unique Features:
- Advanced search
- Featured categories and hot lists
- E-mail notification and want lists

Comments: The Excite portal runs this site. The main Classifieds2000 page has straight sale ads with a nice breakout of collectible and antique categories. There are plenty of listings. Great page navigation links. If you click on "Auctions," you'll reach auctions.excite.com.

www.ewanted.com

Site Name: eWanted Online Auctions
Time Zone: Pacific
Main Interest: Collectibles, Antiques, Computers, Household
Categories: 324

Unique Features:

- Upside down auctions, sellers bid prices down
- Site drawings and special offers
- News and updates on the home page
- New user referral and frequent listing incentive
- Free listings
- Transfer your rating from another site
- Private offers
- Discussion forums

Comments: Buyers list what they want and sellers offer the items, bidding down the prices to earn the business. If you have a friend who's into online auctions, refer him or her to eWanted. You'll receive ten e-coins that you can redeem for gifts. The site has plenty of listings and user action.

www.nobidding.com

Site Name: NoBidding.com – The Online Auction Alternative
Time Zone: N/A
Main Interest: Antiques, Books, Coins & Stamps, Glass, Electronics, Collectibles, Sports Memorabilia, Dolls & Toys
Categories: over 400
Unique Features:

- Wish lists
- Wanted ads
- No listing fees or commissions
- Listings include link to seller's eBay feedback

Comments: At NoBidding.com, all listings are straight sales. You name the price and another user "reserves," or buys, your item. The site uses standard auction software that's easy to use, but they need a better search feature. There are plenty of registered users and many sales.

☞Internet Sites Offering Auction Services

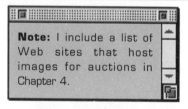

Note: I include a list of Web sites that host images for auctions in Chapter 4.

Certain Web sites offer special auction tools and software. The programs help manage your online auctions. Some of them offer information about the status of all auctions that you have listed at any online auction sites. Others help you format your auction descriptions.

Here's an explanation of the information I include about each site:

Site Name: What's the site called?
Main Interest: The site specialty — counters, auction tracking, auction description formatting, etc.

Services Offered: You'll see what features and services the site offers.
Comments: My thoughts about the site and its usefulness for anyone using online auctions.

Many of these sites offer free auction tools that you can download. Some of them charge a minimal registration fee, and others sell software and auction programs online.

www.auctionmanage.com

Site Name: Auction Manage
Main Interest: Making Internet selling easier
Services Offered:
- Roaming rating system
- Image hosting
- Bulletin board
- Global auction item search
- Wholesale store
- Classifieds

Comments: Auction Manage provides a great online auction site tutorial. The site tour has a sample auction-entry form and search-results page so you can see it all on your screen. Worth a visit if you're new to buying and selling at online auction sites.

www.auctionpatrol.com

Site Name: Auction Patrol for Online Auctions
Main Interest: Educating users about online auctions
Services Offered:
- Message boards
- Practice auctions
- Special sale
- Picture posting and HTML tools
- Tips for successful online auction use

Comments: The HTML tools help you format an auction description in HTML that you can copy and paste into the auction-entry description area. You'll find plenty of great information here. It's worth a look!

www.auctionpix.com

Site Name: Auction Pix Image Hosting

Main Interest: Image Hosting
Services Offered:
  • Image hosting
Comments: Pay a nominal fee to access their image-uploading program. They'll host images for 15, 21, or 30 days.

www.auctionposter.com

Site Name: AuctionPoster.com
Main Interest: Auctions for eBay
Services Offered:
  • HTML creation
  • Image uploading and hosting
  • Free counters
  • Spell check your auction descriptions
  • Create auctions off-line
Comments: Visit AuctionPoster and check out the free auction goodies. Their downloadable programs support all major ISPs. You can create auction descriptions with any of their "themes" so they coordinate with the item you're selling. This one is definitely worthy of a visit. Browse the News link while you're there.

www.auctionsubmit.com

Site Name: Auction Submit
Main Interest: Auction software
Services Offered:
  • Free software download
  • Announcement board
Comments: You can download a free copy of their auction-submit software. Check their Web page for details.

www.auctiontools.net

Site Name: Easy Auction for eBay
Main Interest: Auction tools to organize your online sales
Services Offered:
  • Download their auction management tool for a free trial
Comments: Why not? It's certainly worth a try.

www.auctionwatch.com

Site Name: AuctionWatch.com
Main Interest: Auction add-ons
Services Offered:
- Universal auction search
- Auction counters
- Image hosting
- Message center
- ePostcards
- Collectible spotlight
- News and reviews

Comments: AuctionWatch is loaded with features and links designed to make your online auction experience everything it should be — fun, easy, and safe. You'll find links to many online auction sites, and articles of interest to frequent auction users.

www.bay-town.com

Site Name: Bay-Town.com
Main Interest: Tools for auction management and design
Services Offered:
- Bid sniping tools
- Auction-design programs
- Web page hosting
- Web design
- CGI programs
- Free counters and image hosting
- Auction description templates

Comments: Bay-Town.com offers all kinds of free auction goodies, including an area where you can create your own auction description. You'll get the custom HTML to copy and paste right into the auction description area. You can also get free auction counters and free space on the Web for a home page. Learn about Common Gateway Interface (CGI) programs.

www.blackthornesw.com

Site Name: Blackthorne Software
Main Interest: Software for formatting auction descriptions
Services Offered:
- Download trial software
- Online user guides and tutorials

- News and updates

Comments: Order software online to create auction descriptions that format automatically in HTML. You can also create auction page counters.

www.everysoft.com

Site Name: EverySoft Scripting Co.
Main Interest: Auction software
Services Offered:
- Download auction software and add-ons
- Auction forum

Comments: If you're interested in setting up your own auction site, this is the place to read more about it. You can order their packages online.

www.freemerchant.com

Site Name: Free Merchant
Main Interest: Business Hosting, Auction Tools
Services Offered:
- Business hosting
- Merchant gateway
- Auction tools
- Site traffic logs
- Technical support

Comments: Register at the site and check out Free Merchant's auction tools.

www.honesty.com

Site Name: Honesty Communications
Main Interest: Auction counters, Image hosting
Services Offered:
- Free auction counters
- Auction help
- Message boards
- Announcements
- Online support

Comments: Honesty counters are a fast and easy way to see how many people view your auction listings. Their counters are compatible with eBay and Amazon.com. If you're using another site, Honesty gives you the HTML code for a counter that you can add to your auction description. Honesty Communications is widely used and worth a visit.

www.imagehosting.com

Site Name: ImageHosting
Main Interest: Image hosting, Image management
Services Offered:
- Image hosting
- Scanning
- Image optimization and combining
- User forum
- WebTV friendly

Comments: ImageHosting will give your online auction images a home on the Web. They'll even finish them up so they'll look great with your auction listings.

www.internetauctionlist.com

Site Name: Internet Auction List – Largest Auction Directory
Main Interest: Auction Portal
Services Offered:
- Links to sites with free auction software
- Online auction software downloads
- Links to online auction sites
- News and updates
- Free online newsletter
- Channels for information about collecting

Comments: The Collecting Channel (www.collectingchannel.com) sponsors Internet Auction List. You'll find links to more Web sites than you ever dreamed existed, with the latest information and news about collecting anything — antiques, memorabilia, contemporary collectibles, and so much more. Bookmark this one!

www.little-treasures.net

Site Name: Little-Treasures Image Hosting
Main Interest: Full Service Image Hosting
Services Offered:
- Free graphics to dress up your auctions
- Links to online HTML generators
- Links to online antique malls
- Image hosting
- Competitive pricing
- Auto-uploading

Comments: Little-Treasures is a user-friendly site with plenty of information about how and why free image hosting sites operate and why it might be better to pay for the service.

www.myitem.com

Site Name: MyItem.com
Main Interest: Free Service for Online Auctions
Services Offered:
- Free image hosting
- Informative FAQ

Comments: You can upload as many images as you want, free. The only guideline is that the pictures link to active online auctions.

www.otwa.com

Site Name: Online Traders Web Alliance
Main Interest: Providing help and resources for online auction users
Services Offered:
- Message boards and online auction forums
- Auction resource center
- Patent and trademark resource center
- eBay resource center
- Internet fraud and scam resource center
- Shipping and freight resource center

Comments: This site is full of resource centers! You'll find loads of information about any aspect of buying and selling at online auction sites. There are an HTML practice board, discussion boards for each of the major auction sites, and general interest boards. OTWA uses the Ultimate Bulletin Board (UBB) which has its own quick and easy code for posting links and images. You can even reserve an online conference room and invite attendees to private meetings. This is a new, rapidly growing site.

www.pongo.com

Site Name: Pongo
Main Interest: Auction help, Web page design
Services Offered:
- Tutorials
- Image hosts
- Web design

• Bookstore
• HTML help and practice board

Comments: Any frequent eBay user knows all about Pongo. You'll find links giving hints and tips on making fancy auction listings, taking better pictures, and a large online list of image-hosting sites. They've added a long FAQ to help you even more. Well worth a visit!

www.ricksplanet.com

Site Name: Rick's Planet
Main Interest: Auction Software
Services Offered:

• Download a full-featured auction manager called eAssist™

Comments: Rick's Planet offers an auction submission and tracking tool. Order the package online and download free updates.

www.rubylane.com

Site Name: Ruby Lane Antiques, Collectibles & Fine Art
Main Interest: Online Resource for Finding, Buying, and Selling Antiques, Collectibles, & Fine Art
Services Offered:

• Free auction counters
• Links to articles and chat boards
• Links to online antique malls
• Online news and articles
• Weekly contests and prizes
• Powerful search engine for antiques and collectibles

Comments: Ruby Lane is a vast and wonderful (not to mention popular) Web resource for anyone into the finer aspects of collecting. In addition to free auction counters, you'll find loads of links to online shops that will keep you busy for days on end. You have to check this one out and drop a bookmark so you can come back.

www.sneakydave.com

Site Name: SNEAKYDAVE Enterprises
Main Interest: Web Page Design, Auction Tools
Services Offered:

• Image hosting
• Discussion boards

- Online support
- Auction tools
- The Poor Man's Auction Factory
- HTML Practice Board
- Sneakbay Guestbook

Comments: SNEAKYDAVE has a link to The Poor Man's Auction Factory, now located at Auction Patrol for Online Auctions (www.auctionpatrol.com). For great looking auctions, you just provide some basic information about how you want your auction description to look, and SNEAKYDAVE e-mails you the HTML code to paste right into your auction description. You can also work with it at the HTML Practice Board until it's exactly what you want. As for the Sneakbay Guestbook, you'll have to check that one out for yourself at SNEAKYDAVE.

www.traderjax.com

Site Name: TraderJax.com Picture Hosting
Main Interest: Image Hosting for Online Auctions
Services Offered:

- Image hosting
- Mall stores
- Rent-a-store

Comments: It took some hunting to find the link to set up an image-hosting account, but I finally found it at www.traderjax.com/Login. You'll need to read the FAQ at the main site for further instructions.

☞The Online Auction Experience

With all these auction sites available on the Internet, imagine the chances I'd have to turn Aunt Libby's ceramic Kewpie into cash.

Although they're hugely successful, online auction sites are still in their infancy. As more and more collectors find their way to online auction sites, the venue will continue to develop. Whatever you do, don't let that progress deter you from buying and selling collectibles at auction. To be a smart online auction user and eventually a seasoned participant, I urge you to keep up with online auction formats and features as they advance.

As computer literate as you are now, you'll find new auction programs exciting and even easier to use than previous ones. Remember that the goal of Web site designers is to make their sites more user-friendly with every update. This definitely holds true for auction sites.

The Online Auction Summary

By now, you're well aware of what online auctions offer collectors. You know how to list an auction that will attract prospective bidders, how to format a great-looking auction description, and how to complete the transaction off-line. You know there are hundreds of online auction sites on the Internet ready and waiting for you to register and become a confident, regular user.

The more you surf the sites, the faster you'll realize what thousands of others do every single day. The online auction experience is going, going — and here to stay. :-)

Appendix A — HTML Tutorial

In Chapter 4, you read about the area on the auction-entry form where you insert your auction description. If you enter plain text, that is, text without HTML tags, it usually defaults to some ordinary text when the auction page formats. You probably want your auction to stand out from the rest. Who doesn't? This Appendix provides some simple HTML tags that allow you change the color, font, and size of your descriptive text.

👉What's HTML?

HTML stands for Hyper-Text Markup Language. HTML is a document-layout language we use to make pages for the World Wide Web.

Conventions Used

In these HTML coding examples, I use boldface to indicate text that's not part of the code. When you do your coding, replace my bold text with your own information.

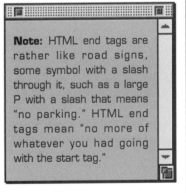

Note: This is in no way a definitive HTML user guide! The HTML code provided here is only a subset of the formatting language, but it's everything you need to know to format great-looking auction descriptions.

Double quotes, slashes, and arrow brackets are important elements of the HTML code. Be sure you include those when you write your code.

👉Formatting Text with HTML Tags

Most HTML tags come in sets, a start tag and an end tag. The start tag indicates that a certain directive occurs after the tag, and the end tag stops the directive. The effected text is between the two tags.

Tags appear inside arrow brackets (< and >). The end tag is the same as the start tag, except the first character after the < is a slash (/) to indicate that the tag's directive stops there.

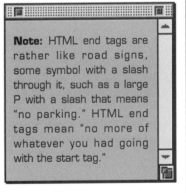

Note: HTML end tags are rather like road signs, some symbol with a slash through it, such as a large P with a slash that means "no parking." HTML end tags mean "no more of whatever you had going with the start tag."

Physical Tags

Tags that change the appearance of the text are *physical tags*. Each tag has an open and close directive. The tags that start and stop bold text are <B> and </B>. Any text included between the two tags appears in boldface font when you view the page.

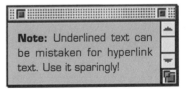

Note: Underlined text can be mistaken for hyperlink text. Use it sparingly!

The following tags create italicized and underlined text, and text that's smaller or larger than the current default size.

HTML Code	Function
<B> </B>	Bold faced text
<I> </I>	Italic text
<U> </U>	Underlined text
<BLINK> </BLINK>	Blinking text
<SMALL> </SMALL>	Text one size smaller than default
<BIG> </BIG>	Text one size larger than default

Here's how the physical tags work:

HTML Code	Output
<B>**For Sale!**</B>	**For Sale!**
<I>**For Sale!**</I>	*For Sale!*
<U>**For Sale**</U>	<u>For Sale!</u>
<BLINK>**For Sale!**</BLINK>	For Sale! (blink! blink!)
<SMALL>**For Sale!**</SMALL>	<small>For Sale!</small>
<BIG>**For Sale!**</BIG>	For Sale!

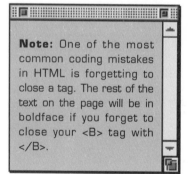

Note: One of the most common coding mistakes in HTML is forgetting to close a tag. The rest of the text on the page will be in boldface if you forget to close your <B> tag with </B>.

Note: The blinking text tag may not work on all browsers and may go away altogether in the future. When blinking text appears on a Web page, it tends to annoy the reader very quickly but for auction descriptions, it might be a great eye-catcher. Of course, I can't demonstrate blinking text on this static hardcopy so you'll have to take my word for it.

You can combine tags for more than one effect. Notice that the tags open and close in mirrored order:

HTML Code	Output
<B><I>**Text that is both bold and italic**</I></B>	***Text that is both bold and italic***

HTML tags are not case sensitive. You can use <B>, <b>, and any combination for start and end tags. Pick one case and stick with it because it makes it easier to differentiate the code from your text when you edit the HTML file later.

Attributes and Values

An *attribute* gives more direction to the function of the tag. Attributes must be included within the main tag and some have a *value* attached to them with an equal (=) sign.

```
<TAG ATTRIBUTE=VALUE>text</TAG>
```

Don't put any spaces between the attribute, the equal sign, and the value.

Assigning Text Color and Font Style

You change the color and font style of the text a little differently. Here you have to use the <FONT> tag. You can use three attributes within the <FONT> tag:

- COLOR – uses any of a hundred or so color names to change the color of the text. You can also use hexadecimal RGB codes if you are familiar with them, but color names are easier. The table that follows lists many color names you can use with the COLOR attribute.
- FACE – indicates what typeface you want the text to be. If the name of the typeface has more than one word, include spaces between the words but enclose the name in double quotes.
- SIZE – changes the size of the text. Your text size can be from 1 to 7 points.

Color

A six-digit hexadecimal code after a pound sign (#) used with the COLOR attribute changes the color of the text. This coding example switches the text color to red:

```
<FONT COLOR=#CC0000>This will be red text.</FONT>
```

Many Web designers include hex codes for colors so they can clearly define hues, but you don't have to. You can use colors by their name instead of trying to figure out hexadecimal codes. It works like this:

```
<FONT COLOR=red>This will also be red text.</FONT>
```

On the next page is a list of color names recognized by most browsers. Notice there are no spaces in the names, so you don't need to enclose the name in quotes.

aliceblue	darkviolet	lightskyblue	paleviolet
antiquewhite	deeppink	lightslateblue	palevioletred
aquamarine	deepskyblue	lightslategray	papayawhip
azure	dimgray	lightsteelblue	peachpuff
beige	dodgerblue	lightyellow	pink
bisque	firebrick	limegreen	plum
black	floralwhite	linen	powderblue
blanchedalmond	forestgreen	magenta	purple
blue	gainsboro	maroon	red
blueviolet	ghostwhite	mediumaquamarine	rosybrown
brown	gold	mediumblue	royalblue
burlywood	goldenrod	mediumorchid	saddlebrown
cadetblue	gray	mediumpurple	salmon
chartreus	green	mediumseagreen	sandybrown
chocolate	greenyellow	mediumslateblue	seagreen
coral	honeydew	mediumspringgreen	sienna
cornflowerblue	hotpink	mediumturquoise	skyblue
cornsilk	indianred	mediumvioletred	slateblue
cyan	ivory	midnightblue	slategray
darkblue	khaki	mintcream	snow
darkcyan	lavender	mistyrose	springgreen
darkgoldenrod	lavenderblush	moccasin	steelblue
darkgray	lawngreen	navajowhite	tan
darkgreen	lemonchiffon	navy	thistle
darkkhaki	lightblue	navyblue	tomato
darkolivegreen	lightcoral	oldlace	turquoise
darkorange	lightcyan	olivedrab	violet
darkred	lightgoldenrodyellow	orange	violetred
darksalmon	lightgray	orangered	wheat
darkseagreen	lightgreen	orchid	white
darkslateblue	lightpink	palegoldenrod	whitesmoke
darkslategray	lightsalmon	palegreen	yellow
darkturquoise	lightseagreen	paleturquoise	yellowgreen

Color Names That Can Be Used with the COLOR Attribute

You might prefer using hexadecimal codes. Lynda Weinman includes full-color hexadecimal charts in *Designing Web Graphics — How to Prepare Images and Media for the Web* (New Riders Publishing, 1996). Weinman's series on Web graphics is excellent for anyone working with images to use on Web pages.

If you want to view colors and their hexadecimal codes right in your Web browser, check out Weinman's "Non-Dithering Colors by Hue" page at www.lynda.com/hexh.html.

Face

Within the <FONT> tag, the FACE attribute means typeface. If the typeface includes more than one word, like Comic Sans MS, you must include the name in double quotes to indicate that it's one value.

In order for a particular typeface to show up in the viewer's browser, it needs to be loaded on his or her PC. To ensure that your text displays the way you want it to, you can include several font names, separated by commas, with the FACE attribute. When the file loads in the browser, it looks at each font name in order until it sees one that it recognizes, and then displays the text in that typeface.

Here's an example:

```
<FONT FACE="Verdana, Arial, Helvetica">
```

Each of these fonts, Verdana, Arial, and Helvetica, is a standard sans serif font. Most PCs are bound to have at least one of them installed. If not, the text displays in the default style.

Size

The SIZE attribute needs a value from 1 to 7, relative to the default font size.

In the following examples, I used the COLOR, FACE, and SIZE attributes and corresponding values to change the color, typeface, and text size:

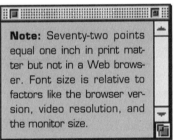

Note: Seventy-two points equal one inch in print matter but not in a Web browser. Font size is relative to factors like the browser version, video resolution, and the monitor size.

HTML Code	Output
<FONT FACE="Tekton">**Text in the Tekton font is cool!**</FONT>	*Text in the Tekton font is cool!*
<FONT SIZE=3>**This text is a size 3!** </FONT>	**This text is a size 3!**
<FONT COLOR=GREEN FACE=Revue> **You can also combine attributes within a tag!**</FONT>	**You can also combine attributes within a tag!**

Text Formatting

Formatting tags allow you to space and center your text, include vertical spacer lines, and add pictures and tables on the page. The first three tags shown in the following table are single tags that don't need an end tag.

HTML Code	Function
<P>	Start a new paragraph. Adds a blank line between the text blocks
 	Line break with no space between the lines of text
<HR>	Makes a horizontal line, usually used in an auction description to set off a photograph
<CENTER> </CENTER>	Anything between the start and end tags appears centered on the page.

Lists

You can create ordered and unordered lists with HTML. Ordered lists contain numbers or letters by each list item. Unordered items have bullets by each item.

You can nest any type of list within another list.

Ordered Lists

Use an ordered list when the order of the items listed is important. Ordered lists start with the <OL> tag and end with </OL>. Indicate list items with <LI>, which is a single-ended tag.

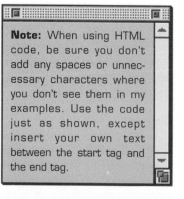

Note: When using HTML code, be sure you don't add any spaces or unnecessary characters where you don't see them in my examples. Use the code just as shown, except insert your own text between the start tag and the end tag.

HTML Code	Output
<OL> <LI>**This is Item One.** <LI>**This is Item Two.** <LI>**This is Item Three.** </OL>	1. This is Item One. 2. This is Item Two. 3. This is Item Three.

The items in an ordered list automatically start with the Arabic numeral 1. You can change that value with the START attribute in the <OL> tag.

HTML Code	Output
<OL START=4> <LI>**This is Item Four.** <LI>**This is Item Five.** <LI>**This is Item Six.** </OL>	4. This is Item Four. 5. This is Item Five. 6. This is Item Six.

Use the TYPE attribute within the <OL> tag to change the numbering style. You can use four values with the TYPE attribute:

- **A** – A, B, C, etc.
- **a** – a, b, c, etc.
- **I** – I, II, III, etc.
- **i** – i, ii, iii, etc.

HTML Code	Output
<OL TYPE=I> <LI>**This is the first item.** <LI>**This is the second item.** <LI>**This is the third item.** </OL>	I. This is the first item. II. This is the second item. III. This is the third item.

Combine attributes within the <OL> tag. In other words, make your list item start with Roman numeral IV this way:

HTML Code	Output
<OL TYPE=I START=4> <LI>**This is Item Four.** <LI>**This is Item Five.** <LI>**This is Item Six.** </OL>	IV. This is Item Four. V. This is Item Five. VI. This is Item Six.

Unordered Lists

Use an unordered list when the order of the items isn't important. Unordered lists start with the <UL> tag and end with </UL>. Indicate list items with <LI>. Items are set off with a bullet.

HTML Code	Output
<UL> <LI>**This is an item.** <LI>**This is an item too.** <LI>**This is another item.** </UL>	• This is an item. • This is an item too. • This is another item.

Tables

Tables are a little more complex than lists but you can do a lot with them, such as:

- Specify the height and width of table cell
- Include photos
- Add borders around text and photos

- Include hyperlinks
- Use colored backgrounds
- Use textured backgrounds
- Span multiple rows or columns

Define a table with the <TABLE> and </TABLE> tags. Just about anything can appear in a table cell — photos, lists, or another table. What's more, you can even give table cells their own background color.

The <TABLE> tag has a few attributes. A set of special table tags defines parts of the table.

Table Tags

- The <TR> tag defines a table row.
- The <TH> tag defines a table header. This may default to bold face type. You don't need to include headers in your tables if you don't want to.
- The <TD> tag defines a cell of table data.

Basic Table Coding

Here is the HTML coding for a basic borderless table:

HTML Code	Output
<TABLE> <TR> <TH>**Heading 1**</TH> <TH>**Heading 2**</TH> </TR><TR> <TD>**Data 1**</TD> <TD>**Data 2**</TD> </TR><TR> <TD>**Data 3**</TD> <TD>**Data 4**</TD> </TR></TABLE>	**Heading 1 Heading 2** Data 1 Data 2 Data 3 Data 4

Borders

As shown in the example above, the border default for <TABLE> is "none," or zero. To get a nice chiseled border around your table and between the rows and cells, use the BORDER attribute within the <TABLE> tag. Use a value of from 1 to 5 with the BORDER attribute to alter the thickness.

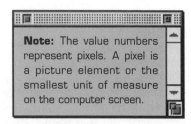

Note: The value numbers represent pixels. A pixel is a picture element or the smallest unit of measure on the computer screen.

HTML Code	Output

`<TABLE BORDER=3>`
`<TR>`
`<TH>`**Heading 1**`</TH>`
`<TH>`**Heading 2**`</TH>`
`</TR><TR>`
`<TD>`**Data 1**`</TD>`
`<TD>`**Data 2**`</TD>`
`</TR><TR>`
`<TD>`**Data 3**`</TD>`
`<TD>`**Data 4**`</TD>`
`</TR></TABLE>`
	Heading 1 Heading 2
	Data 1 Data 2
	Data 3 Data 4

Cell Spacing and Padding

Use the CELLSPACING attribute in the `<TABLE>` tag to control the space between the adjacent cells in a table that are along the outer edges of the cells. The value for the CELLSPACING attribute is a number in pixels.

HTML Code	Output

`<TABLE BORDER=3`
`CELLSPACING=4>`
`<TR>`
`<TH>`**Heading 1**`</TH>`
`<TH>`**Heading 2**`</TH>`
`</TR><TR>`
`<TD>`**Data 1**`</TD>`
`<TD>`**Data 2**`</TD>`
`</TR><TR>`
`<TD>`**Data 3**`</TD>`
`<TD>`**Data 4**`</TD>`
`</TR></TABLE>`
	Heading 1 Heading 2
	Data 1 Data 2
	Data 3 Data 4

The CELLPADDING attribute in the `<TABLE>` tag controls the space between the edge of a cell and its contents. The value for the CELLPADDING attribute is a number in pixels. (See next page.)

Placement Inside of a Cell

The cells used in the examples above are very small. As you enter text, images, and links into the table cells, they expand to accommodate the contents. If you have one cell that has a small image or just a few words, you may want it to appear in the center of the cell. You can control this.

HTML Code	Output
```<TABLE BORDER=3 CELLPADDING=4> <TR> <TH>Heading 1</TH> <TH>Heading 2</TH> </TR><TR> <TD>Data 1</TD> <TD>Data 2</TD> </TR><TR> <TD>Data 3</TD> <TD>Data 4</TD> </TR></TABLE>```	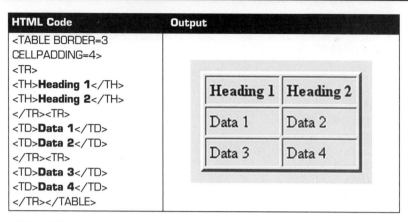

The ALIGN and VALIGN attributes of the <TH> and <TD> tags allow you to control the alignment of the cell contents. The ALIGN attribute controls it horizontally, while VALIGN does it vertically.

The ALIGN attribute has three values:	The VALIGN attribute has three values:
• LEFT • CENTER • RIGHT	• TOP • MIDDLE • BOTTOM

The following figure shows a table formatted using the ALIGN and VALIGN attributes within <TD> tags. Notice that I used the <BR> tag within the "Data Number 1" cell just to expand it. This won't be necessary when you have a lot of text there.

HTML Code	Output
```<TABLE BORDER=3> <TR> <TH>Heading 1</TH> <TH>Heading 2</TH> <TH>Heading 3</TH> </TR><TR> <TD>Data Number 1</TD> <TD ALIGN=RIGHT>Data 2 </TD> <TD VALIGN=TOP>Data 3 </TD> </TR></TABLE>```	Heading 1 / Heading 2 / Heading 3 Data Number 1 / Data 2 / Data 3

Spanning Rows and Columns

Let's say you want one cell to span two rows and another to span two columns. Control this with the COLSPAN and ROWSPAN attributes within the <TH> and <TD> tags. The value for each is a number greater than one, not to exceed the number of rows or columns (depending on what you're spanning) in the table.

This example illustrates a header that spans two columns in the table:

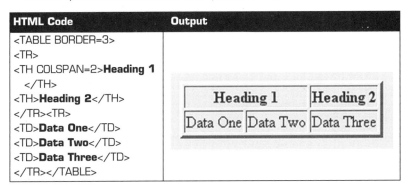

HTML Code	Output
<TABLE BORDER=3> <TR> <TH COLSPAN=2>**Heading 1** </TH> <TH>**Heading 2**</TH> </TR><TR> <TD>**Data One**</TD> <TD>**Data Two**</TD> <TD>**Data Three**</TD> </TR></TABLE>	

Here's an example of a cell that spans two rows in the table:

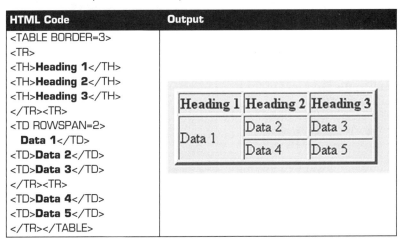

HTML Code	Output
<TABLE BORDER=3> <TR> <TH>**Heading 1**</TH> <TH>**Heading 2**</TH> <TH>**Heading 3**</TH> </TR><TR> <TD ROWSPAN=2> **Data 1**</TD> <TD>**Data 2**</TD> <TD>**Data 3**</TD> </TR><TR> <TD>**Data 4**</TD> <TD>**Data 5**</TD> </TR></TABLE>	

Defining the Color of a Cell

If you want to highlight certain cells or just add a little life to your table, try changing the background color of one or more of the cells. Use the BGCOLOR attribute in the <TH> or <TD> tags:

HTML Code	Output

`<TABLE BORDER=3>`
`<TR>`
`<TH BGCOLOR=GREEN>`
   `Heading 1``</TH>`
`<TH>`**`Heading 2`**`</TH>`
`</TR><TR>`
`<TD>`**`Data 1`**`</TD>`
`<TD BGCOLOR=GOLD>`
   `Data 2``</TD>`
`</TR><TR>`
`<TD>`**`Data 3`**`</TD>`
`<TD>`**`Data 4`**`</TD>`
`</TR></TABLE>`
	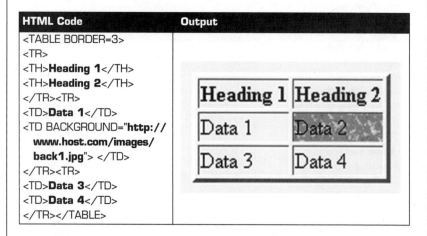

Defining the Background Pattern for a Cell

The BACKGROUND attribute of the `<TH>` or `<TD>` tag adds a pattern image to a table cell. The value is the URL of an image file that will "tile" to fill the background of the table cell. Here's an example:

HTML Code	Output

`<TABLE BORDER=3>`
`<TR>`
`<TH>`**`Heading 1`**`</TH>`
`<TH>`**`Heading 2`**`</TH>`
`</TR><TR>`
`<TD>`**`Data 1`**`</TD>`
`<TD BACKGROUND="http://`
   `www.host.com/images/`
   `back1.jpg``"> </TD>`
`</TR><TR>`
`<TD>`**`Data 3`**`</TD>`
`<TD>`**`Data 4`**`</TD>`
`</TR></TABLE>`	

Adding an Image

The `<IMG>` tag lets you include a picture within your auction description. Use the SRC attribute with the image URL as the value.

Decide where you want your image to appear. At that point, insert the following code just as it appears here:

`<IMG SRC="`**`http://www.domain.com/homepage/images/cobra.jpg`**`">`

I use http://www.domain.com/homepage/images/cobra.jpg as an example. You'll use the image URL you want in your auction description. Note that when you enter the URL, it must contain the full path, including the http:// part.

Positioning an Image

You can control the position of an image with the ALIGN attribute in the <IMG> tag. Use this only when the image is not inside a table. Without this attribute, the image aligns to the left. The values for ALIGN are LEFT, RIGHT, TOP, MIDDLE, and BOTTOM.

The LEFT and RIGHT values flow subsequent text around the image. The others align the image vertically with respect to the surrounding text.

The TOP, MIDDLE, and BOTTOM attribute values only apply to the image relative to any text on the page.

Here's an example of the ALIGN attribute used to position an image to the right of an adjacent paragraph:

HTML Code:
<IMG SRC="**http://www.host.com/images/bearcp.jpg**" ALIGN=RIGHT>
This one-of-a-kind chocolate brown bear is soft and fuzzy from his head to his hand-stitched feet.
<P>
He proudly sports a gold bow around his neck. What a perfect addition to your teddy bear gallery!

Result:

This one-of-a-kind chocolate brown bear is soft and fuzzy from his head to his hand-stitched feet.

He proudly sports a gold bow around his neck. What a perfect addition to your teddy bear gallery!

Of course, the example above is on a small scale, as it would appear in a very small browser. You'll need much more text for it to wrap around the aligned image. Some of the auction description examples in Appendix B use the ALIGN attribute within the <IMG> tag.

Animated GIFs

Since animated icons are GIF files, you add them the same way you do any other image file. You just need to know the URL of the image. You'll find a list of Web sites that offer free animated GIFs in Appendix B.

Remember that large animated images, or those with many frames, take a long time to load. Stick with small, simple animation to dress up your auction description, or to populate the image URL field on the auction-entry form.

Adding Hypertext Links

If you want bidders to visit your home page, include a hyperlink in your auction description. All you need is the URL to your home page.

Hypertext links start with the <A> (anchor) tag and end with </A>. Use the HREF attribute with the page URL as the value. Whatever you enter between <A> and </A> will appear underlined in the browser. When you pass your mouse cursor over it, the arrow will change into a little hand, indicating the text is a hot spot. If you click on a hot spot, the hyperlinked page loads in your browser.

HTML Code:

<A HREF="**http://www.domain.com/~jennyB**">**See Jenny's Page!**</A>

Result: See Jenny ᶠᵐ Page

The underlined text appears as hyperlink text, or a hot spot.

Opening Your Link in a New Browser

You don't want to draw your bidder's attention away from your auction.

You can make the link open up a new browser. This leaves the host browser where your auction description displays undisturbed. Include the TARGET attribute with _NEW as the value within your <A> tag.

> **Note:** Be certain to close the <A> tag because if you don't, the rest of the text (and everything else) on the page will become part of your hyperlink.

HTML Code:

<A HREF="**http://www.domain.com/~jennyB**" TARGET="_NEW">**See Jenny's Page!**</A>

Result:

A new browser opens for the link, leaving the original browser undisturbed.

Making Your E-mail Address a Hyperlink

If you want your viewers to send you e-mail by clicking on your e-mail address, use the <A> tag with the HREF attribute. The value is MAILTO:**address**, as in this example:

HTML Code:

<A HREF="MAILTO:**user@email.com**">**user@e-mail.com**</A>

Result: user@em ᶠᵐ .com

The e-mail address will appear as hyperlink text. Though not all browsers support e-mail links, the ones that do make it very easy for your viewers to contact you.

Including your e-mail address between the start and end <A> tags causes it to be a hypertext link. When clicked on, it brings up an e-mail screen addressed to you.

Making an Image a Hyperlink

If you want your reader to be able to click on a picture to access another site, you must code the <IMG> tag information between the starting and ending <A> tags. This causes a two-pixel wide border to appear around the image by default. If you want a borderless image, use the BORDER attribute with a value of zero. For a thicker border, increase the value to a number larger than two.

HTML Code:

```
<A HREF="http://www.domain.com/~jennyB">
    <IMG SRC="http://www.host.com/images/bear.jpg" BORDER=0>
</A>
```

Result:

The image is a borderless hyperlink.

Learn More About HTML

HTML is a vast and comprehensive coding language. It provides many, many more capabilities than what I describe here. This is enough to help you format eye-catching auction descriptions, though. If you decide to design Web pages, you may want to invest in an HTML reference book or two.

Many great books can teach you to become an expert at HTML coding and Web page design. My personal favorite is *HTML: The Definitive Guide* by Chuck Musciano and Bill Kennedy (O'Reilly & Associates, Inc.).

Writing Your Auction Description with HTML

Open Notepad or another word processing program where you can enter and save plain text. Type in your description along with the URL to any additional image files you want to appear with your item description.

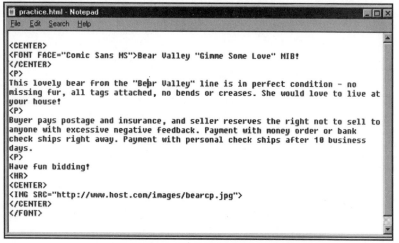

```
practice.html - Notepad
File  Edit  Search  Help

<CENTER>
<FONT FACE="Comic Sans MS">Bear Valley "Gimme Some Love" MIB!
</CENTER>
<P>
This lovely bear from the "Bear Valley" line is in perfect condition - no
missing fur, all tags attached, no bends or creases. She would love to live at
your house!
<P>
Buyer pays postage and insurance, and seller reserves the right not to sell to
anyone with excessive negative feedback. Payment with money order or bank
check ships right away. Payment with personal check ships after 10 business
days.
<P>
Have fun bidding!
<HR>
<CENTER>
<IMG SRC="http://www.host.com/images/bearcp.jpg">
</CENTER>
</FONT>
```

Microsoft Notepad Used to Format an Auction Description

It might be easier to work with Notepad if you select "Word wrap" from the edit menu. This way you don't have to keep using the scroll bars when you want to view text that extends beyond the screen.

Save your description in a file called *practice.html* (or any name you choose) and open it in your browser to see how it looks. You can do this with the File menu on your browser. You'll find detailed instructions for this in Chapter 4.

The formatted file will open in your browser. Keep the file open in Notepad in case you need to make changes or corrections to the description. If you change the file, be sure to save it from the File menu. Hit the "Reload" or "Refresh" button in your browser to view the changes.

Appendix B contains some auction description templates coded in HTML.

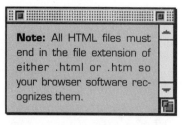

Note: All HTML files must end in the file extension of either .html or .htm so your browser software recognizes them.

Note: When previewing an auction description in your browser, size the browser down to the approximate size of the space in which the description appears on an auction page. This will give you an idea of what the description will look like in a smaller space.

Appendix B — Auction Description Templates

☞Coding Auction Descriptions

This appendix includes examples of auction descriptions coded in simple HTML. I code mine in Microsoft's Notepad and then paste them into the description area of the auction-entry screen. That little space (shown in the Chapter 4 example) where you add the description may look like it's too tiny to fit all this code. Most auction sites, however, don't limit the number of characters you can enter in that field.

Just copy, point, and paste; your HTML code feeds right into the description area.

The following examples show both the HTML code and the result that displays in your browser. Boldface type represents data you have to supply, like your item description, a file name, or a URL.

You might want to make a few practice files before you use the HTML code for auction descriptions. They may take awhile to type in, but once you've saved the text to a file, you can reuse the code just by replacing the old text with the new text when it's time to list another auction.

Color Schemes

The examples in this Appendix will show up better in your browser. The background colors I chose looked fine to

Note: Some auction sites include horizontal lines between the auction description and the picture you include. Watch for any automatic formatting done by the site program. Look carefully at other active auction pages, and review your description before you submit it so the page doesn't end up being cumbersome with lines and spaces.

Note: When you find a description style you like, type it in one time and save it to use as a template file. Whenever you list an auction, simply replace the previous information with new information, change a background color or two, and you'll have another great-looking auction.

me when I tested them, but others may find them hideous. If you decide to use other colors, simply replace the names within the appropriate tag.

Since this book is in grayscale, I tried to use background colors and backgrounds that would contrast well. In doing so, I discovered some color combinations of dark and light that go well together. This table lists some suggestions:

Light Color	Dark Color
cyan	darkcyan
salmon	orangered
violet	darkviolet
skyblue	royalblue

lightpink	indianred
peachpuff	salmon
palegreen	forestgreen
gold	darkgoldenrod
tan	sienna
violet	darkviolet
royalblue	lightslateblue
lightskyblue	darkblue
burlywood	maroon
turquoise	cadetblue
tomato	firebrick
springgreen	seagreen
dodgerblue	lightslateblue
lightslategray	darkslategray

Contrasting Colors

Icons Used in These Examples

Though I show the URL to icons and background patterns used in the examples that follow, they are not actual URLs to those icons. I simply included them in the HTML code to illustrate how to include images with the descriptions.

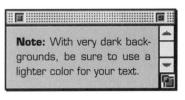

Note: With very dark backgrounds, be sure to use a lighter color for your text.

You can find many of the icons that appear in these examples at image banks all over the Web. Just do a search for "images" or "icons" and you're bound to find many sites with images you can use.

Image Banks on the Web

These Web sites have collections with hundreds of images that you can use in your auction descriptions. To maintain control over images you want to use (site owners can and often do move files around), copy the icon to your hard drive, and upload it to your Web directory later. You can then code the URL to the image into your auction description.

Remember that linking images back to another host puts a lot of traffic on that server.

Note: If you have a home page on the Web, you might want to build your own index of images. Then you can source them right from your own page when you format your auction descriptions.

Uniform Resource Locator	Site Name
pixelplace.com	The Icon Factory
www.hlt.uni-duisburg.de/Icons	Anthony Thyssen's Icon Library
www.animationlibrary.com	Animation Library
www.andyart.com	Andy's Art Attack
www.iconbazaar.com	IconBAZAAR
www.clipartconnection.com	The Clip Art Connection
www.arttoday.com	ArtToday
www.barrysclipart.com	Barry's Clip Art Server
people.delphi.com/nlopez/anim.htm	Cat GIF Animations
www.netmegs.com/~animate	Animation Shack
www.rewnet.com/bbb	Buttons, Bullets, and Backgrounds
www.specialweb.com/original	Celine's Original .GIFs
www.efn.org/~trentj/useless1.html	The Useless Button Universe
web2.airmail.net/lrivera	FOUR bEES Free Web Graphics
members.tripod.com/~nutty747/	Free Web Art
www.theshockzone.com	TheShockzone

Copying an Icon

The Web gives us a great function for "borrowing" icons from other pages. You can copy and save any icon on any page, unless the image is part of a program. Just place your mouse cursor over the picture, right-click, select "Save Image As" or "Save Picture As" from the menu, and tell your computer where to keep the file.

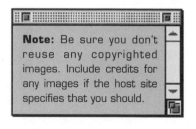

Note: Be sure you don't reuse any copyrighted images. Include credits for any images if the host site specifies that you should.

To keep track of your image files, build a "web-pix" directory (or something similar) for storing them. Then you won't have to hunt them down later.

Adding a Link to Your Current Auctions

If you have other auctions running, you may want to code a link to them in your auction descriptions. Bidders can save on shipping charges if they buy several items from you at the same time.

To get the URL for your current auctions, do a seller search on yourself. When that page comes up, copy the URL from the address line of your browser and paste it into Notepad. Then you can include that URL in the <A> tag.

☛Auction Description Formats

These examples are relatively easy to code and they look wonderful. Once you get the hang of coding in HTML, designing your own auction descriptions will be easy.

As I mentioned before, you'll only have to type in the code file once, and test it by opening it in your browser. Then, you can save it to a file and reuse it each time you enter an auction. Just replace the previous auction's information with the new data.

The HTML code for each example appears in the section following the formatted descriptions.

Example 1

You saw this handbill style auction description in Chapter 4. Notice that I use the ALIGN attribute in my <IMG> tag to move the photo to the left, leaving room for the text to wrap around it.

Bear Valley "Gimme Some Love" Exclusive!

Here's a unique item from the creator of the Bear Valley line. Rita Brodsky, the artistic designer for Bear Valley Unlimited, created "Gimme Some Love" solely for her daughter's use in her books about Collecting on the Internet. Now you can own it!

This one-of-a-kind chocolate brown bear is soft and fuzzy from his head to his hand-stitched feet. He proudly sports a gold bow around his neck. What a perfect addition to your teddy bear gallery!

Item will ship in its original shoebox. One adult non-smoking owner. No rips, teeth marks, or other defects. Modest reserve to protect seller from site malfunction. You're bidding on the exact item shown in this photo.

North American bids only please. Buyer pays shipping and insurance, seller reserves the right not to sell to anyone with excessive negative feedback. I do leave positive feedback for all successful transactions. Payment with money order. **Personal checks accepted if you have a 25 or higher positive feedback rating.** Check out my other auctions to save on shipping. Have fun bidding!

Example 1. Auction Description

Example 2

Following is the table style auction description you saw in Chapter 4. Notice the balance of large text for the heading with smaller paragraph text. My terms of sale are down near the bottom in text. It's readable, yet it doesn't draw attention away from the item I'm selling.

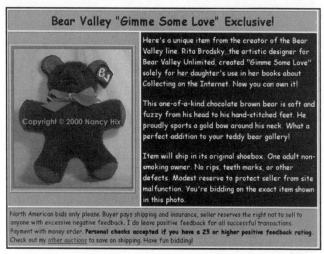

Example 2. Auction Description

Example 3

This description style includes a few bullet items and places the item information and the terms of sale side by side. The photo and the text under it share the same table cell. I also added some cell padding and spacing to define the cell borders.

Example 3. Auction Description

Example 4

This example includes two images showing the item from different angles. Notice how the photos appear "framed" because each one is in its own table within a table cell. The table cells are padded and spaced. I also used a few symbols around the heading to add some life to it.

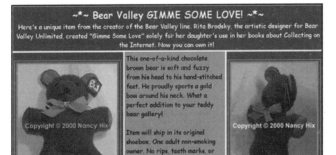

Example 4. Auction Description

OurBusiness.com

Bear Valley "Gimme Some Love" Exclusive!

Here's a unique item from the creator of the Bear Valley line. Rita Brodsky, the artistic designer for Bear Valley Unlimited, created "Gimme Some Love" solely for her daughter's use in her books about Collecting on the Internet. Now you can own it!

This one-of-a-kind chocolate brown bear is soft and fuzzy from his head to his hand-stitched feet. He proudly sports a gold bow around his neck. What a perfect addition to your teddy bear gallery!

Item will ship in its original shoebox. One adult non-smoking owner. No rips, teeth marks, or other defects. Modest reserve to protect seller from site malfunction. You're bidding on the exact item shown in this photo.

North American bids only please. Buyer pays shipping and insurance, seller reserves the right not to sell to anyone with excessive negative feedback. I do leave positive feedback for all successful transactions. Payment with money order. **Personal checks accepted if you have a 25 or higher positive feedback rating.** Check out my other auctions to save on shipping. Have fun bidding!

Example 5. Auction Description

Example 5

The example at the bottom of page 337 is something plain and simple that adds color text to a standard white background. I've also added a link to the seller's business Web site at the top, so bidders can stop by and do more shopping.

Example 6

This example combines the handbill and table auction description styles, with some interesting results. A fancy border image sets off the heading and balances the page at the bottom. This works great if you're using a small image.

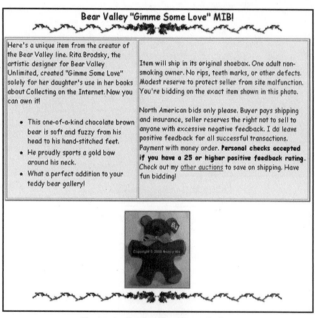

Example 6. Auction Description

Example 7

The simple description at the top of page 339 uses a table with a thicker, chiseled border with the same light-colored background for each table cell. I left off a heading in order to draw more attention to the descriptive text.

Example 8

This chiseled-border table at the bottom of page 339 is an excellent style if your picture is large, or particularly wide. I added some cell spacing to separate the text blocks with thicker borders. Again, there's no heading. The image is the main attraction.

Here's a unique item from the creator of the Bear Valley line. Rita Brodsky, the artistic designer for Bear Valley Unlimited, created "Gimme Some Love" solely for her daughter's use in her books about Collecting on the Internet. Now you can own it!

This one-of-a-kind chocolate brown bear is soft and fuzzy from his head to his hand-stitched feet. He proudly sports a gold bow around his neck. What a perfect addition to your teddy bear gallery!

Item will ship in its original shoebox. One adult non-smoking owner. No rips, teeth marks, or other defects. Modest reserve to protect seller from site malfunction. You're bidding on the exact item shown in this photo.

Buyer pays shipping and insurance, seller reserves the right not to sell to anyone with excessive negative feedback. I do leave positive feedback for all successful transactions. Payment with money order. **Personal checks accepted if you have a 25 or higher positive feedback rating.** Check out my other auctions to save on shipping. Have fun bidding!

Example 7. Auction Description

Here's a unique item from the creator of the Bear Valley line. Rita Brodsky, the artistic designer for Bear Valley Unlimited, created "Gimme Some Love" solely for her daughter's use in her books about Collecting on the Internet. Now you can own it!

This one-of-a-kind chocolate brown bear is soft and fuzzy from his head to his hand-stitched feet. He proudly sports a gold bow around his neck. What a perfect addition to your teddy bear gallery!

Item will ship in its original shoebox. One adult non-smoking owner. No rips, teeth marks, or other defects. Modest reserve to protect seller from site malfunction. You're bidding on the exact item shown in this photo.

Buyer pays shipping and insurance, seller reserves the right not to sell to anyone with excessive negative feedback. I do leave positive feedback for all successful transactions. Payment with money order. **Personal checks accepted if you have a 25 or higher positive feedback rating.** Check out my other auctions to save on shipping. Have fun bidding!

Example 8. Auction Description

☞HTML Code for the Descriptions

Here's the HTML code for each of the auction descriptions in the previous section. The text shown in boldface is what you'll replace with your own information.

Once you find a description you want to use, you only have to type it once into Notepad or another text-processor. Once you have the file, you can use it again. Simply replace the text with the new information, change some colors, and you'll have a brand new auction.

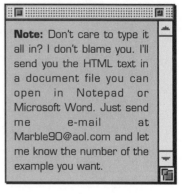

Note: Don't care to type it all in? I don't blame you. I'll send you the HTML text in a document file you can open in Notepad or Microsoft Word. Just send me e-mail at Marble90@aol.com and let me know the number of the example you want.

Example 1

```
<CENTER>
<FONT FACE="Comic Sans MS" SIZE=5>
<B>Bear Valley "Gimme Some Love" Exclusive!</B></FONT><BR>
<IMG SRC="http://www.host.com/images/border01.gif">
<BR>
<IMG SRC="http://www.host.com/images/bearcp.jpg" ALIGN=LEFT>
<FONT FACE="Comic Sans MS" SIZE=3>Here's a unique item from the cre-
   ator of the Bear Valley line. Rita Brodsky, the artistic designer for Bear
   Valley Unlimited, created "Gimme Some Love" solely for her daughter's
   use in her books about Collecting on the Internet. Now you can own it!
<P>
This one-of-a-kind chocolate brown bear is soft and fuzzy from his head
   to his hand-stitched feet. He proudly sports a gold bow around his
   neck. What a perfect addition to your teddy bear gallery!
<P>
Item will ship in its original shoebox. One adult non-smoking owner. No rips,
   teeth marks, or other defects. Modest reserve to protect seller from site
   malfunction. You're bidding on the exact item shown in this photo.
<P>
<FONT FACE="Comic Sans MS" SIZE=2>North American bids only please.
   Buyer pays shipping and insurance, seller reserves the right not to sell to
   anyone with excessive negative feedback. I do leave positive feedback for
   all successful transactions. Payment with money order. <B>Personal
   checks accepted if you have a 25 or higher positive feedback rating.</B>
   Check out my <A HREF="http://www.auction.com/site/allmine">other
   auctions</A> to save on shipping. Have fun bidding!
</CENTER>
```

Example 2

```
<TABLE BORDER=2 CELLPADDING=3 CELLSPACING=3>
<TR>
<TD COLSPAN=2 BGCOLOR=tan ALIGN=MIDDLE>
<FONT FACE="Comic Sans MS" SIZE=5>
<B>Bear Valley "Gimme Some Love" Exclusive!</B></TD>
</TR><TR>
<TD BGCOLOR=tan>
<TABLE BORDER=1>
<TR>
<TD><IMG SRC="http://www.host.com/images/bearcp.jpg"></TD>
</TR></TABLE>
</TD>
<TD BGCOLOR="#330000">
<FONT FACE="Comic Sans MS" COLOR=white SIZE=3>Here's a unique
item from the creator of the Bear Valley line. Rita Brodsky, the
artistic designer for Bear Valley Unlimited, created "Gimme Some
Love" solely for her daughter's use in her books about Collecting on
the Internet. Now you can own it!
<P>
This one-of-a-kind chocolate brown bear is soft and fuzzy from his head
to his hand-stitched feet. He proudly sports a gold bow around his
neck. What a perfect addition to your teddy bear gallery!
<P>
Item will ship in its original shoebox. One adult non-smoking owner. No rips,
teeth marks, or other defects. Modest reserve to protect seller from site
malfunction. You're bidding on the exact item shown in this photo.
</TD>
</TR><TR>
<TD COLSPAN=2 BGCOLOR=tan><FONT FACE="Comic Sans MS" SIZE=2>
<P>
<FONT FACE="Comic Sans MS" SIZE=2>North American bids only please.
Buyer pays shipping and insurance, seller reserves the right not to sell to
anyone with excessive negative feedback. I do leave positive feedback for
all successful transactions. Payment with money order.<B>Personal
checks accepted if you have a 25 or higher positive feedback rating.</B>
Check out my <A HREF="http://www.auction.com/site/allmine">other
auctions</A> to save on shipping. Have fun bidding!
</TD>
</TR></TABLE>
```

Example 3

```
<TABLE BORDER=2 CELLPADDING=3 CELLSPACING=3>
<TR>
<TD COLSPAN=2 BGCOLOR=tan ALIGN=MIDDLE>
<FONT FACE="Comic Sans MS" SIZE=5>
<B>Bear Valley "Gimme Some Love" Exclusive!</B></TD>
</TR><TR>
<TD BGCOLOR=tan ALIGN=CENTER>
<IMG SRC="http://www.host.com/images/bearcp.jpg">
<BR>
<FONT FACE="Comic Sans MS" SIZE=2>North American bids only please.
    Buyer pays shipping and insurance, seller reserves the right not to sell to
    anyone with excessive negative feedback. I do leave positive feedback for
    all successful transactions. Payment with money order. <B>Personal
    checks accepted if you have a 25 or higher positive feedback rating.</B>
    Check out my <A HREF="http://www.auction.com/site/allmine">other
    auctions</A> to save on shipping. Have fun bidding!</TD>
<TD BGCOLOR="#330000">
<FONT FACE="Comic Sans MS" COLOR=white SIZE=2><B>Here's a unique
    item from the creator of the Bear Valley line. Rita Brodsky, the artis-
    tic designer for Bear Valley Unlimited, created "Gimme Some Love"
    solely for her daughter's use in her books about Collecting on the
    Internet. Now you can own it!
<UL>
<LI>
This one-of-a-kind chocolate brown bear is soft and fuzzy from his head
    to his hand-stitched feet. He proudly sports a gold bow around his
    neck. What a perfect addition to your teddy bear gallery!
<LI>
Item will ship in its original shoebox. One adult non-smoking owner. No rips,
    teeth marks, or other defects. Modest reserve to protect seller from site
    malfunction. You're bidding on the exact item shown in this photo.
</UL>
</TD>
</TR></TABLE>
```

Example 4

```
<TABLE BORDER=2 CELLPADDING=3 CELLSPACING=3>
<TR>
<TD COLSPAN=3 BGCOLOR="#990033" ALIGN=MIDDLE>
<FONT FACE="Comic Sans MS" SIZE=5 COLOR="#ffffff"><B>~*~ Bear Val-
    ley GIMME SOME LOVE! ~*~</B><BR>
```

```
<FONT FACE="Comic Sans MS" SIZE=3>Here's a unique item from the cre-
ator of the Bear Valley line. Rita Brodsky, the artistic designer for Bear
Valley Unlimited, created "Gimme Some Love" solely for her daughter's
use in her books about Collecting on the Internet. Now you can own it!
</TD>
</TR><TR>
<TD BGCOLOR="#990033">
<TABLE BORDER=1>
<TR>
<TD><IMG SRC="http://www.host.com/images/bearcp.jpg"></TD>
</TR></TABLE>
</TD>
<TD BGCOLOR="#CC9999"><FONT FACE="Comic Sans MS" SIZE=3>This
one-of-a-kind chocolate brown bear is soft and fuzzy from his head to
his hand-stitched feet. He proudly sports a gold bow around his neck.
What a perfect addition to your teddy bear gallery!
<P>
Item will ship in its original shoebox. One adult non-smoking owner. No rips,
teeth marks, or other defects. Modest reserve to protect seller from site
malfunction. You're bidding on the exact item shown in this photo.
</TD>
<TD BGCOLOR="#990033">
<TABLE BORDER=1>
<TR>
<TD><IMG SRC="http://www.host.com/images/bearcp.jpg"></TD>
</TR></TABLE>
</TD>
</TR><TR>
<TD COLSPAN=3 BGCOLOR="#FFCCCC">
<FONT FACE="Comic Sans MS" SIZE=2>North American bids only please.
Buyer pays shipping and insurance, seller reserves the right not to sell to
anyone with excessive negative feedback. I do leave positive feedback for
all successful transactions. Payment with money order. <B>Personal
checks accepted if you have a 25 or higher positive feedback rating.</B>
Check out my <A HREF="http://www.auction.com/site/allmine">other
auctions</A> to save on shipping. Have fun bidding!</TD>
</TR></TABLE>
```

Example 5

```
<CENTER>
<FONT SIZE=4 FACE=Verdana>
<A HREF="http://www.ourbusiness.com">OurBusiness.com</A></FONT>
<P>
```

```
<IMG SRC="http://www.host.com/images/bearcp.jpg">
<BR>
<HR>
<FONT SIZE=4 COLOR=purple FACE=Verdana>
<B>Bear Valley "Gimme Some Love" Exclusive!</B></FONT>
<BR>
<FONT FACE=Verdana SIZE=2 COLOR=purple>Here's a unique item from the
    creator of the Bear Valley line. Rita Brodsky, the artistic designer for Bear
    Valley Unlimited, created "Gimme Some Love" solely for her daughter's use
    in her books about Collecting on the Internet. Now you can own it!
<P>
This one-of-a-kind chocolate brown bear is soft and fuzzy from his head
    to his hand-stitched feet. He proudly sports a gold bow around his
    neck. What a perfect addition to your teddy bear gallery!
<P>
Item will ship in its original shoebox. One adult non-smoking owner. No rips,
    teeth marks, or other defects. Modest reserve to protect seller from site
    malfunction. You're bidding on the exact item shown in this photo.
<P>
<HR>
<FONT FACE=Verdana SIZE=1>North American bids only please. Buyer pays
    shipping and insurance, seller reserves the right not to sell to anyone with
    excessive negative feedback. I do leave positive feedback for all successful
    transactions. Payment with money order. <B>Personal checks accepted
    if you have a 25 or higher positive feedback rating.</B> Check out my
<A HREF="http://www.auction.com/site/allmine">other auctions</A> to
    save on shipping. Have fun bidding!
</CENTER>
```

Example 6

```
<CENTER>
<FONT FACE="Comic Sans MS" SIZE=4>Bear Valley "Gimme Some Love"
    Exclusive!<BR>
<IMG SRC="http://www.host.com/images/border02.gif">
<BR>
<TABLE BORDER=2>
<TR>
<TD BGCOLOR=beige><FONT FACE="Comic Sans MS" SIZE=2>Here's a
    unique item from the creator of the Bear Valley line. Rita Brodsky,
    the artistic designer for Bear Valley Unlimited, created "Gimme Some
    Love" solely for her daughter's use in her books about Collecting on
    the Internet. Now you can own it!
<UL>
```

<LI>This one-of-a-kind chocolate brown bear is soft and fuzzy from his head to his hand-stitched feet.
<LI>He proudly sports a gold bow around his neck.
<LI>What a perfect addition to your teddy bear gallery!
</UL>
</TD>
<TD BGCOLOR=beige><FONT FACE="Comic Sans MS" SIZE=2>Item will ship in its original shoebox. One adult non-smoking owner. No rips, teeth marks, or other defects. Modest reserve to protect seller from site malfunction. You're bidding on the exact item shown in this photo.
<P>
North American bids only please. Buyer pays shipping and insurance, seller reserves the right not to sell to anyone with excessive negative feedback. I do leave positive feedback for all successful transactions. Payment with money order. <B>Personal checks accepted if you have a 25 or higher positive feedback rating.</B> Check out my
<A HREF="http://www.auction.com/site/allmine">other auctions</A> to save on shipping. Have fun bidding!</TD>
</TR>
</TABLE>
<P>
<IMG SRC="http://www.host.com/images/bear.jpg">

<IMG SRC="http://www.host.com/images/border02.gif ">
</CENTER>
</FONT>

Example 7

<TABLE BORDER=5>
<TR>
<TD BGCOLOR=beige>
<IMG SRC="http://www.host.com/images/bear.jpg"></TD>
<TD BGCOLOR=beige><FONT FACE=Verdana SIZE=3><B>Here's a unique item from the creator of the Bear Valley line. Rita Brodsky, the artistic designer for Bear Valley Unlimited, created "Gimme Some Love" solely for her daughter's use in her books about Collecting on the Internet. Now you can own it!
<P>
This one-of-a-kind chocolate brown bear is soft and fuzzy from his head to his hand-stitched feet. He proudly sports a gold bow around his neck. What a perfect addition to your teddy bear gallery!
<P>
Item will ship in its original shoebox. One adult non-smoking owner. No rips,

teeth marks, or other defects. Modest reserve to protect seller from site malfunction. You're bidding on the exact item shown in this photo. </B>
</TD>
</TR><TR>
<TD COLSPAN=2 BGCOLOR=beige><FONT FACE=Verdana SIZE=2>Buyer pays shipping and insurance, seller reserves the right not to sell to anyone with excessive negative feedback. I do leave positive feedback for all successful transactions. Payment with money order. <B>Personal checks accepted if you have a 25 or higher positive feedback rating.</B> Check out my
<A HREF="http://www.auction.com/site/allmine">other auctions</A> to save on shipping. Have fun bidding!</TD>
</TR></TABLE>

Example 8

<TABLE BORDER=5 CELLSPACING=4>
<TR>
<TD BGCOLOR=beige ALIGN=center>
<IMG SRC="http://www.host.com/images/bear.jpg">
<FONT FACE=Verdana SIZE=2><B>Here's a unique item from the creator of the Bear Valley line. Rita Brodsky, the artistic designer for Bear Valley Unlimited, created "Gimme Some Love" solely for her daughter's use in her books about Collecting on the Internet. Now you can own it!</B></TD>
</TR><TR>
<TD BGCOLOR=beige>
<FONT FACE=Verdana SIZE=2><B>This one-of-a-kind chocolate brown bear is soft and fuzzy from his head to his hand-stitched feet. He proudly sports a gold bow around his neck. What a perfect addition to your teddy bear gallery!
<P>
Item will ship in its original shoebox. One adult non-smoking owner. No rips, teeth marks, or other defects. Modest reserve to protect seller from site malfunction. You're bidding on the exact item shown in this photo.</B>
</TD>
</TR><TR>
<TD COLSPAN=2 BGCOLOR=beige><FONT FACE=Verdana SIZE=1>Buyer pays shipping and insurance, seller reserves the right not to sell to anyone with excessive negative feedback. I do leave positive feedback for all successful transactions. Payment with money order. <B>Personal checks accepted if you have a 25 or higher positive feedback rating.</B> Check out my
<A HREF="http://www.auction.com/site/allmine">other auctions</A> to save on shipping. Have fun bidding!</TD>
</TR></TABLE>

Appendix C — E-mail Samples for Online Auction Transactions

Since online auction sites face us with varied personalities and temperaments, you're likely to encounter all types of people. By their nature, online auction sites put people in touch though e-mail, which is the best way to communicate with your buyers and sellers. You can keep records of auction correspondence.

For people just starting out with electronic communication, e-mail can be a tough horse to break. It's still a "faceless" medium. We miss important components of human interaction such as body language, voice inflections, and even handwriting. All we have are words on a screen, so we must word our messages carefully to avoid misunderstandings.

The Internet is teeming with nice people, particularly when they're about to do business with you and trust you'll uphold your end of the deal. Most of the e-mail that transpires between the buyer and seller is very friendly. Good communication is essential to successful online auction transactions, because it impresses people. They'll want to mention it as part of your buying and selling practice when they leave feedback for you.

In this appendix, I include some sample e-mail "letters" designed to smooth any rocky waters you may encounter along the online auction route. I hope that some of these examples help you avoid unpleasant experiences and negative online auction feedback.

☞E-mail Etiquette

Our main electronic communication medium has its quirks, but manners are manners. Remember that with e-mail, anything you send can be saved — indefinitely — and used against you later. A furious insult intended for an audience of one could end up in far wider circulation than you intended.

Here are a few things to think about when sending e-mail, especially when tempers are flaring:

- If this message displayed publicly, would it embarrass you?
- Would you say the same thing face-to-face?
- Remember that you're dealing with people from all walks of life. Is your message easy to understand?
- Did you proofread your e-mail? A small typo could cause a gross misunderstanding or make you seem foolish.
- Are you sending the equivalent of an electronic punch in the stomach? If so, it will be received that way and may be responded to in kind.
- Did you include the text of the original message, so the person knows what raised your hackles?
- If an e-mail message provokes a strong emotional response in you, did you take time to read it over to be sure you clearly understood the intended meaning?
- If your message is "just kidding," do you include the proper emoticons? Should you be "kidding" with someone in online auction communication? :-)

☛Normal Transactions

A "normal transaction" is one in which you're dealing with someone of an even, predictable temperament. Always assume that the person you're writing to is as nice as you are. I include some examples of e-mail you might send at various times throughout the online auction transaction.

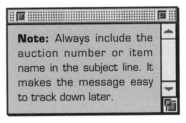

Note: Always include the auction number or item name in the subject line. It makes the message easy to track down later.

For the Seller

For the initial contact, and hopefully thereafter, the seller should be exceptionally personable. Remember that you're asking a total stranger for money, and that person is likely to judge you by the e-mail you send.

If you're terse or rude, there's a good chance the payment will never arrive. I included a few examples here to help you and your new customer get off on the right cyber-foot.

Initial Message to High Bidder

Be polite and friendly and include everything the buyer needs to know to prepare and mail the payment to you.

Here's an example of an introductory message from the seller to the high bidder:

> Hi! Congrats on being the high bidder for the set of eight Peaceables Plush collectibles. That was some fancy last-minute bidding! I hope you enjoy the items.
>
> Your high bid was $65. Please add $6.50 for shipping and insurance for a total of $71.50. Since you have excellent feedback, a personal check is fine. Please send payment to:
>
> Starr Cellore
> PO Box 31416
> Bidville, Illinois 57432
>
> Be sure to include the auction number and item name (or a copy of this e-mail) with your payment so I can leave feedback for you and ship your items promptly. Let me know when you have sent payment so I can watch for it. Thanks for bidding on my auction!
>
> -Starr

This tells the buyer everything he or she needs to know, and adds a nice personal touch. It also helps the buyer feel confident about sending payment to a stranger.

Payment Receipt

The payment arrived today. It's both important and courteous to let the person know that it reached you. Be sure to tell the buyer when you plan to ship the item.

It's also time to post positive feedback for the buyer. Once the payment arrives, he or she upheld the agreement, as long as the payment wasn't drastically late.

Mary,

Your payment arrived today. Thanks for including all of the auction information with it! I loved your remittance letter. I just posted positive feedback for you and I hope you do the same for me if you like the Avon Collector Plate.

I'm packing it up now to ship on Tuesday. Please let me know when the item arrives!

Thanks,

-Starr

If the buyer sent a personal check, indicate when you'll deposit the check and include a date that's ten days later as your expected ship date.

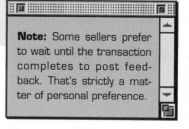

Note: Some sellers prefer to wait until the transaction completes to post feedback. That's strictly a matter of personal preference.

Notification of Shipment

Now Starr needs to let Mary know that she shipped the item. Here's a quick note to tell her it's on the way.

Hi Again Mary!

I shipped out your item this morning via Priority Mail. You should receive your collector plate in three to five days. I insured it for the full amount you paid, per our agreement.

Please let me know when the plate reaches its new home.

-Starr

Now Mary can watch for the package to arrive and alert Starr if it doesn't.

For the Buyer

If you send e-mail to an auction seller asking for information about an

active listing, keep the tone positive. Your message will reach someone you plan to send money to, and that person is likely to judge you by the e-mail you send.

Be as "upbeat" as possible.

Request for Item Clarification

Maybe you want a better description of the item's color, or you need to know a particular model number. Here's one way to get the information you need:

Dear User ID "marble,"

I'm interested in bidding on your auction for the Victorian birdhouse. Can you tell me if the bottom plate is removable? I seem to remember that model having a hinged door, but I can't tell from your photo.

I'm very interested in bidding on this auction. It closes tomorrow evening, so please send me the information as soon as possible, so I have time to bid!

Thank you,

-Jeff (User ID "surreal")

You'll probably get the information in time to enter a bid, especially if there are no other bids on the item.

Initial Message to Seller at Auction Close

It's reassuring for sellers to hear from the high bidder right after the auction closes. That means you're a serious buyer. Here's an example of a message you can send once your last-minute loading and reloading is over and you're the winner:

Hi! I was the high bidder on auction #435512957. Please let me know where to send payment. I can have it in the mail tomorrow.

Tom Piper, Jr.
1234 Stealer Street
Pigville, NY 00000

Thanks for listing this great piece! I can't wait to see it.

Tom

I'm sure you'll get a quick response. The seller will probably post feedback for you that mentions your nice communication.

Payment Dispatch Message

Let the seller know when you've sent the payment. This message doesn't need to be too long:

> Shavani,
>
> I just wanted to let you know that I mailed the payment for auction #435512957 to you today. Please let me know when it arrives.
>
> Thanks,
>
> -Leandra

This also assures the seller that you're a conscientious auction participant, and payment is on its way.

Notification of Item Receipt

Once the package arrives and you're satisfied with the item, be sure to e-mail the seller after you post the appropriate positive feedback:

> Dear Linda,
>
> I received the music box from auction item #435512957 today and I'm absolutely thrilled with it. I left positive feedback for you and I hope we can do business again in the future. It's been a pleasure.
>
> -Jim

Who knows — maybe your cyber-paths will cross again.

☞Sticky Situations

Sometimes the transaction doesn't follow the plan. When unexpected events hamper the natural course of the online auction process, you'll need to contact the other party in e-mail.

How you write is how you represent yourself (says the author, for the umpteenth time). There may be situations where words fail you, such as when the person you're dealing with exemplifies the mustard-gas rhetoric often used behind the sterility of a computer monitor.

Hopefully, these e-mail templates will keep you on a steady seat at the keyboard during sticky situations so your e-mail expresses your message — without drawing cyber-blood.

I've included here some sample messages to send when things run afoul of the rules.

Buyers

On those rare occasions when you receive an item that isn't what you expected, you need to contact the seller right away. Remember two things when drafting your e-mail:

- If your e-mail assumes it's an honest mistake, you have a good chance of getting the right item.
- A nasty-gram *always* makes the situation worse.

Initial contact is usually easy. Just assume the person you're contacting is as nice as you are. Remember, too, that there's a person with feelings and emotions at the other end reading the e-mail. He or she might be upset or embarrassed when your e-mail arrives, especially if it was an honest mistake. Please be nice.

With that said, let's explore some unfortunate situations.

Seller Has No Prior Feedback

You didn't notice this until you ended up the high bidder on a closed auction? Well, you can't do much at this point. Just send your payment as the seller directs, and then send a nice e-mail message saying it's on the way. Remember that this new seller is probably as nervous as you are about the transaction. Here's how you can ease the tension:

Dear Louise,

I ended up as the final high bidder on your auction #435512957. Please let me know the total amount I owe you, and include an address where I should send the payment.

I see by your lack of user feedback that you're new to this auction site. Welcome! If you have any questions, I'd be happy to help. Meanwhile I'm looking forward to posting your first positive feedback comment when this transaction completes successfully.

-Vaclav

This also gets the point across that you're watching this transaction closely because the user has no reference point of good practice.

You Received Warnings About Seller

We talked about this in Chapter 5. You're the final high bidder on an item and now your inbox is full of e-mail from other users warning you about the seller.

You're worried and you want to let the seller know. Here's a diplomatic way to relay the message:

Dear Deanna,

Since auction #435512957 ended with me as the high bidder, I've received three e-mail messages from people who claim they've had problems with you. I like to make my own judgments about online sellers and therefore intend to honor my bid and carry out this transaction. I'd prefer to use an escrow service to ensure that we'll exchange positive feedback when our deal successfully completes.

Please let me know if you agree with this. I'll initiate the escrow account and cover all expenses associated with it.

Sincerely,

-Boris

Now you need to send e-mail to all those who warned you about the seller. Thank them, and ask them to let you know *before* the auction closes next time. With any luck, Deanna will welcome the chance to improve her online auction reputation and agree to use escrow. If not, cross your fingers for good luck when you mail that payment, and stay in touch with her via e-mail throughout the transaction.

You Received the Wrong Item

The package arrives, but when you open it expecting a Golden Jubilee Barbie® doll, you find several hanks of glass beads. The shipping note is addressed to Charlynn, but you're Angie. Several states away, Charlynn unwraps an unexpected Barbie® doll and wonders who Angie is.

Send the seller e-mail right away so he or she knows about the mix-up:

Dear Monica,

Today I received your package but instead of the Golden Jubilee Barbie, I found glass beads and a note to "Charlynn." I'm afraid you mixed up two shipments! The fastest remedy is for Charlynn and me to simply exchange packages. If you don't think she'd mind, please send me her e-mail address; I'll arrange the exchange and let you know shipping and insurance expenses.

If you prefer, I can repack and return the package to you right away. Please let me know how you want to handle this.

-Angie

Monica may prefer to contact Charlynn and handle the exchange herself. Be sure you stay in touch with her until the correct item arrives at your house. Hopefully, she'll reimburse both of you for postage.

You Want a Refund for Non-Mint Item

You carefully unwrapped the antique cuckoo clock and found damage on the minute hand. The seller listed the item as "mint; no missing parts or flaws." Nobody wants to pay top dollar for a less-than-perfect item. Contact the seller right away, within the 3-day inspection period, and ask for a refund:

Dear Heather,

I received the Bavarian cuckoo clock today and I regret to inform you that it's damaged. Only half of the minute hand is present and the missing part is not in the packaging. The shipping container shows no apparent damage. I trust this was an unintentional oversight on your part. I'm returning the item to reverse the transaction.

I plan to ship the clock back to you tomorrow morning. Please let me know when you have sent my refund.

Sincerely,

-Barry

If you're lucky, the seller will claim it's an honest mistake and issue a refund. If he or she instead responds with an accusation that *you* chipped the piece, don't play into the hostile hand. This could be a ploy to stage a cyber-battle and stick you with a damaged item. Nobody wins those. If you send rude or insulting mail, you'll just give the seller leverage to build a case against you. It might make your palms itch, but remain professional.

You Never Received the Item

More than enough time has passed for payments to arrive, checks to clear, and items to be packed and shipped. You need to stay in contact with the seller:

Dear Laura,

According to your last e-mail message (which I attached below), you sent my folk art Panda two weeks ago. I have not received it. Please let me know the status of my shipment.

-Charmian

If it's determined that the item was lost in shipping, Laura should have the package traced. In this situation, Charmian needs to stay in touch with Laura, daily if possible, until the package turns up or Laura sends a refund.

Seller Says You Sent Wrong Type of Payment

The auction description specified that payment should be with a money order, but you sent a personal check. The seller wants to know why you ignored the instructions. This is a good time to be humble:

Hi Claire,

I'm so sorry about the personal check I sent. I had several other payments going out and completely forgot that you wanted a money order. I'll get one this afternoon and have it in the mail tomorrow morning. I'll let you know for sure when it's in the mail.

Meanwhile, please let me know when you've sent my check back. I'll enclose a postage stamp to reimburse you. Again, I'm sorry about the oversight.

-Donna

Claire probably won't hold it against you, since enclosing a stamp is a small but meaningful gesture on your part.

Your Check Bounced

Oops. Nobody expects this to happen. Blame it on your spouse, blame it on the bank, blame anyone, but whatever you do, get a money order for the payment amount and include whatever charges the seller accrued because of your overdraft. Apologize profusely. Here's help:

Dear Jane,

I received an overdraft notice from my bank today and I'm mortified with embarrassment. The check I sent to you for auction item #435512957 bounced. I've had a little trouble with my account lately but that shouldn't be your problem. I intend to make good on this payment and heartily apologize for any inconvenience this causes you.

I purchased a money order today for my high bid. I added shipping charges and an additional ten dollars to cover any fees your bank charges you for the overdraft. Please delay shipping the item to me until we're both certain that I've covered all the expenses.

Again, please accept my most sincere apology for this incident.

-Fanny (User ID "boing")

Now get that money order in the mail — immediately. An experienced seller will understand that nobody's perfect.

Sellers

As the seller, you might also face a few sticky situations. Again, it's important to maintain a professional attitude. Remember that an occasional misanthrope could forward copies of your e-mail to people who bid on your auctions. Don't send anything you wouldn't want a future customer to judge you by.

Buyer Never Sent Payment

You waited over a week and the buyer's payment never arrived. As irritating as this is, give the buyer the benefit of the doubt. The payment may be lost in the mail.

Bert,

It's now ten days since auction #435512957 closed and I have not received your payment. Please let me know if you sent it.

-Nan

This message assumes that the buyer still plans to uphold the agreement and simply asks for the status of the missing payment.

Buyer Sent Wrong Type of Payment

You asked for a money order and you instead received a personal check. You have two choices:

- Return the check and ask for a money order.
- Deposit the check and wait ten days for it to clear the bank before you ship the item.

You decide which option is best for you. Let the buyer know the direction you're taking:

Dear Freddie,

Your payment arrived today, thanks for sending it so fast! You sent a personal check, though, so I'll have to wait until it clears the bank before I ship the item.

Or...

> Thanks for your prompt payment, but I'm afraid I can't accept your personal
> check. I'm sure this was an oversight on your part since my auction descrip-
> tion asked for a money order. I'll return your check in tomorrow's mail; mean-
> while, please send a money order for the same amount. I'll let you know when
> it arrives.
>
> -Flossie

Either way, you're not jeopardizing the way you prefer to manage your online auction selling.

Buyer's Check Bounced

Good thing you held up shipment until the check cleared the bank. When
you receive an overdraft notice, here's how you can gently ask for a new
payment:

> Dear Ralph,
>
> My bank informed me that your check bounced, and charged ten dollars to my
> account. I'm afraid I have to ask for a money order in the amount of the origi-
> nal payment, plus the overdraft charge, before I can ship the item.
>
> I understand how these things can happen. Please let me know when you've
> sent the new payment.
>
> -Meggie

An honest person will respond in a horrified manner and claim it's a bank
error, of course.

Forget It, You're Re-listing the Item

You waited long enough, you never heard from the buyer, and you're giving
up. It's time to re-list the item, and you need to let the high bidder know. I
suggest keeping it civil, though. You never know what's going on in someone's life.
Here's what I recommend:

> Dear Blaire,
>
> I contacted you two weeks ago about paying for the Civil War stamp col-
> lection and I haven't heard back from you. The auction ended a month
> ago. I assume this means you have changed your mind about the sale. I

will leave the appropriate feedback for you. I re-listed the collection today.

If you have unforeseen circumstances, I wish you well.

Sincerely,

-Tootie

You're obviously not getting any money from the high bidder, so annoy him or her with kindness. Unfortunately, negative feedback is warranted in this situation.

You'll also need to report the incident to the site administrators so they can refund the site commission. They may want a word with the defaulting buyer, so include the person's name and user ID.

You Sent the Wrong Item

You're busy, you had many auctions running, and you mixed up a few address labels. One of your buyers expected an antique dog muzzle but you sent him a Precious Moments plush lion instead.

Contact the plush lion recipient immediately and explain what happened. Offer a plan for quick resolution:

Dear Luke,

I just discovered that I shipped you the wrong item. I accidentally sent a plush lion and your muzzle is on its way to Omaha. I'm contacting both of you to see if you'd be willing to ship the items directly to each other instead of back to me. You'll get them faster.

Let me know if you'd be willing to do this. If not, you can send the lion back to me and I'll handle the reversal.

I'm so sorry about this. Please keep a record of all postage and insurance fees because I intend to reimburse both of you.

-Laura

Send a similar note to the person about to receive the muzzle.

Based on my personal experience with online auction sites, discord between buyers and sellers doesn't happen that often. Most transactions, even those in which the buyer returns the item, complete without problems.

You can significantly affect the outcome of your own online auctions with carefully worded e-mail messages.

Glossary

The world of online auctions carries its own lexicon of terms. This glossary will help you identify them when you encounter them online. Also, as with any hobby or interest, followers adopt a special language as a form of "shorthand" when referring to the type, style, or condition of a collectible. Keep this list nearby as you manage your collecting with online auctions.

This glossary also provides Internet terms. If you can't find one you're seeking here, visit www.whatis.com for a huge index of terms.

Accessories – Anything originally included with the item.

Alias – Another name you're known by, such as a user ID.

Americana – Antiques or other items that reflect early American culture or history.

Antique – Traditionally, anything over 100 years old. This varies, however, within the collecting world. Cars over 20 years old are eligible for antique license plates in some states, yet fossils and gemstones aren't usually considered antiques. An antique is more broadly defined as "something old within its class."

Applied decoration – A design added to an item after manufacture by soldering, painting, or gluing.

As is – Indicates item has a flaw, variation, or aberration.

Art glass – Decorative glass made for display rather than function.

Art pottery – Pottery made for display rather than function.

ARPAnet – Advanced Research Projects Agency network, which was the precursor to today's Internet.

Attribute – Defines the way an HTML tag operates.

Auction – Presenting something for sale for a pre-determined period with the intent of selling it to the highest bidder.

Auction description – See "Description."

Auto-ship – When a dealer agrees in advance to buy a certain number of each item that the collectible company produces.

Background file – A JPEG or GIF image which, when tiled, makes up the background of a Web page or a table cell.

Bid – An offer to buy an item listed for auction.

Bid increment – The amount by which the bid increases each time a new one is placed.

Bid retraction – Canceling a bid when the auction is active.

Bisque – Porcelain with no applied glaze.

Buyer – The winning bidder who actually buys the item at his or her high bid price.

Category – Main classes or sections for items on auction sites.

Cell – See "Table cell."

China – Fine porcelain and earthenware dishes.

Collectible – Any collected item for which there is a secondary market.

Collecting buddy – Someone you met in an Internet chat room or bulletin board with whom you share your collecting passion.

Collector membership – An offer available through dealers or directly from the company. It includes a kit with one or two pieces, and the option to purchase additional pieces only available to members. Members usually receive a newsletter or periodical dedicated to the collectible line.

Collector quality – An item in mint or excellent condition that would be acceptable for a collector.

Conservator – One who restores collectible items to or close to the original condition.

Crazing – Minute cracks on the surface or in the glaze. Usually applies to ceramics or pottery.

Dated – A mark added to an item to indicate its year of manufacture.

Deadbeat bidder – Winning bidder who never pays for the item. Auction sites revoke their user privileges.

Dealer – One who buys and sells antiques and/or collectibles for a profit.

Description – The text part of the auction page that is formatted and entered by the seller.

Double-click – Two rapid-succession clicks of a mouse button.

Disneyana – Any item produced by Walt Disney Productions or Disney Studios.

Disparate parts – Parts from one or more items applied to make another.

Dutch auction – An auction in which multiples of the same item are sold with one auction listing.

Dynamic auction format – An auction format in which the information is current up to the minute when you reload the page.

E-mail – electronic mail. A message sent through cyber-space from one user to another.

E-mail mining – Collecting e-mail addresses from online auction sites for the sole intent of spamming. (See Spam)

Emoticon – a little face made out of keyboard symbols that illustrates the writer's intent or emotion.

Encryption – Scrambling data sent over the Internet so it can't be read if it's intercepted.

English auction – In online format, an auction that stays open as long as the seller wants it to.

Estate auction – An auction in which a collection of items owned by a recently deceased person is sold, usually one by one.

Event piece – See "Special Event Piece."

Excellent condition – Usually means near-mint condition, for example, if the item itself is in issue condition except for a flaw in the packaging that doesn't affect the piece.

Fake – In collectibles, a counterfeit or forgery. Selling a fake as an original constitutes fraud.

Feedback – Also called "Rating;" a comment left for one person by another after completing an online auction transaction with one another.

Featured auction – One for which an extra fee is usually paid to have the listing appear on the auction site home page, or first in the list of search results or category listings.

Fine art – Art produced for aesthetic purposes.

Folk art – Primitive art, usually that which was produced in the early 1900s.

First in series – Either item #1 in a series of items by the same collectible company, or items in a collectible line that were made before there was a market demand for the collectible. Usually the prime pieces in any collectible line.

Flame – A hostile remark toward another person made on a bulletin board or in a chat room.

Flame war – A barrage of hostile remarks by several users directed at each other.

Gently loved – A previously used item, for instance, an ornament hung on a Christmas tree for a few seasons, or a child's toy. Frankly, if all items in your collection are in mint condition, this one will be of noticeably poorer quality.

GIF – Stands for Graphic Interchange Format and is a type of image file used for Web icons.

Giftware – An item purchased to give as a gift, with no intent for collecting any more of that type.

Glaze – A thin glossy coating usually applied to pottery or porcelain.

Guestbook – A program that allows Web page visitors to enter information into an on-screen form and type in a line or two of a message.

Hairline crack – A thin, almost invisible crack in porcelain, earthenware, or ceramic.

Handle – Your nickname in cyberspace.

Home page – The main page in a Web site, usually contained in a file called index.html.

Home page builder – A program at a home page site that helps you build your first page with the help of a menu-driven program. It then lets you convert your page to HTML so you can edit and update the file.

Hot item – An auction that draws a considerable amount of bids.

Hot spot – A string of text or an image that changes the mouse cursor into a little hand. This indicates a hyperlink which takes the user to another page (or a different place on the current page) with a left-click.

HTF – (Hard-to-Find) Signifies the item is in limited production and/or availability and cannot easily be found at retail.

HTML – (Hypertext Markup Language) The coding language used to create Web pages.

Hypertext links – Same as hyperlink text. Hypertext links connect Web documents. Hypertext links are underlined, colored text that may change to a different color once you have visited the page that the hypertext links to. When you pass your mouse cursor over hyperlink text, the arrow changes into a little hand, indicating you're on a hot spot. If you click the left mouse button while on a hot spot, the linked page opens in your browser window.

Hypertext Markup Language – See "HTML."

Icon – An image.

Image file – A JPEG or GIF file that contains an icon or a photograph. A JPEG file ends in .jpg and a GIF file ends in .gif. GIFs are usually graphic files, whereas JPEGs are usually photos.

Impression – A design or monogram made by pressure on the surface of the item.

Inlay – A design made by cutting out a pattern and replacing it with a different material in the same shape as the cut pattern.

Internet – or more simply "the Net," is a collection of networks, or a network of networks, that allows computers all over the world to communicate with each other.

JPEG – Stands for Joint Photographic Experts Group and is a type of image file used for photographs.

Left-click – Clicking on the left mouse button.

Limited edition – Collectible items produced in a specific quantity. They are marked with a serial number.

Link – See "Hypertext Links."

Listing – Another term for "auction," or the act of entering an item at an online auction site.

Listing fee – Small assessment for starting an auction.

Lurk – To participate in a "read-only" mode on a bulletin board or in a chat room.

Maximum bid – The most you'll pay for an item that's up for auction. Once you enter a maximum bid, you can raise the amount, but you can't lower it.

Membership – See "Collector Membership."

Memorabilia – Nostalgia items collected to remind one of a time passed.

META tag – A code element used in an HTML document for use by search engines to categorize and index a Web site. They include keywords and short descriptions about the contents of the page.

MIB – (Mint in Box) Offers a way of being more specific about the term "mint." It means not only is the item itself in its original condition, but remains in its original box.

Minimum bid – The amount at which bidding starts in an online auction.

Mint – Means that the item is in the same condition it was the day it left the manufacturer. There is no degree of mint; an item is either mint or it isn't mint, period. There is no such thing as "mint, except for…"

Some conditions that void the mint status of an item are:

- Placement of or damage caused by a price sticker
- Broken or dented packaging
- Missing or damaged product labels
- Chips or dents, even if repaired
- Incomplete set

MIP – (Mint in Package) Means the item never has been out of the original packaging. This usually means items sold in packaging that breaks when opened, like a piece mounted on a card. Since the item left the manufacturer in the package, it's mint only if it's still in the original package.

MOC – (Mint on Card) Means same as MIP, only the item remains mounted on the packing card. The item, card, and any accessories are in perfect condition.

Motif – Design or style that earmarks an era.

Museum quality – An item in mint or issue condition suitable for setting a standard of perfection.

MWMT – (Mint With Mint Tags) means that not only was the Beanie Baby™ in issue condition with both of the tags attached, but both tags were in mint condition with no bends, dents or price sticker residue on them. It's another way of saying "mint."

MWT – (Mint With Tags) Started with Beanie Baby™ traders to establish that not only was the item in issue condition, but it also had both the heart-shaped swing tag and the sewn-in product tag in their original places. Again, just another way of saying "mint."

Near-mint – A term used by refreshingly honest sellers. Used to describe an item with a small chip, dented box, bend in the product tag, price sticker damage, or any other aberration from the issue condition of the item.

Net – See "Internet."

NRFB – (Never Removed From Box) Is another term for "mint." Be wary of this term, because it could mean the seller never opened the box to inspect the piece for damage or to ascertain that all product documentation was included. Be sure to ask if the seller at least checked the item before putting it up for sale.

Numbered edition – Numbered collectible item not produced in a specific quantity.

Open-ended auction – Any auction system that adds a specific amount of time, like five minutes, onto the end of an auction following any bid entered in the last hour.

Ordered list – A text list in which a sequential number or letter sets off each item.

Outbid – When someone else bids more than your maximum bid and becomes the new high bidder for an auction.

Password – Private set of characters you must enter along with your user ID when you use an online auction site.

Patina – Normal signs of age, usually used to describe wood or metal.

Physical tags – HTML tags that change text to boldface, italics, underline, or a few other options.

Plush – The soft fabric used to make stuffed animals, or soft toys made from a furry fabric.

POAT – Stands for Prime Online Auction Time, which are the hours between 7:30 PM and 11:30 PM in any US time zone.

Porcelain – A hard, fine-grained white ceramic ware.

Pottery – Earthenware produced with low-temperature firing.

Post – To enter a comment on a bulletin board or in a Usenet newsgroup.

Primary market – Buying an item from a dealer for the suggested retail price.

Primitive art – See "Folk art."

Proxy bid – When your bid automatically raises to your maximum bid if someone tries to outbid you.

Rare – Difficult if not impossible to find; very few in existence.

Registered user – One who has an active user ID and password at an online auction site who can list and bid on auctions.

Repaired – When an item is fixed using the original parts or material.

Reserve auction – One at which the seller has determined a minimum bid required to purchase the item.

Reserve price – The lowest amount you'll accept for an item in an online auction.

Restored – When an item is fixed using material or parts that were not part of the original piece.

Re-strike – A new item made from an original mold or plate.

Retirement – When a collectible company ceases manufacture of a particular piece.

Right-click – Clicking on the right mouse button. Some actions require a fast double-click.

Search – The online auction site feature used to locate specific listings by certain criteria, such as the collectible item or the manufacturer's name.

Search engine – A database of URLs linked to certain keywords. Excite, Alta Vista, and Lycos are some search engines. Yahoo is often called a search engine but technically is a directory because people, instead of Web-bots, index the entries.

Secondary market – Selling an item purchased at the suggested retail price for more or less than the retail price.

Secondary-market price – The resale value of an item. This can be either above or below the suggested retail price.

Secure Sockets Layer – (SSL) also called a "Secure Server." A program that encrypts data so it can't be understood if intercepted.

Seller – The person who enters an auction and receives payment from the winning bidder.

Shareware – Software programs you download from the Web that you try for a certain amount of time.

Shill – An illegal activity involving bidding on your own auction or encouraging someone to bid up your item with the intent of raising the price.

Site – See "Web Site."

Sniping – Bidding at the very last second in order to secure the winning bid.

Spam – Sending the same e-mail message to a multitude of users in an effort to generate business. Also, posting to many Usenet news groups at once. Always considered obnoxious.

Special-event piece – A special piece you can only buy at special events, like in-store shows. Usually produced in a limited quantity.

Stoneware – A strong opaque ceramic ware that is high-fired, dense, and nonporous.

Super special-event piece – A special piece you can only buy at a major special event, like the International Collectible Exposition. Usually produced in a limited quantity.

Super-duper special-event piece – A special piece you can only buy at an exclusive event hosted by the collectible company. Always produced in a very limited quantity.

Surfing – What you do when you click on hypertext links to bounce from Web page to Web page.

Swap meet – A gathering of secondary vendors who sell or trade collectibles with admission-paying customers.

Table cell – Component of a table in which text or an image appears. Table cells can also appear empty if you code only a <BR> tag (and nothing else) within the <TD> tag.

Tag – An element of HTML code contained within <brackets>.

Traffic – The volume of visitors to a particular page.

Uniform Resource Locator – (URL) An address that identifies the location of a page on the Web.

Unordered list – A text list in which a bullet sets off each item.

Usenet – A network that allows people to share messages. Another part of the Internet.

Value – Determines how an HTML tag attribute will function. Also, the price at which an item is expected to sell.

VHTF – (Very Hard To Find) Usually describes a nostalgia item, an early variation, or a super-duper special-event piece that was severely limited in quantity.

Visited link – A hypertext link that you've previously accessed.

Web – See "World Wide Web."

Web-bots – Robot-like programs that scan the World Wide Web and build site indexes.

Web page – An HTML document containing text, images, and other online elements. It may be a stand-alone HTML document or one contained within a browser frame.

Web ring – A collection of linked URLs that are accessed in succession by visiting each page in order.

Web site – A collection of Web pages on a server that follow a common theme or belong to the same person or organization.

Webmaster – The person in charge of managing the Web site and often the writer of the HTML code for the individual Web pages.

Wimp feedback – Waiting for the other party to enter user feedback for you before you'll enter a comment in return.

Winner's curse – The tendency for the high bidder at auction to pay too much for an item because last minute bidding drives the price up.

World Wide Web – Also called "the Web." A subset of the Internet. A system that uses the Internet to connect multimedia documents by way of hypertext links.

About the Author

Nancy L. Hix collects online and frequents many Internet bulletin boards and collector chat rooms. She's a founding member of the Harmony Kingdom House of Peers, a collector's society that raises money for charity by auctioning artist prototypes on eBay.

Her first book, *Collector's Guide to Buying, Selling, and Trading on the Internet* (Collector Books, 1999), drew great reviews from collectible and antique publications. She's also been published in *Mary Beth's Beanie World* and *The Queen's Courier*.

As a technical writer for a major telecommunications company, she wrote numerous freelance articles for internal employee publications. She is also an accomplished Web page designer and teaches the HTML code both in person and online.

Born in Chicago, she's a graduate of Illinois State University in Normal, where she specialized in Media Communications. She holds a master's degree in human resource management from National-Louis University in Evanston.

She and her husband Jeff live in Warrenville, Illinois, with their two sons, a cat named Mindy, and definitely too many collectibles.

Contact the author via her personal home page at http://www.angelfire.com/il/marble9. She accepts correspondence via electronic mail at Marble90@aol.com.

Index